Valuation of a
Medical Practice

Valuation of a
Medical Practice

Reed Tinsley, CPA
Rhonda Sides, CPA
Gregory D. Anderson, CPA, CVA

John Wiley & Sons, Inc.
New York • Chichester • Weinheim • Brisbane • Singapore • Toronto

Library of Congress Cataloging-in-Publication Data:

Tinsley, Reed.
    Valuation of a medical practice / Reed Tinsley, Rhonda Sides, Gregory D. Anderson.
        p.   cm.
    Includes index.
    ISBN 0-471-29965-0 (cloth : alk. paper)
    1. Medicine—Practice—Valuation.   2. Medical economics.
I. Sides, Rhonda.   II. Anderson, Greg, 1961 Sept. 5–   III. Title.
    [DNLM: 1. Practice Valuation and Purchase—methods.   W 80 T592v 1999]
R728.T553   1999
610'.68'1—dc21
DNLM/DLC
for Library of Congress   99-10467
                                                                    CIP

Printed in the United States of America.

10   9   8   7   6   5   4   3   2   1

About the Authors

Reed Tinsley, CPA, serves as shareholder in charge of Horne CPA Group's Houston, Texas office and is instrumental in the firm's Physician Services Division. He works closely with other health care consultants to assist in providing quality services to physicians, medical groups, hospitals, and other managed care organizations as they develop strategies for sound management for the future.

Reed has published numerous articles in national and regional publications and is frequently asked to speak on a variety of health care topics, including managed care contracting, physician affiliations, practice operations, and capitation. He is a member of the Editorial Advisory Board for *Physician's Marketing and Management* and editor of the *CPA Health Niche Advisor*. He is also a member of the Medical Group Management Association and National Health Lawyers Association. His articles have been published in the *Journal of Medical Practice Management*, *MGMA Journal*, *Hospital Physician*, *Texas Medicine Family Practice Journal*, and *Group Practice Journal*.

Rhonda Sides, CPA, has become associated with Horne CPA Group as Senior Manager in Nashville, TN. She specializes in practice valuations, cost accounting, operational assessments and financial feasibility issues related to group and integrated delivery system development. Rhonda has experience in all aspects of individual and corporate taxation, retirement plans, and cost accounting. She lectures nationally for various health care and financial organizations, and is actively sought for her ability to combine the practicality of accounting with the needs of health care practice management. A Certified Public Accountant, Rhonda is a member of the Georgia and Tennessee Societies of CPAs, the American Institute of CPAs, and the Healthcare Financial Management Association. Rhonda is also a candidate member of the American Society of Appraisers.

Gregory D. Anderson, CPA, CVA, a shareholder in the Horne CPA Group's Hattiesburg office, is a member of the firm's Physician Services Division and the firm's Business Valuation/Litigation Support Division. He works directly with the firm's team of health care consultants, providing services to physicians, medical groups, hospitals, and other managed care organizations in physician and managed care fee analysis, physician compensation, valuation of health care entities, and development of ambulatory surgery centers.

Greg has published various articles in local and regional publications and has presented programs on medical practice valuation topics to organizations of physicians, health care managers, and attorneys. He has served on the Valuation Quality Control Committee of the American Medical Advisory Group and on the Editorial Board of *Healthbeat*, the firm's physician services publication.

Greg graduated from the University of Southern Mississippi with a bachelor's degree in business administration in 1983. He earned the designation of Certified Valuation Analyst in 1997. His professional affiliations include the American Institute of Certified Public Accountants, the Mississippi Society of Certified Public Accountants, and the National Association of Certified Valuation Analysts.

Contents

CONTENTS

Introduction

What is a medical practice worth? *It depends!* And once you understand this sole fact, you can begin to concentrate on how to get to the answer.

There is a great misunderstanding in the medical community as to what constitutes the value of a medical practice. Purchasers often think it is valued based on what they plan to bring to the table. Sellers often think it is a simple formula that is applied uniformly across the board.

While there are guidelines and formulas that are used to ascertain values, there are many unique and individual circumstances related to a practice that set it apart from all the others. These circumstances are where the valuator focuses on making assumptions that affect the value of the practice. These assumptions are applied numerically to the valuation "formulas" to determine a dollar amount that represents the value.

All valuations are not performed in the same manner. It depends on the purpose of the valuation. Two key points should be stressed here, as we will build upon these throughout each chapter.

Key Point #1: The strength of the practice's income stream and what it produces for the owner(s) is what creates true value in a medical practice.

Key Point #2: The key to a successful valuation is deciding whether the practice's future income stream will mirror its present income stream.

SECTION 1: PURPOSE OF THE VALUATION

Sale to Another Physician

The valuation may be for the purpose of selling the practice to another physician, typically in the form of a purchase of ownership from an employed physician to join the practice as an owner. In some cases, this occurs with a retiring physician who sells his or her ownership to the existing shareholders.

Acquisition by a Hospital

During the past few years, acquisitions of practices have been happening at an accelerated pace. Due to the impact of managed care, hospitals have been compelled to purchase practices to maintain their patient referral base. Many hospitals have been building physician practice networks primarily with primary care practice acquisitions. Many of these hospitals are nonprofit hospitals. Therefore, the hospitals have been under regulatory guidance not to overpay for the practices. Because it is the taxpayers' money that the hospital is expending, regulations prohibit the nonprofit hospital from what is called "inuring" the physicians to bring referrals to the hospital.

Acquisition by a Physician Practice Management Company (PPMC)

Again due to managed care, companies known as PPMCs have begun to emerge as an alternative for physicians for dealing with the increasing challenges associated with managed care and the management of the practices as a business. Typically, the PPMCs have various procedures for structuring a purchase of a medical practice. Other reasons for valuing a practice are for estate and gift tax planning, strategic and management planning, physician estate and retirement planning, shareholder dispute resolution, and assessment of property damages.

Practice Merger

When practices are valued for mergers, it should be determined among the parties to the transactions as to how the equity interests will be handled. For example, if the subject practice is to own a 50 percent stake in the merged entity following the transaction, then should its investment in the newly formed entity also equal 50 percent of the total value of the new entity? If so, what happens in the case where the value of the practice falls short of reaching 50 percent? Is the subject practice to ante up cash to equate the difference? These are issues that should be discussed initially, preferably before the valuation process begins.

Questions may arise between physician groups and purchasing entities that should be addressed prior to the acquisition or merger transaction date. We have unfortunately seen too many instances whereby this process was not well thought out. It's like a marriage: you'd better address your major differences before the wedding because after the honeymoon your chances are slim to none for a peaceful resolution. If you are a physician contemplating a sale of your practice, the following checklist of factors would be useful in your planning.

- Employment status of the physicians following acquisition

Will the physicians become employed by the purchasing entity or will they remain self-employed or as owner/employees of their practice corporation? There is no right or wrong answer to this question. The answer, as is true for many of the following questions, depends on the goals of the two parties to the transaction and could be a negotiating point for either party.

Retention of autonomy is always a very important aspect for the physicians. If you are the purchaser, much regard should be given to this if you are to have a successful relationship with your physicians.

- Compensation plan

There are as many questions to ask regarding the compensation plan as there are variations in physician compensation plans. Again there is no right or wrong answer and the physicians must decide what they need. Much of this may depend on their age, retirement goals, college tuition, and so on, and whether much of their compensation is to be deferred. Physicians should consult with their professional advisors for guidance.

A physician's "go-forward" compensation plan is a very important part of the value. The variations of physician compensation plan calculations can be mindboggling. Many of them have become very cumbersome with lots of minute detail that can cause anguish, argument, and dissent. The goal of the physician compensation plan should be to compensate all parties equitably for what they contribute. If you are the physician, you will want to know what your compensation will be based on—whether it is gross charges, net cash receipts, accrual-based receipts, deduction for direct expenses, physician benefit expenses, corporate overhead, and so forth.

This is one of the stickiest points for most physician groups. The physician does not want to take a cut in pay, nor does anyone else for that matter. However, much of what we have seen does just that. Some compensation plans entertain the physicians with only 80 to 90 percent of previous years' compensation with additional qualitative and quantitative measurement incentives to make the remaining percentage just to be where they were last year. An argument for this is, "Don't we all have to improve to keep our job?" But in some respects it seems unfair depending on the circumstances of a physician, his or her practice, patient market area, and so on. If you are a physician facing this scenario, make sure you understand what is required of you to attain any incentive goals.

Issues that should be understood include the basis of salary structures, bonus and incentives, performance reviews, frequency of bonus calculations and distribution, and the effect on compensation of qualitative measurements such as administrative incentives, utilization reviews, quality assurance, and clinical measurements.

- Governance structure

Will there be a joint governance structure whereby physicians will have representation on a board of directors? The physicians should be involved in the management of their practices and should also be included in future strategic planning and recruiting discussions and decisions.

- Business plan

The purchaser's business plan should be presented to the physicians so that they have sufficient information with which to make their decisions about joining forces with the purchasing entity. Some physicians may not be comfortable that their practice will be run from Wall Street, for example. If a purchaser has immediate or intended plans to become a publicly traded company, it should be upfront with the physician group. Any immediate plans for growth, recruitment, and relocation of facilities should be discussed with the physicians.

- Growth plans

Adding practices/specialties: Are there plans to add specialties that may change the way the physicians currently do business (i.e., ancillary services), and will these specialties add a significant referral base to the existing practices?

- Financial strengths/backing

Physicians should inquire about the strength of the purchaser's capital especially if the purchaser is a company backed by venture capitalists. What will the venture capitalists require from them?

- Internal support system

Much of the time this is used as an additional carrot to relieve the physicians of their administrative and management burden. And many times, the purchaser's infrastructure is not quite prepared to handle the load required to deal with physician practices. Physicians are not accustomed to what is sometimes "corporate bureaucracy" just to get approval to purchase a piece of equipment. The purchaser should work hard at training its internal staff to handle physician practice operational issues. Likewise, the physicians must understand that this is a bigger company now and the hoops and red tape are for their protection and the company's.

Operational areas of hospitals, health systems, and PPMCs that sometimes fail to adequately support the acquired practices are human resources, billing and collection, accounting (and in particular purchasing), computer system conversion training and support, and transcription services.

- Physician contract terms

It is important for all parties to the transaction to fully understand the terms of contractual provisions, especially with regard to restrictive covenants and termination clauses.

- Management fee structure

Typically, this is structured as a percentage of net collections. In the event that physicians are not employees, there would be a management fee paid by the physicians to the purchaser as payment for the management of the practice—which usually includes billing and collection and employment of practice staff.

What is the management fee based on and is it subject to change? The physicians should inquire of the purchaser whether and to what qualifications the management fee will change.

What items are not in the control of the physicians? Once the physician relinquishes control of his or her practice, there are issues as to whether the physician really has control over certain expenses. If you are the physician, find out what you are being held responsible for and how that will be measured.

Will the practice's employees become employees of the purchaser? If the employees of the practice become employees of the purchaser, what control, if any, does the physician still have in hiring, firing, salary reviews, performance reviews, training, disciplines, and scheduling?

Compensation and benefits: Issues often encountered with regard to practice staff are their concern over continuity of their job and the changes they will face. Their first question will be whether they will still have a job. Their next question will be whether their salary and benefits will change. Purchasers and physicians alike should recognize that this whole process is usually very traumatic for practice staff. One PPMC we have had the opportunity to work with always involved the practice staff at the earliest possible time in the acquisition process. Prior to the due diligence process, the PPMC holds informal meetings with the staff (usually over a lunch brought in by the PPMC) in which a representative (who will be an active part of the acquisition process as well as after the honeymoon and during ongoing operations) will explain what is taking place, answer questions, and put their immediate fears to rest. He or she is also part of the due diligence process and is available on site throughout the process for staff to (1) ask questions as things are thought out and (2) become accustomed to the new regime (gradually). This is a win-win situation for both parties.

- Managed care contracting

If you are a physician contemplating this situation, speak with physicians that are already affiliated with the purchasing entity to get feedback on their experiences. Ask what things should be addressed prior to the deal that may not have been brought up already.

If you are a physician selling or merging your practice and if, for some reason, you have not been involved with the valuation process, it is recommended that you ask to review the valuation. You should ask questions to be sure that you understand the assumptions used in the valuation. This process sometimes creates animosity toward the purchasing entity. Ultimately, the purchasing entity's desire is for an amiable negotiation and transaction with the physicians. It is in their best interest to involve the physicians at the earliest point possible. We're still talking about "marriage" here. And there is nothing in the valuation report to which the target practice owners should not be privy.

With regard to managed care contracting, whether the situation is a merger, acquisition, or a buy-in by a new physician, discussions should take place regarding what is required after the transaction to effectively maintain existing or obtain new managed care contracts. (What is required to place a new physician on an existing contract?)

In the event of a merger, have issues such as antitrust been addressed? In the event of an acquisition, what issues are at hand that could endanger the revenue stream of the target practice? We have seen one situation where the current relationship between the purchaser and a large managed care insurer significantly endangered the revenue stream of the practice being purchased. Because the practice had a large percentage of its revenue from the Managed Care Organization (MCO), and the purchaser had a bad track record with this MCO, what does that do to the value? Does the purchaser have experience and successes at effectively obtaining and negotiating managed care contracts?

Buy-In/Buy-Out

In instances where a physician is ready to retire or is withdrawing from the practice, the practice will be valued in order to determine the departing physician's share. In instances where there is to be a new owner to buy into the practice, the existing practice must be valued in order to determine a fair asking price for the new owner.

Buy/Sell Agreements

This will typically be based on the provisions set forth in a buy/sell agreement already in place at the practice. The agreement should stipulate the manner in which the value should be determined— where the value is based on fair market value (FMV), net book value, or some other definition of value. It should also stipulate the formula or method(s) to be used to determine the value and whether accounts receivable (A/R) and goodwill will be a part of the value and under what circumstances.

Divorce

Valuations for purposes of divorce are different from valuations for business purposes. It is important for the valuator to refer to all related state law and precedent cases with regard to the valuation of professional practices. It is typical in the case of a divorce valuation that the physician or the physician's spouse retains an attorney to handle the valuation. In turn, the attorney engages the valuator for valuation services.

SECTION 2: MARKETING VALUATION SERVICES

Even if a valuator is not a member of a valuation society or organization and is not bound by membership to uphold specific valuation standards, the courts look to examples of valuation work exemplified by these societies and organizations. If you are a consultant or accountant breaking into offering valuation services, it is recommended that you become a member of one or more of these organizations. They are very helpful in the initial and ongoing education required to be a competent valuator.

Hospitals

For the most part, hospitals are not acquiring practices as fast as they were a few years ago. However, depending on the level of managed care penetration in a particular market, hospitals may be just beginning an acquisition phase to build a hospital-affiliated physician network. Chances are they are in need of a qualified valuator to provide valuation services for their targeted practices. And in most cases, these hospitals are nonprofit hospitals and will need an independent valuation to assess fair market value.

Attorneys

The valuator should market his or her services to family law and health care attorneys. As mentioned above, the attorneys are typically the physician's professional advisors that handle divorce cases and will engage the services of the valuator. Additionally, attorneys will handle many other valuation-related issues of their physician clients such as estate tax, gift tax, and shareholder disputes.

Physician Community and Your New Clients

As discussed earlier, there are various reasons that physicians would need the services of a valuator. But often they do not know whom to call when the time comes, or even the right time to do so. Educating your physician audience about the services you provide helps to create an awareness of your services. You may receive a call from a physician you met more than a year ago at a seminar. When it is time

9

for a physician to prepare for retirement and turn over the helm to a junior physician and other partners, they will be familiar with you, the valuator, as one of their trusted advisors—one that understands the habits and circumstances of their client.

Many of us get in the groove of servicing our clients in the same way, doing the same thing day in and day out, year after year. We don't always do a good job of letting our clients know all the other things we do. One of the best sectors to which we can market is to our own clients. And think about how many referrals you currently get from your own existing client base.

How to Market Valuation Services

The valuator should write valuation articles for newspapers and magazines on health care business that can reach the medical community audience. The articles should cover topics that are current issues of concern to physicians and purchasers of medical practices as well as other valuators engaged in the business of valuing medical practices. Volunteer to speak at business and health care society meetings on the topic of medical practice valuations. Participating in such activities forces the valuator to continue to learn, stay current, and refine his or her valuation skills.

SECTION 3: TAX ISSUES INVOLVED IN THE VALUATION PROCESS

Structure of the Transaction

Asset Sale versus Stock Sale

In our experience, the purchasers of medical practices have typically preferred to purchase assets (both tangible and intangible) as opposed to stock. This is one of the most common forms of structuring a practice purchase transaction. Purchasers prefer this because they can choose which assets they wish to acquire.

In an asset sale, the purchaser has the luxury of assuming all or none of the practice's liabilities. An asset purchase is not typically the preferred transaction structure from the selling physician's point of view because of the potential tax consequences of the transaction, especially if the practice is incorporated as a regular corporation, a professional corporation (PC), or a professional association (PA). When a practice is incorporated, it is subject to double taxation of the gains associated with the sale of assets. Additionally, in some states, sales tax is required on asset sales.

The purchaser is allowed to record the practice's assets on its books at the time of transaction at the price they paid for it (commonly referred to as the step-up basis). What this means is that typically the price paid for an asset is more than the practice's net book value as of the closing date of the transaction. Consequently, the purchaser records the assets at the purchase price (the higher price) and is allowed to depreciate this higher amount.

The selling practice and physicians would usually prefer a sale of the practice's stock because there is only one level of taxation and the gain is based on the difference between the purchase price and the physicians' basis in the practice, including tangible assets.

As a comparison, if the selling practice is a corporation, a PC, or a PA, then it will be subject to two levels of taxation in an asset sale. First, the practice will be taxed at the corporate level on the sale of the business assets. Then, the owners of the practice will be taxed individually on the gain from the sale. This is the main reason that sellers would rather sell stock than assets of the practice.

As a way to counter the effects of taxation from an asset sale, many transactions are structured such that a portion of the sales price can be assigned to a contractual arrangement: typically a covenant not to compete or an employment contract. This may also constitute an earnout provision (a deferred price arrangement) for this portion of the sales price. In earnout provisions, it is important that the seller effectively negotiate the portion of the price he wants now versus what he'll agree to in an earnout. Also, the seller must negotiate the length of time of the earnout.

Tax consequences should be projected by the selling physicians' accountants and attorneys to determine the impact of the sale on their personal finances. This is especially important given the recent changes to tax law, especially the capital gains rate. It is important that the physicians analyze their liability of capital gains, which are now 20 percent, and ordinary income with the highest marginal tax bracket being 39.6 percent.

If the seller is an S-corporation, then the sale is not subject to double taxation. However, all gains are taxed to the owners of the practice at the individual level with the application of the same rules for business gains/losses and categorization of short-term and long-term capital assets.

In summary, with regard to asset sales the major advantages to the purchaser are the ability to pick and choose which assets and liabilities will be purchased and the ability to record and depreciate the step-up tax basis of assets purchased as well as the amortization of goodwill. With the asset transaction, the purchaser cannot be held liable for hidden and unknown liabilities of the seller. The major disadvantages are the selling physicians' consequences from double taxation and the differences in tax treatment of ordinary income versus capital gains.

With regard to stock sales, one advantage to both parties to the transaction is that it is usually a much simpler transaction to structure and carry out than an asset transaction. For the selling practice, it eliminates the consequences of double taxation. The biggest disadvantage for the purchasers is that they will automatically assume all liabilities of the practice, even the ones that may not surface until after the transaction is a done deal.

Mergers

In a merger transaction, one practice's net assets are merged into the other's. The "other" party is the merger's survivor. Unlike asset sales, a merger transfers all assets and liabilities. This is possibly a double-edged sword. There are advantages and disadvantages of assuming the entirety of the selling practice. However, a major disadvantage is that it is an automatic assumption of all liabilities. This could be an unfortunate situation for the purchaser if the appropriate due diligence was not performed prior to the transaction. Consequently, the surviving entity will assume any undesirable or unwanted assets.

Section 1060 Tax Reporting Requirement

As a result of each asset sale transaction, the purchaser and the seller are required to report details of the transaction to the Internal Revenue Service (IRS). This is mandated by Section 1060 of the Internal Revenue Code (IRC).

To report the transaction, each party is required to complete and submit IRS Form 8594; Asset Acquisition Statement. This form is to be completed for the tax year of the transaction. This form requires both parties to report the allocation of the purchase price among various asset categories. The information reported by both parties should be identical.

The asset allocation is defined by the IRS to be reported in five categories. (Prior to 1998, there were only four categories.) These categories are defined as Classes I through V. Each class is designated as follows:

Class I: Cash, demand deposits, and similar accounts in banks, savings and loan associations, and other depository institutions

Class II: Certificates of deposit, U.S. government securities, readily marketable stock or securities, and foreign currency

Class III: Tangible assets such as furniture, fixtures, land, buildings, equipment, and accounts receivable; also includes intangible assets that are not Class I, II, IV, or V assets

Class IV: All amortizable Section 197 intangible assets, except goodwill and going-concern value; includes workforce in place, business books and records, operating systems, patents, copyrights, formulas, processes, designs, patterns, know-how, formats, customer-based intangibles, supplier-based intangibles, licenses and permits, covenants not to compete, franchises, and trademarks

Class V: Section 197 intangibles, goodwill and going-concern value

The selling physicians' motivation is usually to allocate as much as possible to the assets that will produce a capital gains tax rather than a tax on ordinary income, which is usually the higher of the two for the physicians.

Definitions of Value

The definition of value must be appropriately applied to the valuation as well as the purpose of the valuation.

Fair Market Value

As defined in the Internal Revenue Service Revenue Ruling 59–60, it is "the amount at which the property would change hands between a willing buyer and a willing seller when the former is not under compulsion to buy and the latter is not under any compulsion to sell, both parties having reasonable knowledge of the relevant facts."

Fair Value

The definition of "fair value" differs from "fair market value" in that it has a legal meaning that addresses what is rightfully fair to award as the value of an asset or entity. It is the amount that will "fairly" compensate a party who has been deprived of a benefit of an asset or an entity. This would be in cases where there is no purchaser or seller, and consequently, no transaction.

Investment Value

This definition of value is best described as the value that can be calculated by injecting the invested capital and influences that the investor had planned for the purchased entity. It is particular to a specific purchaser, a specific seller, and a specific set of business and economic circumstances.

Intrinsic Value

Intrinsic value is often confused with or used synonymously with investment value. Intrinsic value differs in that it is not the representation of just one investor but a cross section of typical investors. This value represents the most likely result of a business's value according to the investors' perceived risks and circumstances inherent in the investment.

Going Concern Value

Going concern value is defined as the assumption that the practice will continue to operate in the future in an ongoing manner essentially the same as on the valuation date. Assets that are valued under the going-concern premise are also referred to as valued based on the assets' "in-use value." (In-use value should not be confused with the premise of "highest and best use.")

Liquidation Value

Liquidation value is the valuation of tangible assets of the practice as a result of the business's forced or voluntary closure. This value is usually the lowest value assigned to the business's assets. They are priced for bargain sales and quick disbursement. The assets may be sold separately or as a lump sum.

Which Is the Most Appropriate Definition of Value for the Engagement?

For example, situations that warrant a liquidation value estimate are those practices that are worth more as a liquidation of fixed asset value than as a going-concern practice. In other words, from a business standpoint, the practice has no future and, consequently, no future earnings stream. The only things left are its fixed assets. This may occur in the case of a solo physician who has prematurely announced his or her retirement to the practice's patients, and whose patients have migrated elsewhere. If the physician has not made plans to recruit a replacement physician, there is no patient base he or she is leaving behind. An incoming physician purchasing this practice would be purchasing nothing but fixed assets. In our experience, we have seen this exact scenario.

In this example, basing a value on history would overstate the value whereas basing the value on the practice's future revenue stream would understate the value if the practice, in fact, had a material fixed asset value and it is likely that it would continue. This exemplifies the point made above that this approach estimates value as of a point in time with no regard for past or future. In this case, this would be an appropriate measurement of value.

One of the biggest differences in the valuation of medical practices that is misunderstood is the difference between the definition of *fair market value* and *investment value*. Too often, medical practice valuations that are performed for the purpose of estimating fair market value are confused with the required (or "desired") return on investment (ROI) of the purchaser. Again, while the purchaser's ROI is important to the purchaser, it has nothing to do with the value of the subject practice. For example, if the purchaser requires a rate of return of 25 percent and the medical practice's risk is 16 percent, then maybe it is not an attractive investment to the purchaser since she desires more than the practice may give her. In this case, if the purchaser valued this practice assuming a 25% risk rate, then the value becomes "investment value" as opposed to "fair market value."

Generally speaking, the risk associated with a practice that is being acquired or merged rests solely with the practice being valued. However, many valuations, especially valuations that are prepared internally by the potential purchaser, are based on factors that are relevant only to the purchaser. In other words, if not for this specific purchaser's set of circumstances, these factors would be irrelevant to the subject practice's value. While certainly, from the purchaser's standpoint, this type of estimation is recommended for prudent investing, it is not inherent in the value of a medical practice until *after* the acquisition has taken place. In most acquisition or merger cases, the value estimate should be based on "fair market value." Therefore, this requirement negates specific investment "synergies" relevant to a given purchaser.

To illustrate this difference in perspective, suppose an investor is considering purchasing 5,000 shares of common stock of a major soft drink manufacturer. The risk associated with this stock may be determined by such factors as the effectiveness of the company's management, sales and marketing efforts, international monetary exchange rates, new product development, competition, market demand, seasonality, and the current commodity price of sugar and corn syrup. The risk associated with the soft drink company's stock has *absolutely nothing* to do with the required rate of return of the investor. It is imperative that the valuer understands this difference— the *wrong risk* can result in the *wrong value.*

Regulatory Issues and the Valuation Process

When performing a medical practice valuation, you must be aware of federal regulatory issues that might impact the valuation process and the final calculation of practice value. The greatest concern you as the valuator should have is what could happen if there is an overvaluation of the medical practice that you are valuing. Depending on the specific reason you are conducting the valuation, an overvaluation might cause someone to get in trouble with the federal government. With this in mind, this chapter will cover three specific regulatory areas: Medicare fraud and abuse, Internal Revenue Service private inurement, and the Stark law.

MEDICARE FRAUD AND ABUSE

As a valuator, you must be aware of Medicare's antikickback statute. This statute makes illegal the payment, offer, or inducement of any remuneration in exchange for patient referrals. For example, a hospital cannot pay a physician money directly in exchange for his or her patient referrals to the hospital. As such, an overvaluation of a medical practice could raise major concerns if a hospital is buying a physician practice because this looks like the hospital might be paying for the doctor's referral patterns. The same can be said of any third party acquiring a physician practice to which the doctor makes patient referrals.

A consistent trend in the health care industry is the development of integrated delivery systems by hospitals. To accomplish this task, hospitals have been acquiring physician practices, resulting in the need for valuation of the practices it is acquiring. The government has specific concerns about integrated delivery systems under the antikickback statute.

The main concern relates to the price paid for the physician practice. Often what the hospital is really interested in is "locking up" the referral patterns of its referring practices. Many hospitals have had to acquire medical practices to eliminate a competitor from trying to buy the same practices. The government also is concerned that the price paid for the practice is really a payment for the future flow of patient business to the hospital. It is obviously illegal to pay a doctor now (i.e., when the practice is purchased) for the flow of referrals in the future. This is why you never see the purchase price allocated to any portion of the future referral stream.

However, a portion of the purchase price is allocated to intangibles, such as goodwill. It is an inflated goodwill or other intangible figure that will catch the eye of the government. So in the case of an overvaluation, the government could try to make the case that the excess payment was in fact in exchange for future patient referrals.

PRIVATE BENEFIT/PRIVATE INUREMENT

This regulatory issue usually applies when a tax-exempt entity acquires a physician practice. The typical example is when a tax-exempt hospital acquires a physician practice. Under federal tax law, no part of a Section 501(c)(3) organization's net earnings may inure to the benefit of any private shareholder or individual. The transaction cannot benefit any specific individual. So if a benefit or inurement is found, a tax-exempt entity could lose its tax-exempt status or be fined.

Spiraling increases in health care costs have spawned innovative solutions to reduce the price, increase the quality, enhance the efficiency, and improve the availability of medical services. The integration of hospitals and physicians into single organizations with the common goal of benefiting the community is part of this movement. This marriage is how integrated delivery systems are formed. Health Care Financing Administration (HCFA) estimates that $175 billion a year is spent on physician services. Thus, hospitals have a monetary incentive to participate in this marriage.

A tax-exempt hospital that purchases a physician practice generally does so in order to provide a charitable service to the community, as well as to obtain the direct and indirect revenues from that business. Direct revenues come from providing outpatient services. The economic return to the hospital from direct revenues of an acquired medical practice may be nominal, however, and direct revenues are often not the only source of anticipated economic return.

Indirect revenues flowing from the referrals of the clinic's patients to the hospital for services often provide significant returns on the acquiring hospital's investment. At any given time, 60 percent of hospital beds could be empty. Thus, an important factor in hospital acquisitions of outpatient facilities such as physician practices is the hospitals' desire to position themselves for referrals of inpatients. The importance of this factor is expected to increase as health care services are increasingly shifted from inpatient to outpatient settings, under the influence of managed care payment systems.

As previously mentioned, federal (and state) laws prohibit payments for referral of Medicare (and Medicaid) patients. For this reason, valuation appraisals of medical practices do not reflect the indirect value of referrals to hospitals.

An organization cannot be organized or operated exclusively for charitable purposes unless it serves a public rather than a private interest. Thus, to meet the requirements of IRC 501(c)(3), an organization must establish that it is not organized or operated for the benefit of private interests. This private benefit prohibition applies to physicians who, either individually or in a medical group, sell their assets to an exempt organization and subsequently perform services for it. Benefits to the physicians must be balanced against benefits to the public in deciding if private benefit is present.

Private inurement generally involves persons who, because of their relationship with an organization, can control or influence its activities. Such persons are sometimes referred to as "insiders." In some circumstances, physicians may be insiders with respect to an organization to which they sell their practices. In that case, the inurement applies in addition to the prohibition on private benefit. The payment of amounts *exceeding fair market value* for the medical practice assets acquired from physicians may thus cause an organization not to qualify for IRC 501(c)(3) status.

In deciding if an organization providing healthcare services qualifies for exemption under IRC 501(c)(3), the Service applies a "facts and circumstances" approach based on Revenue Ruling 69-545, *supra*. An important factor in determining if an organization operates exclusively for the benefit of the community, as opposed to private interests, is whether the organization's acquisition of assets from physicians confers private benefit on, or causes its earnings to inure to, the sellers. If the organization pays more than fair market value, private benefit, and possibly inurement, is present, and as such the organization will most likely not qualify for exemption or be subject to some sort of sanction by the Service.

The Service defines fair market value as the price on which a willing buyer and a willing seller would agree, neither being under any compulsion to buy or sell, and both having reasonable knowledge of the relevant facts (Rev. Rul. 59-60, 1959-1 C.B. 237). Whether the price paid for assets exceeds fair market value may be determined in various ways. It is the exempt organization's burden to establish this fact.

Generally, where the sales transaction involves unrelated parties bargaining at arm's-length, the actual sales price may be assumed to be fair market value. However, when hospitals acquire practices owned by physicians who are on their medical staffs, and who continue to provide services through a new affiliated organization, the existence of arm's-length bargaining may be questionable according to the Internal Revenue Service. In the absence of an arm's-length transaction, the best determinant of fair market value is a *properly performed, unbiased valuation* of the medical practice.

As you can readily see, if the valuation of a medical practice being acquired by a tax exempt entity is overstated, the consequences could be severe. This is why you must be extremely careful when valuing a medical practice when the reason for the valuation is due to an anticipated acquisition, especially one by a hospital entity.

THE STARK LAW

Stark II is a federal statute that became effective January 1, 1995. Like Stark I, it is intended to curb the abuses inherent in physician self-referral arrangements. While the Stark I regulations clarified many issues related to Stark II, Stark II regulations have yet to be issued, so little guidance is available to practicing physicians. Like Stark I, Stark II prohibits physicians who have a financial relationship with an entity from referring their patients to the entity for designated health services.

A financial relationship consists of an ownership or investment interest in the entity or a compensation arrangement with the entity. If the physician does not own any portion of the entity, and does not pay the entity or receive any kind of payment from the entity for the referral or for anything else, there is no financial relationship. A financial relationship can exist between a physician and an entity even if that relationship does not involve designated health services or the Medicare or Medicaid programs. For example, a compensation arrangement is defined in Stark II as, in general, any arrangement involving any remuneration between a physician (or family member) and an entity. This remuneration can involve payments for anything, such as payments for rent, payments for nonmedical types of items or services, or payments for housing or travel expenses. Therefore, the purchase of a practice by an entity and the related payment to the physician or physicians could constitute a financial arrangement.

Section 1877(e)(6) of the Stark II regulations provides that an isolated transaction, such as a onetime sale of property or a practice, is not considered to be a compensation arrangement for purposes of the prohibition on referrals if the following conditions are met:

- The amount of remuneration for the transaction is consistent with fair market value and is not determined, directly or indirectly, in a manner that takes into account the volume or value of referrals by the physician.

- The remuneration is provided under an agreement that would be commercially reasonable even if no referrals were made to the entity.

- The arrangement meets any other requirements the Secretary may impose by regulation as needed to protect against Medicare program or patient abuse.

An "isolated transaction" is defined as one involving a single payment between two or more persons. A transaction that involves long-term or installment payments is not considered an isolated transaction.

Therefore, to comply with the Stark law, the valuator's appraised figure must represent fair market value and the payment of the purchase price cannot be made in installments. Like Medicare fraud and abuse and the Internal Revenue Service's private benefit/inurement statutes, an appraisal that overvalues a medical practice could have severe legal consequences.

Special Issues Pertaining to the Valuation Process

When conducting any medical practice valuation, it is important to identify and analyze certain key factors. All of the factors that will be discussed in this chapter may at some time affect the valuation process and the ultimate determination of fair market value. If these factors are not properly evaluated before and during the valuation process, the end result could be an overstatement or understatement of practice value. The following factors apply to large practices as well as small practices.

GROSS REVENUES

Which Revenue Years to Include in the Valuation

When valuing a medical practice, you will have to determine which years to include in your calculation of excess profits generated by the practice. As such, it is important to keep in mind that what really generates the value of the practice is the revenue stream generated by the practice. It is the revenue stream that generates the "profit" for the practice's owner or owners. This is why it is so important to determine exactly which year or years to include in the valuation, in other words, which financial years represent the true "current" income stream of the medical practice.

Exhibit 2.1 is an example of calculating the profit of a medical

Exhibit 2.1

Profit calculation for a medical practice

	12-31-94	12-31-95	12-31-96
Revenue	9,060,070	9,562,956	10,615,691
Expenses	9,141,209	9,746,376	10,346,688
Net Income	(81,139)	(183,420)	269,003
Reductions:			
Comparable Compensation	2,431,091	2,699,690	2,952,155
Adjustments	2,674	4,878	13,242
Addbacks:			
Actual Owners' Compensation	2,433,901	2,688,605	3,021,432
Service Coding Adjustment			50,000
Retirement Contribution Adjustment			100,000
Excess Earnings	**0**	**0**	**475,038**
Weights	0	0	1

practice. In this example, the valuator would have to decide which year best represents the income stream of the practice. In this particular case, investigation by the valuator finds that doctors had been added to the practice in years 1994 and 1995, as well as doctors having departed during these same years. There were no doctor changes in the 1996 financial year. Based on this and other factors, the valuator determined that 1996 best reflected the true income stream of the practice and, as such, used only 1996 in the calculation of practice value.

If revenue has been declining in the past three years, the valuator will have to decide if he or she should include some of those years in the valuation. For example, a practice might be experiencing a continuing decline in what it gets paid by insurance companies. As a result, earnings have declined over the years. In this case, the valuator might want to consider using only the latest financial figures in the calculation of practice profit. If revenue has been increasing each year, the appraiser might want to take a conservative approach and include the current year and the previous three to four years in the valuation and weight each year from highest (current year) to lowest. Remember these two points:

1. Do not obtain years'-worth of financial figures and automatically assume they are to be included in the ultimate calculation of practice value, because you will need to

2. Decide which year or years best reflect the true earnings stream of the practice.

Onetime Revenues Included in Gross Revenues

Remember that the strength of a medical practice is the income stream it produces. This is what creates true value. As such, you must make sure during the practice valuation that the revenues the practice generates will transfer to a potential buyer or any person or entity taking over the practice. One of the most important issues in a medical practice valuation is this: *never take a revenue stream for granted!* The biggest mistake made by many valuators is that they take the gross collections of the practice and immediately use these numbers to calculate practice value. Most valuators don't even look to see what makes up the practice's revenue stream and decide whether adjustments must be made *before* calculating practice value.

Revenues that would not transfer to a potential buyer or transferee should not be included in the valuation. Why would a buyer pay for something he or she will not receive or get the benefit of? Would you? Of course not. Therefore, these revenues should be removed from the practice's revenue stream before calculating its net profit and then its ultimate value.

Based on our experience, the following are the most common onetime revenues you should try to detect to determine whether they should be removed from the revenue stream; all will be included in the gross collections or revenues shown on the practice's tax return or accounting income statement:

*   *Teaching honorariums.* It is doubtful a buyer or transferee could generate these same revenues.

*   *Special service programs.* One example of this type of revenue is an internist who developed a weight-loss program. The question the valuator should ask is whether anyone who

25

takes over the practice is capable of implementing or taking over the same program. If not, the valuator has to decide if the revenues could be replaced (using the discounted cash flow method) or if they should be removed altogether from the revenue stream.

- *Subsidies.* Always look for subsidies in the income stream. There could be rental subsidies by a third party or possibly subsidies from a hospital from a new doctor income guarantee. If the revenue does not or cannot continue into the future, it should be removed from the income of the practice.

- *Specific services.* During the valuation process, make sure there are no special services that cannot be transferred to a third party. If these revenues cannot be transferred, they should be backed out of practice income. Let's suppose you must value an orthopaedic practice. You find that 50 percent of the income was generated by reviewing workers' compensation medical records. Your first priority must be to determine whether these revenues can be transferred to a third party. The solution: contact the Workers' Compensation Commission to inquire whether these services can be transferred to a third party. If not, these revenues must be removed.

- *Royalties.* These revenues do not usually get transferred and therefore should be removed from the revenue stream.

To determine whether certain revenues should be removed from the practice's gross revenues, you should first review the service frequency report. This report can be produced by the practice's medical billing software system and is the report that usually shows practice production and revenues broken down by individual Current Procedural Terminology (CPT) code. Look to see if any of these revenues are not transferable. In addition, you should review month-end computer-generated reports by specifically looking closely at the "debit adjustments" shown on the report. If the practice is posting these revenues into its medical billing system, it must offset the credit by posting a revenue-based "debit adjustment." Review these categories for onetime or nontransferable revenues. Finally, inquire of practice management and the physician(s) whether there are any revenues that will not or cannot be transferred to a third party. Make sure this portion of the valuation interview process is properly documented.

Missing Revenues

As mentioned above, you should never take a medical practice's gross revenue stream for granted. The valuator must perform a detailed investigation of what makes up this revenue stream and determine whether additional adjustments are warranted. When investigating the income stream, you will also need to look for missing revenues as well as the onetime revenues previously discussed. *As an independent valuator,* it is your objective to include in your valuation process the accurate income stream of the practice. There may be situations where revenues must be added to the gross revenues shown on the tax return or accounting statement.

The following are the three most common situations we have found in the medical practice valuation process that might cause the valuator to make an increase adjustment to the gross revenue figure.

1. Undercoding of Visit Services

The services the doctor or doctors render and how these services are billed to the patient and the patient's insurance company produce a medical practice's gross revenues. The coding of clinical services rendered is the critical link between a medical practice providing the services and getting paid for them. It is common knowledge that physicians do not receive adequate education in medical schools on how to code their services, how to bill their services, and the importance of medical record documentation. This fact alone highlights the need to investigate for missing revenues.

Physicians code their services utilizing a set of five-digit codes referred to as Current Procedural Terminology (CPT), which is copyrighted by the American Medical Association (AMA). Physicians use these codes to bill their services to insurance companies and other third-party payers. These codes cover services from office visits and consultations to brain surgery. Each year, the AMA issues updates to the CPT manual with new additions, deletions, and modifications.

During the valuation process, you should investigate the doctor's or each doctor's (in a group practice) coding of visit services, called evaluation and management services. In our experience, we have found that many doctors do not code their visit services correctly. In most cases, these services are "undercoded," resulting in lost revenues to the practice. The following is a simple example of undercoding:

Sue Mulligan wakes up one morning with severe abdominal pain and calls Dr. Tinsley, a gastroenterologist, for an appointment for that same day. Dr. Tinsley performs a detailed examination of Ms. Mulligan and diagnoses the problem. Since Ms. Mulligan is an established patient, Dr. Tinsley can choose from one of five visit codes to bill this service: 99211 to 99215. Due to the nature of the presenting problem and the type of exam performed by Dr. Tinsley, the code billed would probably be 99213 or even 99214. If Dr. Tinsley bills CPT code 99212, he has undercoded the service.

To identify possible visit undercoding, you will need to obtain a copy of the most recent year-to-date CPT frequency report and the prior 12-month CPT frequency report. If you are experienced in or have a good knowledge of CPT coding, scanning these reports will probably identify an undercoding situation. If not, complete the form in Exhibit 2.2 for each physician. Once this form is completed, do the following:

1. Scan the report to see if the coding distribution makes sense based on the doctor's medical specialty and the type of patients he or she sees (i.e., treats). Some medical specialties treat sicker patients than others (e.g., a critical care pulmonologist versus a family practitioner). For these types of doctors, you would expect to see the distribution weighted toward the higher code numbers.

2. Present the completed form to the administrator, billing personnel, and the doctor. Inquire of them during your interview process whether undercoding is occurring and why.

If you find that visit services have in fact been undercoded, your next decision is to decide whether to make an adjustment to the

Exhibit 2.2
Evaluation and management CPT review

CPT CODE:	TIMES DONE	PERCENTAGE
99201	_____	_____
99202	_____	_____
99203	_____	_____
99204	_____	_____
99205	_____	_____
Total		100%
99211	_____	_____
99212	_____	_____
99213	_____	_____
99214	_____	_____
99215	_____	_____
Total		100%
99221	_____	_____
99222	_____	_____
99223	_____	_____
Total		100%
99231	_____	_____
99232	_____	_____
99233	_____	_____
Total		100%
99241	_____	_____
99242	_____	_____
99243	_____	_____
99244	_____	_____
99245	_____	_____
Total		100%
99251	_____	_____
99252	_____	_____
99253	_____	_____
99254	_____	_____
99255	_____	_____
Total		100%
99291	_____	_____
99292	_____	_____
Total		100%

amount gross revenues reported by the practice. Making increases to the practice revenue stream is often a difficult decision because the valuation does not want to overstate the amount of gross revenues, which then could result in an overstatement of practice value. It is also a difficult decision because the valuation must assess whether such an adjustment is warranted to begin with.

Investment Value or Fair Market Value? Whether or not this type of revenue adjustment is warranted is based on the following issue: *If the adjustment is made, is the valuator then calculating investment value instead of fair market value?* Investment value represents what a medical practice might be worth to a potential investor. As such, investment value represents individual investment requirements and opportunities; it reflects the worth of the practice to a particular investor for his or her own reasons. Investment value is often predicated on the future return to the investor and, as such, investment value is often measured by cash flow since this is where the investor will look for a return on his or her investment.

Therefore, the question is, if you increase practice gross revenues to reflect proper visit coding practices, are you really calculating investment value instead of fair market value? This is because these are "potential" revenues and potential revenues are often evaluated by the investor or any other person or entity interested in the business. For example, a medical practice or any business is attractive to any investor where revenues can be increased over and above past financial performance with very little effort. Since these are investor-type issues, should an independent valuator be involved with them?

We say yes. The objective of a medical practice valuation by an independent valuator is to place a value on the *true income stream of the medical practice.* Missing revenues resulting from the undercoding of services should be included in this income stream because the need to change coding practices is so obvious that any investor or buyer would immediately require this change. In other words, these are not "potential" revenues but real additional revenues that can and will be collected.

However, as a valuator, *you cannot automatically assume these revenues can be produced and collected.* This is why you must have very involved discussions with practice management, billing personnel, and the doctors themselves to determine why the undercoding has taken place. Can the doctors in fact change their coding behavior? This is one of those judgment calls that must be made in every medical practice valuation.

2. Incorrect Coding of Consultative Services

In addition to finding missing revenues resulting from the undercoding of visit services, you might also find missing revenues resulting from not billing consultative services correctly. A doctor (almost always a medical specialist) can bill a consultation instead of a regular office visit if the doctor's clinical opinion is needed by another doctor and the doctor meets all the appropriate CPT guidelines for consultative services. When a consultation occurs in the office, the doctor should bill one of the following CPT codes: 99241–99245; in the hospital: 99251–99255. These codes pay higher than regular office visit codes. Use the coding form shown previously in this chapter to evaluate whether the practice is properly billing for consultative services. You will do the same evaluation as you do for undercoding: determine whether the coding makes sense depending on how the patients are referred to the practice, and make inquiries of management, billing personnel, and the doctor(s).

If incorrect usage of consultation codes has occurred, you should increase practice gross revenues if your investigation determines that these errors can easily be corrected and implemented by the practice. For both undercoding and consultative coding situations, you will have to calculate the amount of missing revenue. This is usually done by multiplying visit encounters by a conservative estimate of average payer reimbursement for each level of service. Average payer reimbursement can be calculated by reviewing actual reimbursements from the practice's major payers or by obtaining an estimate from the billing staff.

3. Overstated Revenues

An independent valuator should also look for overstated revenues as well as missing revenues. If overstated revenues are included in the calculation of practice value, the result is often an overstatement of value. To reiterate, the objective is to determine the real income stream of the practice. There are often three types of overstatement situations: (1) the commitment of fraud and abuse by the practice, (2) utilization abuse by the practice, and (3) upcoding of visit services normally due to a lack of coding education by the doctors.

It will be difficult for you to detect fraud and abuse situations in a medical practice, except in the intentional upcoding of visit services. For example, it would be almost impossible for the valuator to detect the billing of services that were never rendered. This is a classic form of health care fraud. If you are engaged to perform the valuation, make sure your representation letter includes language stating the practice is not aware of any fraud and abuse violations and is currently not under investigation for the same. This representation letter must be executed before releasing the valuation report.

Utilization abuse by a practice is a little easier to detect but is still quite difficult. The objective is to find out if the doctor is somehow "gaming" the health care system by performing services that really might not be necessary. There are surgeons who will perform a surgery on practically anyone who walks in the door or primary care doctors who will order every lab test in the world. This type of behavior can often be found in service areas where the payer mix is mostly comprised of fixed-fee payers, such as Medicare, Medicaid, and managed care plans. Since reimbursement for these payers is declining, some doctors try to make up the difference by increasing the amount of services rendered to the patient.

To detect possible utilization abuse, you will need to review closely the CPT frequency report that was previously mentioned in this chapter. It will be easier to detect utilization abuse in group practices than it will in solo physician practices. Unless the valuator has access to independent utilization data for comparative purposes or has enough health care experience so as to be able to detect possible overutilization situations, the representation letter should contain appropriate language making the practice "represent" that in its opinion it is not overutilizing services. In group practice valuations, take the CPT frequency report and compare each doctor's utilization side by side. Differences in utilization patterns should become obvious, and once detected the issue should be discussed with management, billing personnel, and the doctors themselves.

The process to detect visit upcoding is the same as trying to detect the downcoding of services as discussed earlier in the chapter. Complete the evaluation and management coding worksheet and review it carefully. Based on the doctor's medical specialty and the types of patients he or she sees, does the visit coding distribution make sense? If the distribution of codes leans toward the higher levels of service (e.g., 99204, 99205, 99214, 99215), further investigation will be warranted. Like undercoding, discuss this issue with practice management, billing personnel, and the doctor. If the coding pattern has errors, an adjustment to gross revenues might be warranted.

Like missing revenues, if you detect an overstatement situation, you will need to decide whether to record a reduction adjustment to gross revenues. Failure to do so likely will cause an overstatement of the final calculated practice value. If this type of adjustment is warranted, calculate the amount using the same modeling techniques discussed in the missing revenue portion of this chapter.

OPERATING COSTS

When calculating true net profits for a medical practice, it is important that the appraiser include only reasonable and necessary practice operating expenses in the calculation. The appraiser must identify those costs included in the financial statements and tax returns that exceed standard expense norms. The objectives here are to:

- Look for and identify operating costs whose amounts appear to exceed what would be considered normal for a medical practice.

- Look for and identify personal and other nonoperating costs.

- Look for missing operating costs.

- Make the appropriate adjustments to operating costs so that the appraisal reflects true, normalized expenses for the practice.

As a starting point, many appraisers use surveys, such as the ones produced by the American Medical Association and the Medical Group Management Association, to determine the expense norms. A worksheet is usually prepared comparing actual operating costs to these related survey amounts. If any expense category appears out of line, the appraiser will want to investigate each further for determining whether an adjustment is warranted.

The following is a brief discussion of common medical practice operating cost categories, including what you should look for and what adjustments you might need to make.

Continuing Medical Education (CME)

This expense category is often overstated. Physicians at times take their family members and relatives on CME trips and charge the entire trip to the practice. Some doctors take extravagant education trips. A reasonable CME expense is around $2,500 per physician.

Retirement Plan Contribution

The conservative approach is to assume a buyer of the practice will continue or implement a retirement plan and, as such, there is often no adjustment made to this expense category. This is often the case in the physician industry. In a divorce valuation, obviously you would not make an adjustment because the doctor or doctors with the plan still retain the practice.

But what if you know for a fact the buyer does not and will not implement a retirement plan? In this case you may want to eliminate by adjustment the retirement plan expense in the calculation of excess earnings and in the discounted cash flow calculations. What if you know for a fact the buyer has a different retirement plan than the practice's and, as a result, retirement contributions will either increase or decrease after the purchase? For example, what if the practice has a simplified retirement plan but the buyer has an age-weighted retirement plan? What if a hospital acquires a practice and as a result contributions for practice employees and physicians will decrease? These are common issues in acquisition transactions.

In these situations, it is often recommended not to make an adjustment if it is known that plan contributions will increase or decrease after the acquisition. The fact these expenses may increase or decrease after an acquisition is an economic issue assumed by a buyer and an independent appraiser should not take this into account in the valuation process.

Auto Expense

Look for excess costs here. There could be multiple automobiles on the books of the practice, including those of family members. There could even be a very expensive automobile on the books of the practice, resulting in higher maintenance and operating costs than what is considered the norm.

Salaries

This is an interesting expense category. To assess salary costs, the appraiser will need to obtain a listing of all employees, their job duties, and their salaries. The first step is to check to see if there are any "obvious" employees that are not necessary to the daily operations of the practice. This leads you to look for paid family members and/or relatives. These salary figures and their benefits should be eliminated from each related expense category if the job duty is not necessary. Remember it is the job duty of each employee that drives your analysis. The fact that a wife is employed as the office manager should not make a difference since most practices need an office manager.

The next step is to analyze what each person is paid and has been paid if multiple practice years have been included in the valuation process. An issue that often arises in the valuation process is what you do when a practice has employees who are getting paid way above what is considered the norm for that area or the norm according to salary surveys. Excess compensation often can be tied to employees having long lengths of service at the practice. What about the employee that has been with the practice for 15 years? Some practices have the tendency to give annual salary raises each year and as a result, base compensation at some point will exceed what their counterparts are getting in the marketplace.

In this situation, we believe no adjustment is warranted, *unless* the excess compensation obviously applies to a family member or relative. You cannot and should not increase the net earnings of the practice by adjusting salary expense downward because the physician owner(s) have decided to pay their employees a certain amount. The assumption is that current employees cannot be replaced by an equivalently talented individual at a lower salary. This is just not the case in most practices since hiring competent personnel can be quite difficult.

In addition, the impact of employee changes also has to be considered since this often affects the operations and eventually the cash flow of the practice. For example, it sounds simple to replace a highly paid front desk person with someone of equal ability but at a lower salary. Unless the person who gets hired can demonstrate equal ability, most likely front desk operations can be compromised, which often results in a problem in the billing/collection processes. So again, the main point to be made here is not to assume a highly paid employee can be easily replaced by another person of equal talent at a lower salary. In these situations, the salary cost should not be adjusted downward.

Rental Costs

Review rental costs to make sure the rent being paid is in fact fair market value rent. You want to make sure the practice being valued is not overstating its operating costs by paying in excess of fair market value. This often occurs in the following two situations we have found:

1. The doctor or doctors own the building where the practice operates. In this situation, many times you will find the practice paying in excess of fair market value because the doctors want to convert what would normally be ordinary taxable income (in the form of salary) into passive income (in the form of rental income). This is a common tax technique used by many doctors.

2. The office medical equipment is owned by a trust, which in turn rents the equipment back to the practice. You will see this mainly in solo medical practices but may see it in multiple physician practices as well. This is another common tax technique whereby the trust is usually owned by the doctor and/or the doctor's family members. This is one way cash flow is transferred to family members to pay for other expenses, such as college education.

√ When rental expense exceeds fair market value, you should reduce rental expense to this amount and transfer the difference to physician compensation.

SAME SERVICE UTILIZATION

As mentioned above, one report you will look at during the valuation process is the *CPT Frequency Report.* The issue of service utilization in this context is different from our prior discussion of adjustments to gross revenues. Here we are talking about the following: Can a buyer or transferee perform the same services as the doctor or doctors owning the practice? If not, an adjustment to revenue might be warranted.

This factor will obviously depend on the specific scope of the valuation. In most situations, the doctor will transfer the practice to another doctor or entity that can perform the same services as those indicated on the CPT frequency report. However, there might be cases when this might not occur, as best illustrated by the following example.

A valuator is engaged by a hospital to value a family medical practice consisting of one physician. The reason for the valuation is that the family physician is moving to the East Coast and the hospital is recruiting another family practitioner to buy and take over the practice. When the valuator calculates a profit generated by the practice that is over and above what is a reasonable compensation figure for family practitioners, the valuator finds that profit was over $400,000. When excess profit appears high, the valuator must immediately investigate why this is so. In this instance, the valuator found that practice production was much higher than the average family practice. A review of the practice's CPT frequency report revealed why.

Most family practitioners treat many patients in the office, and order ancillary services such as lab tests and X rays, but most do not perform many procedures. When the CPT frequency report was reviewed, it showed many procedures, such as colonoscopies, endoscopies, and some ear, nose, and throat (ENT) procedures. In reality, this family practitioner was practicing as an internal medicine physician, one who typically performs these types of procedures. So the question presented to the valuator is this: Based on the specific scope of the engagement, can a recruited family practice doctor perform the same services as the practice being valued?

When this was discussed with the hospital administrator and the practicing family physician, the conclusion was that unless the hospital recruited an internist, a recruited family physician most likely would not perform the same procedures. In this situation, based on the specific scope of the engagement (the recruitment of a family practice physician), the procedures would have to be eliminated from the gross revenues of the practice during the valuation process. A failure to do so would have resulted in a large overstatement of practice value and even more importantly, a major problem by whomever purchased the practice because the revenues would automatically decline simply because the same services could not be rendered by the new doctor servicing the practice.

PRODUCTIVITY

How does the valuator handle the situation where the doctor does not work very hard? What if a doctor of a specific medical specialty would normally see 20 to 30 patients in the office every day, but for the practice you are valuing, the doctor or doctors are only seeing 10 to 15 per day? As a valuator, you must find out why this is so. In most cases, you won't make an adjustment to the gross revenues of the practice. Instead, you will evaluate whether productivity can be increased and, if so, this fact would be used in the calculation of practice value using the discounted future cash flow methodology. Under this model, you might increase *future* gross revenues if in fact physician productivity can easily be increased. The ability to increase production will be based on the facts and circumstances of each practice valuation and will also be based on interviews with practice management, billing personnel, and the doctor(s).

A common mistake made by valuators is when the valuator increases productivity based on a particular assumption and there is no provision in the valuation process that the assumption might not occur in the future. This is best illustrated by example:

A valuator is engaged by a 66-year-old otolaryngologist (ENT physician) to place a value on his practice for purposes of selling the practice to another ENT physician or ENT group practice. During the valuation process, it is found the doctor works three days a week and, due to eye surgery two years ago, no longer does surgery. The doctor states that he still treats patients in the office but if the patient needs surgery, he refers them to a fellow ENT physician. This referral pattern has lasted since the eye surgery. The doctor's take-home salary the previous year was $100,000.

Since the $100,000 salary is far below current reasonable compensation for this medical specialty, it appears the practice does not have value beyond book value or possibly even hard asset value. The issue the valuator must address is whether a new ENT physician will be able to pick up as production the surgeries the doctor is now referring out. The valuator will be able to find out the number of surgeries being referred out and should be able to quantify this figure. So how should this figure be incorporated into the valuation and calculation of final practice value?

In this situation, the valuator must first investigate the current referral patterns, both by the practice primary care referring physicians and those by the doctor to the other ENT physician for surgeries. This is the type of situation where an inexperienced valuator may say to himself or herself: "I should increase the gross revenues of the practice because any ENT physician acquiring this practice will be able to keep and perform the surgeries that are now being referred out." This type of thought process is dangerous because obviously there is no guarantee the new doctor can garner the surgeries now being referred out. If not, and an increase in gross revenues is made, there might be a large overstatement of practice value.

In this specific instance, the first step is to determine whether the referrals can be in fact garnered by any new ENT physician stepping into the practice. This is done by analyzing very carefully what surgeries the doctor is currently referring out and the number of them. Next, assess whether the primary care referrals would continue. If a doctor has not been doing surgeries for two years, it is likely that the primary care doctors are referring directly to the surgeon if a person needs surgery. Can these referral patterns be switched to the new doctor? To answer these questions, the valuator might interview the following individuals (each would probably have insight into the referral process): the hospital administrator, the doctor selling the practice, billing personnel, the practice administrator, and possibly even some of the primary care referring physicians.

Assuming the valuator is confident a new doctor can garner the surgeries now being referred out to the other physician, the valuation report must take into account the fact that productivity might not increase as planned. In this specific situation, the valuator will increase surgical productivity using the future discounted cash flow model. Each year this method will show an increase in practice revenues because now the new doctor is able to perform surgeries that are now being referred out. The valuator will of course have to quantify how many surgeries a new ENT physician will be able to perform. But what if the surgical assumption is wrong? The result will be an overstatement of value. This is why the valuator must also increase the capitalization rate for some type of utilization risk; in other words, the valuation takes into account the possibility the number of new surgeries shown in the future discounted cash flow calculation might not occur.

MEDICAL SPECIALTY

The medical specialty or specialties of the practice being valued can have an impact on the valuation process. As part of the valuation, you will need to ask yourself the following question: What could happen now and in the future that could impact the revenues of this particular practice specialty? If external factors affect the income stream, then you as the valuator must take them into account in your valuation. These factors will most likely impact your computation of a capitalization rate or your modeling of future revenues as part of the future discounted cash flow model.

The most obvious external factor is reimbursement. Are there current events occurring that could impact practice reimbursement? Are there potential future events that could impact reimbursement and thus the future income stream of the practice? The following are examples of current events impacting practice reimbursement for a medical specialty:

- Congress enacts changes to the Medicare payment system; as such, Medicare reimbursement is expected to decline 15 percent for medical specialists in the current year. In this situation, you will either have to factor in a "reimbursement risk factor" as part of the capitalization rate or determine the impact on the estimation of future revenues in the future discounted cash flow model. For specialties that treat many Medicare patients, such as cardiology, the impact on the financial model will be greater than for those that do not. In other words, the model might actually show revenues declining in some of the future years.

- A state enacts Medicaid managed care legislation. This means that most of the state's Medicaid recipients will be transferred to managed care plans. The impact of managed care is usually a decline in utilization because the referral process is now managed. As such, you as the valuator may show a small decline in revenues in the future discounted cash flow model for those practices that treat a large number of Medicaid individuals.

These are simple examples of current events that could impact the valuation process. It is important during the practice interview to ask management and the doctors about specific events that are impacting the practice now or in the very near future.

Future events are somewhat harder to predict and therefore harder to "dial in" to the valuation process. Again, a detailed practice interview is critical to finding out this information. A knowledge of the health care industry and its current and future trends is also important. The following are examples of future trends that could impact the valuation process:

- You find out that managed care penetration in the service area has been growing steadily and is predicted to continue to gain marketshare. It is pretty much a given that as managed care grows, practice revenues stagnate or decline because patients are moving to plans that often reimburse less than their prior insurance coverage. Managed care reimbursement often pays less to medical specialists than other insurance plans. If you were valuing a medical specialty in an area where managed care is growing, you would have to assess the impact on either the capitalization rate (reimbursement risk) or the future discounted cash flow model (modeling future revenues).

- Health management organization (HMO) penetration is high in a particular service area. When there is high HMO penetration, there is always the potential of an exclusive single specialty contract arrangement awarded to an Independent Physician Association (IPA) or other delivery system. For example, an HMO might want to carve out its cardiology services by awarding the contract to a group practice in the area. With this knowledge, you would need to do the following as part of your valuation: (a) find out what percentage of the practice is HMO business and break this down by specific HMO (see discussion of payer mix below); (b) if a large portion of the practice's revenues are received from HMO plans and from one or two payers in particular, you might need to find out each HMO's contracting philosophy to make sure the practice is not vulnerable to a carve out situation; (c) find out if there are any competing practices or delivery systems in the area (see discussion of competition below); and (d) determine whether the capitalization rate should be increased for competition risk if you feel the practice and its income stream may be vulnerable in this area.

REFERRAL PATTERNS

If a practice is reliant on referrals from other doctors to generate its production, you then must assess if these referral patterns will continue into the future if the practice is transitioned to another doctor or doctors. When assessing this factor, always keep in mind the particular scope of your valuation. This factor specifically impacts medical specialists because they receive most of their patients by referral from other doctors. Therefore, if you are valuing a medical specialty practice, or even a multispecialty practice that includes medical specialists, the first step is to obtain a copy of the year-to-date and 12-month prior year *Referring Doctor Report*. Almost all medical software billing systems can produce this report. Next, review the report to see where the referrals come from and whether the majority of referrals are concentrated in a small number of doctors. The objective here is to make sure these referrals will continue into the future; if not, the practice's future revenue stream could be at risk and this risk must be included in the valuation if it is applicable.

For example, you find that 80 percent of all of the practice's production is generated from patient referrals from only five doctors. At first blush it would appear the practice might be at risk because if anything happened to one of the five doctors (death or disability for example), future referrals could decline. As such, you might want to include a "referral risk" factor as part of your capitalization rate. In addition, you would probably also want to get the ages of each of these referring doctors. This is important because you want to make sure there is not a risk of one of the doctors retiring and the practice losing her referrals. Referrals could be lost if the doctor retired, her practice was bought by the hospital, and the hospital moved the referrals to other similar specialists who were not as busy.

As stated, the reason (or scope) of the valuation is important. If the reason for the valuation is the sale of the practice, you as the valuator will need to find out who potential buyers might be. This is because you will want to assess whether the purchaser of the practice will be able to maintain the current practice's referral patterns. For example, some referring physicians may not want to immediately refer their patients to a much younger physician unless the older physician assists in the transition for a period of time (see discussion of the transition factor below). Any doubt on the valuator's part of the ability of the practice to maintain the current referral pattern will most likely impact the development of an appropriate capitalization rate. The rate will take into account some sort of "future referral risk."

PAYER MIX

A valuator must always assess the practice's payer mix and determine what impact this payer mix may have on the future income stream of the practice or whether certain risks exist. This is important because from where a practice receives its revenues often defines its financial performance. For example, suppose a practice treats mainly Medicare patients. Knowing this, the valuator could assess the impact on the practice if Medicare payment methodologies and billing rules change.

Exhibit 2.3 is a sample breakdown of a practice's payer mix. The total should equal 100 percent. The figures should be based on production generated, not production collected. "FFS" in the exhibit stands for *fee for service;* the commercial payer class applies to indemnity type of plans. Most medical software billing systems can produce some type of report that can give you an actual or good idea of the practice's payers. If not, ask the administrator or a billing person to give you their best "guesstimate" of the payer mix breakdown; some information is better than none.

The objective here is to see if the practice's production is concentrated in one or a few payers. If the percentage is high for managed care payers, such as Preferred Provider Organizations (PPO)s and HMOs, you will then need to find out if the production is concentrated in a few managed care plans. As stated above, you should then assess the potential impact of changes in the payer's reimbursement payment structure. This could be recent changes or predicted changes in the future.

For example, suppose you find that the majority of the practice's production is concentrated in PPO fee-for-service plans. You then find out the majority of these revenues come from one plan—Blue Cross/Blue Shield. After further investigation, you become aware that Blue Cross has just adopted Medicare's payment methodology to pay its contracted doctors and, as such, reimbursement is

Exhibit 2.3

Payer mix percentage of patients in each insurance class

Medicare	_____ %
Medicaid	_____ %
Champus	_____ %
Workman's Comp.	_____ %
HMO FFS	_____ %
PPO FFS	_____ %
Capitation	_____ %
Blue Cross	_____ %
Commercial	_____ %
Self-Pay	_____ %
	100 %

expected to decline 20 percent. In the valuation, this fact would impact the modeling of future practice revenues in the future discounted cash flow methodology.

If a large portion of practice production is from capitated plans (i.e., the practice receives a fixed dollar amount per patient per month from the payer), you should assess past profitability on the contract or contracts. If profitability has been declining over a number of years, this might impact the future financial figures you place in the future discounted cash flow method. Profitability can be assessed by comparing the capitated payments to the related fee-for-service equivalent for services rendered to these patients. If you can, profitability can be assessed by comparing the total capitation payments received to the costs incurred to render these same services.

Finally, if a large portion of the practice's production is from capitation contracts, you will need to find out if any of these contracts are exclusive arrangements. Since many of the practice's patients are steered to it because of this contracting relationship, you as the valuator must assess the impact on the practice should this contract ever be terminated. While you cannot assume a contracting relationship will ever end, the amount of revenue generated by the relationship might cause you to include some sort of "contract risk" ✓ as part of your capitalization rate.

COMPETITION

As briefly mentioned in the discussion above on referral patterns, competition can impact the future income stream of a medical practice. The valuator should determine if the practice's future income could be affected by current competition and if it is at risk from future competition. Say, for example, that a specialty physician's service area is underserved, and the physician treats most of the patients in the area. If another physician of a similar specialty is recruited into the area, he could take patients (i.e., income) away from the current physician. This would impact either the development of the capitalization rate (i.e., inclusion of a competition risk component) or the modeling of future revenues if it is known that competition will have a future impact (e.g., the valuator knows a doctor of the same medical specialty is already planning to set up a new practice). The following are real-life examples:

- You are engaged to value a pediatric oncology practice. This is the only pediatric oncology practice in a nine-county service area. In this situation, you will have to assess whether a competing practice could be started in the area (i.e., the service area is underserved for this oncology subspecialty). In addition, you will have to make inquiries into whether there are any plans for a doctor of the same specialty to be recruited to the area. This is done through interviews with the practice as well as possibly hospital administrative personnel. If no plans exist but the practice is vulnerable to this type of competition, likely the most conservative approach would be to increase the capitalization rate for some type of future competition risk factor.

- You are asked to value a neurotology practice. This is the only neurotologist in the city. During the valuation, you find the largest ear, nose, and throat group practice in the city has just recruited a neurotologist and the new doctor will start employment in six months. In this situation, you would have to sit down with the doctor whose practice is being valued to assess what impact if any this recruitment will have on the future income of the practice. At this interview you would review with the doctor his referring doctor list to make sure this referral pattern will remain unchanged. If the income stream will or might be impacted, this would impact the future revenues you place in the future discounted cash flow method. If the future impact cannot be quantified but you know there is or could be one, you might just increase the capitalization rate for this competition risk factor.

These two cases are obvious examples of the impact of real or potential competition. However, keep in mind that competition can take many other forms. This is why you, the valuator, should always assess competition risks when you look at the practice's payer mix. After reviewing the payer mix, you need to satisfy yourself that "there is nothing occurring in the service area in the form of competition that could take patients away from the practice." We discussed above the impact of an exclusive capitated contracting relationship. Here are some other examples:

- There is an increase in the number of Medicare senior plan products in the area and the payers are moving these patients into exclusive physician contracting relationships. The practice so far has not been asked to participate in these relationships. The risk here is that the practice may lose some or a majority of its Medicare patients.

- There is a physician practice management company buying primary care practices in the area. Could this impact future referrals to a specialist practice? How would this competition affect other nonacquired primary care practices since the PPMC will be able to add a significant amount of capital to the acquired practices?

- Hospitals are buying physician practices in the service area. For the practice that is being valued, what might be the future effect on the practice's income stream? Referrals could decline or basic competition could make the practice lose patients to the hospital-supported group practice.

REIMBURSEMENT

We have talked at length in this chapter about how certain factors and situations can affect practice reimbursement. Reimbursement is what the practice gets paid for the services it renders to insurance or other third-party-payer insurance plans. Any actual or potential change in physician reimbursement must be accounted for in the valuation. This is because what a doctor gets paid for his or her services obviously has a major impact on the revenues of the practice. If reimbursement declines, practice revenues will decline accordingly. As we have previously discussed, if changes in reimbursement are known, the estimations in the future discounted cash flow method will be impacted. If not, the valuator may want to increase the capitalization rate for a known, but unquantifiable "reimbursement risk."

PRACTICE EFFICIENCIES

This issue applies to those medical practices that are very poor managers of the billing and collection process. How do you value the practice whose majority of accounts receivable are over 90 days old?; whose financial statistics such as the gross collection percentage and the net collection percentage are far below industry standards? In other words, the financial performance of the practice would be much better than that shown on the accounting records if the practice did a better job at its billing and collection process.

We believe this situation cannot and should not impact the valuation process. How a future buyer or anyone taking over the practice might handle the billing and collection process is pure speculation. We do not see how speculation can be handled in the preparation of a valuation report. You cannot reward a practice (by increasing revenues in the valuation report in the future discounted cash flow model) for its failures.

PRACTICE TRANSITION

How a practice is transitioned has a direct impact on the future income stream of the practice. The valuator should determine if the physician selling or transitioning out of the practice will help the new doctor or owner with the transition into the practice. Experience has shown us that if a doctor transitions out of the practice quickly, revenue in the near term has a tendency to decline. This is because patients and referral sources are often left in limbo when a doctor suddenly departs.

Here is a real-life example. A primary care doctor wants to move as soon as possible to Sante Fe, New Mexico. The hospital has decided to recruit a new physician to the practice and assist in the acquisition. The hospital knows that as soon as a new doctor (i.e., buyer) is found, the existing doctor will move to New Mexico. In other words, there will be no transition. In this situation, it is somewhat like "pitching the keys" to a buyer and saying "good luck."

When there is little or no transition, revenue will surely decline in the near term. Without transition, referring doctors will need to get acquainted with the new doctor, which in turn slows the referral process. Patients will not know how to act toward primary care physicians without a transition. The practice is basically asking the patient to make an appointment with a new doctor he or she does not really know much about. Taking all of this into account, it is easy to see why revenue declines in the near term. It is also easy to see why some patients will not return to the practice or why some doctors will not refer to the practice.

If the departing doctor will transition the practice, usually by staying around for at least three to six months, the valuator probably will not make too many adjustments to either the capitalization rate or the future discounted cash flow method. This is because most patients and referrals will continue with the practice. On the other hand, if the departing doctor leaves quickly, the impact will be on the future discounted cash flow model. The valuator should reduce revenues in at least the first year and then slowly increase revenues in years thereafter.

As we have previously mentioned, the reason for the valuation will often impact the valuation process. The impact on transition is equally great, as can be seen by the following real-life examples.

Death of a Physician

Suppose you are asked to value a practice soon after a physician dies. The impact on the valuation will most likely depend on whether the doctor is a medical specialist or a primary care physician, as well as whether the doctor is in solo practice or in a group practice. The most serious impact concerns a solo medical specialist. This person most likely derives most of his revenue by referrals from other doctors. Upon a death, there is no one to transition these referral patterns to. In other words, there is no "market" for the practice. The referring doctors will immediately start to refer their cases to the other doctors in the area of the same medical specialty. Therefore, a practice in this situation will probably have little or no goodwill value, simply because the strength of the income stream (the referral patterns) has moved on. Minimal goodwill value might be derived from those patients the doctor has treated that may be coming back for treatment in the future (i.e., nonreferral encounters).

On the other hand, if the medical specialist is a member of a group practice, and if the group has in it another doctor of the same medical specialty, the impact is lessened. In this situation, practice value will be higher because the referral patterns most likely can be transferred to the remaining doctor or doctors in the group. In other words, revenue will not be lost.

The same applies to a primary care physician in a group practice as long as there is another doctor in the practice of the same medical specialty. But unlike the case of a solo medical specialist, there is probably a greater chance that value could be retained by a solo primary care practice. Most primary care practices do not generate their patients from referrals by other doctors. Most of these patients will make an appointment with the doctor when they feel sick or at the time of their next scheduled checkup. In this situation, a large part of practice goodwill could be retained if the valuator feels or knows that the practice could be transitioned quickly to a third party. If not, value decreases dramatically because the patients needing immediate treatment will find another doctor and those that do not will find out the doctor has passed away and will begin to make plans to find another primary care physician.

So let us look at a few real-life solo practice examples. Suppose you are asked to value the practice of a solo practice general surgeon who has just passed away. As the valuator, your first job is to perform a detailed review of the practice referral patterns and assess whether the referral patterns can be retained in any way. If it is likely that the primary care physicians will immediately start to refer to the other general surgeons in the area, practice value begins to drop immediately and any goodwill value may be lost for good. This is especially true if you are asked to value the practice months after the death has occurred.

A spouse calls you to assist her in the disposition of her deceased husband's obstetrics/gynecology (Ob/Gyn) practice. The death occurred two months ago and she wants to know if there is any value that can be sold to another Ob/Gyn physician. In this situation, you must find out how many of the current obstetric patients know about the death and have found another obstetrician to continue their care. In other words, this portion of the revenue stream has been lost. How many of the patients have actually asked the estate for a copy of their medical records for their new physician? This is another indicator these patients have a new doctor.

On the other hand, the gynecological patients might be retained if a buyer could be found quickly. Many of these patients come back in for an annual physical exam and, as such, might be able to be retained. Gynecologists also receive referrals from other doctors and these referral patterns must be analyzed to assess whether they could be retained somehow. If it can be shown a buyer could be found pretty soon, maybe some practice value could be sold since a portion of the income stream could be retained.

Permanent Disability

The same issues apply here as they do for the death of a physician. However, the only difference is that the disabled doctor might be able to assist in the transition of the practice, if the doctor's practice is a solo practice. The retention of value will obviously depend on whether the practice could be sold to a third party fairly quickly. The longer it takes to transition a practice, the more likely patients and referral patterns will be lost for good. If the practice can be transitioned quickly, and if the disabled doctor can participate in the transition, most likely a greater portion of practice value can be retained.

As the valuator, you must always keep one thing in mind as it applies to this issue of referral sources and how quickly a practice can be transitioned to a third party. There will be times you are asked to value a solo practice and there are other doctors in the service area of the same medical specialty. You may think there is a ready market for the practice and you might then have a tendency to place full or near full value to the practice. This is a common mistake. Why? Simply because in almost all of these situations a competing practice is not going to pay full value for a patient base or a referral pattern that it might get anyway. Would you? We doubt it. This is particularly true of referral-based practices. However, there may be some situations where a competing practice may want to get its hands on the medical charts and try to transition some or all of these patients. In this situation, the competing practice will try to "buy the practice" for chart value but little else.

Terminal Illness

There may be a time when you are asked to value the practice of a doctor who has been diagnosed with a terminal illness. Like death and disability, full value will most likely be retained if the doctor is a member of a group practice and the patients or referral sources can successfully be transitioned to another doctor in the group of the same medical specialty. This is not the case for the solo physician.

As long as the terminal illness has not been disclosed, there is an opportunity to place a full value on the practice. This is because the doctor continues to practice "business as usual" and is able to assist with any transition of the practice. However, as soon as the illness is disclosed or known, practice value begins to deteriorate. When patients or referral sources find out about the illness, they will continue with the doctor as long as the doctor is able to practice. However, as soon as the illness is known, any potential market for the practice begins to dwindle. This is because any doctor or practice wanting to acquire this doctor's practice will use the issue of the illness as leverage in the negotiations. Again, why would you buy something at full value that you are probably going to get anyway once the physician finally quits practicing medicine?

There may be a better opportunity to transition the value of the practice to an outside third party if the party is from out of town (i.e., the hospital recruits a new doctor to buy and take over the practice—this is the scope of the valuation). This is because the impact of the illness on the revenue stream might not be as great and the new doctor may not use this leverage as much in negotiations. So in this situation you must find out if any disclosures of the illness have been made and what impact these disclosures have on the value of the practice. You cannot place full value on a practice if it is known, for example, that the referral patterns have or will be impacted. If you know they will but cannot quantify it, you might want to increase the capitalization rate for this specific risk factor.

CONTRACTING RELATIONSHIPS

The objective here is to find out if a majority of the practice's revenue stream is tied to a contractual relationship. The special issue applies to most hospital-based physicians. Most hospital-based medical practices have a contractual relationship with the hospital where they practice. These contracts do have termination clauses in them. If the contract is ever terminated by the hospital or even by the practice, the revenue stream is lost because the practice has lost access to the patient base. This is a simple concept—if the physician(s) cannot practice in the hospital, they cannot treat patients who need care in the hospital setting.

So a common question is whether goodwill actually exists for a hospital-based medical practice, since all of its revenues are tied to a contractual relationship with the hospital or hospitals where they practice. If goodwill does exist, it is probably minimal for these types of practices. One could make the case that if the practice has held the hospital contract for a long period of time, then it is unlikely the contract would be terminated. Unfortunately, these contracts do get terminated, especially when conflict arises between the practice and the hospital or if the hospital is sold to another health care system. The point to be made here is that, more likely than not, hospital-based practices will have less goodwill than non-hospital-based medical practice. To be conservative, you might want to increase the capitalization rate to account for this significant risk factor.

Finally, keep in mind there might be situations where the practice's patients are received by "referral" but not necessarily from doctors. For example, a large amount of the practice's revenue may come from a joint program with another party (e.g., a vestibular center joint venture with another health care provider). In these situations, assess the contract relationship and determine all external factors that could impact the relationship (e.g., managed care). This can be done during the physician interview process. Like hospital-based physicians, you will want to consider increasing the capitalization rate for the risk that the contract relationship might end in the near future.

SUMMARY

When valuing a medical practice, you will need to assess every one of these special issues. A failure to do so could have a major impact on your final valuation figure. This is arguably one of the most important parts of the valuation process and one where valuators, especially inexperienced ones, usually "stub their toes." Exhibit 2.4 is a checklist of these special issues that you can use during your valuation engagement. As you look at each one and determine its impact or potential impact on the valuation, make sure that each is properly documented in your valuation file.

Exhibit 2.4
Medical practice valuation special issues checklist

Practice name: _____

Prepared by: _____

1. Gross Revenues
    1.1. Determine which year or years should be included in the valuation's calculation of practice profits
        1.1.1. Consider most recent year if it best reflects the practice's true income stream
        1.1.2. If revenues and profits have been increasing each year, consider conservative approach of including each year in valuation and weighting each year
    1.2. Review revenues to determine whether any onetime revenues exist
        1.2.1. Determine if these revenues can be transitioned to a potential buyer
        1.2.2. Determine if these revenues should be removed from the net profit of the practice
        1.2.3. Look specifically for
            1.2.3.1. Honorariums
            1.2.3.2. Medical directorships
            1.2.3.3. Subsidies
            1.2.3.4. Special service or program revenues
            1.2.3.5. Hospital income guarantee payments
    1.3. Determine if there are any missing revenues that should be added to the net profit of the medical practice
        1.3.1. Review the CPT frequency report
        1.3.2. Review practice fee schedule
        1.3.3. Review visit coding patterns
        1.3.4. Review billing for consultative encounters
        1.3.5. Look for utilization abuse
        1.3.6. Look for overcoding situations
2. Operating Costs
    2.1. Look for and identify operating costs whose amounts appear to exceed what would be considered normal for a medical practice
    2.2. Look for and identify personal and other nonoperating costs
        2.2.1. Payroll costs
        2.2.2. Rental costs
        2.2.3. Automobile and travel costs
        2.2.4. Continuing medical education costs
        2.2.5. Miscellaneous costs
    2.3. Look for missing operating costs
        2.3.1. Rental costs
        2.3.2. Employee costs
        2.3.3. Shared costs with another practice
    2.4. Make the appropriate adjustments to operating costs so that the appraisal reflects true, normalized expenses for the practice

Exhibit 2.4
(*Continued*)

3. Same Service Utilization
    3.1. Review CPT frequency report
    3.2. Determine whether a buyer or transferee performs the same services as the doctor or doctors owning the practice
    3.3. If not, determine whether an adjustment to revenue is warranted
        3.3.1. In calculation of current practice profit
        3.3.2. In calculation of future revenues to be included in the discounted cash flow method
4. Physician Productivity
    4.1. Review CPT frequency report and number of patient visits by individual physician
        4.1.1. If productivity appears low, determine the cause
        4.1.2. Assess impact on estimation of future revenues to be included in the discounted cash flow method
    4.2. Determine if situation exists where a buyer can increase productivity (based on past performance) simply by being able to render services the current owner cannot
        4.2.1. Assess impact on estimation of future revenues to be included in the discounted cash flow method
            4.2.1.1. If future revenues are increased, determine if the capitalization rate should be increased to take into account risk that increased productivity may not occur
5. Medical Specialty
    5.1. Assess external factors (current and future) that may impact future income stream of the specific medical specialty (e.g., reimbursement patterns)
        5.1.1. Identify practices that treat
            5.1.1.1. Significant number of Medicare patients
            5.1.1.2. Significant number of managed care patients
    5.2. Determine impact on estimation of future revenues to be included in the discounted cash flow method or if capitalization rate should be increased for the related risk factors
6. Referral Patterns
    6.1. If applicable, obtain and review referring doctor report for current and prior years
    6.2. Determine if same referral patterns will continue into the future and what external factors could impact the referral process
    6.3. Determine impact on estimation of future revenues to be included in the discounted cash flow method or if capitalization rate should be increased for the related risk factors
7. Payer Mix
    7.1. Obtain current practice payer mix
    7.2. Based on payer mix, determine events that could occur in the future that could impact the future income stream of the medical practice (e.g., adoption of the Medicare RBRVS payment system by managed care companies)

Exhibit 2.4

(Continued)

    7.3. Determine impact on estimation of future revenues to be included in the discounted cash flow method or if capitalization rate should be increased for the related risk factors

8.   Competition

    8.1. Determine if the practice's future income could be affected by current competition and if it is at risk from future competition

    8.2. Define identity of the potential competitors

        8.2.1. Hospitals acquiring practices

        8.2.2. Physician practice management companies

        8.2.3. The possibility of another doctor of the same medical specialty establishing a new medical practice in the service area

        8.2.4. Integrated delivery systems that are competing for exclusive managed care contracting relationships

    8.3. Determine impact on estimation of future revenues in the discounted cash flow method or if capitalization rate should be increased for the related risk factors

9.   Reimbursement

    9.1. Determine any actual or potential changes in physician reimbursement

    9.2. Determine impact on estimation of future revenues to be included in the discounted cash flow method or if capitalization rate should be increased for the related risk factors

10. Practice Transition

    10.1. If applicable, determine if the departing doctor will help transition the practice to the acquiring doctor or entity

        10.1.1. Determine impact of following departing events

            10.1.1.1. Death

            10.1.1.2. Disability

            10.1.1.3. Retirement or practice sale

                10.1.1.3.1. Determine if departing doctor will execute a covenant not to compete; if not, assess need to increase capitalization risk for this risk that departing doctor may practice again in the service area

    10.2. If not applicable, determine impact on production and related revenues included in the discounted cash flow method

11. Contracting Relationships

    11.1. Determine if a significant portion of the income stream is received as the result of a specific contractual relationship

        11.1.1. Hospital contract

        11.1.2. Managed care contract

    11.2. Determine how long practice has had contractual relationship

    11.3. If significant relationship exists, assess potential impact on future revenues of the practice

    11.4. If necessary, increase capitalization rate for risk that contract may be terminated and practice will lose related revenues

Beginning the Valuation Process

The valuation process is much more than a simple or random analysis of value; therefore, an understanding of the planning process is essential to successfully starting the project. As with any project that requires experience, judgment, and analytical ability, the planning stages of the process are often as critically important as the use of judgment and the financial assessment of the practice. This chapter deals with the early stages of the valuation engagement and includes discussion on selection of the valuator, the engagement acceptance process, the steps involved in successfully planning the project, and the process of gathering the necessary information. Each of these sections is vitally important to the success of the project. The lack of emphasis in any one area can lead to undesirable results.

The rationale behind the valuation process has been established in the previous chapters. This will be the foundation from which the engagement process begins. While in these early stages of the project, very little is known about the detailed operational and financial characteristics of the practice. Greater experience in the techniques of valuing a medical practice will increase your comfort level and will result in a smoother preplanning of the engagement. It is important to understand that there is no substitute for the judgment and analytical abilities that come with experience in these projects.

How do we define the successful engagement? Is it the determination of a precise number that will be considered correct by all parties? Will the report be so comprehensive and self-contained as to answer all questions of all parties? Likely it will not. In most cases, the goal is to reach an independent and objective conclusion of value for the practice and provide a comprehensive report with sufficient detail to substantiate the analyses, judgment, and conclusions of the valuator.

In the planning stage of the engagement, our objective is to focus on independence, objective judgment, and preliminary analysis to develop a foundation from which reasonable assessment of value may be derived and a comprehensive report prepared.

Understanding the identity and needs of the parties to the engagement is also key to understanding the planning process. For the professional who is engaged to conduct the valuation, the preplanning and planning aspects of the process involve client acceptance, confirming engagement arrangements, planning the calculations and report, gathering the necessary information, and conducting preliminary inquiries. For the prospective users of the report, the process is quite different.

The physician has a vested interest in the successful completion of the project. Whether as a candidate for a buy-in or buy-out, or as a party to an acquisition, divorce, dissolution, or merger transaction, the physician is especially concerned with the economic outcome, often without regard for the details surrounding the value conclusion. Concise information, sufficiently presented in support of the conclusion, is critical, and the valuator must be capable of demonstrating accuracy in the report, as well as an understanding of the nature of the physician's practice.

The hospital administrator deals with the process of selecting an individual or firm to conduct the valuation and determines whether the valuator has the requisite experience level and knowledge of valuation theory and practice to successfully and accurately complete the process. The administrator is concerned with facilitating the process and, because the transaction is usually on a fast track, quite often finds it necessary to prepare an offer to the owners of the target practice before a competing hospital does. The administrator expects a report that is sufficiently detailed and accurate to withstand scrutiny by federal agents or tax examiners, as well as a valuator who can successfully document his judgment and findings and successfully testify in support of his opinion of value. The central focus of the administrator is protection of the hospital and the physician and to make certain that sufficient evidential matter is available to develop a valid foundation for negotiating the transaction with the target physician group.

In the mind of the attorney, the selection of an independent and objective valuator is critically important, as are the skills of the valuator in a possible expert witness role. Although the attorney may have specific objectives in a case, such as in a divorce setting, the attorney recognizes the importance of the objectivity of the independent valuator. The valuator should always be an advocate for his objective and independent opinion of value. To serve as an advocate of either side in litigation is to seriously damage the credibility of the expert witness. Bias has no place in a report on the valuation of a medical practice. Therefore, the attorney and the valuation expert both rely on independence and objectivity, and the attorney expects the valuator to avoid bias or client advocacy.

With these objectives clearly in focus, we can now turn to the specific steps involved in beginning the valuation engagement.

PREPLANNING THE ENGAGEMENT

Assessing the Valuation Need

From the very inception of the proposed or litigated event, whether divorce, dissolution, merger, or practice acquisition, the users of the valuation will recognize the need for this service and will contemplate the use of a provider of this service. At this point, one or more prospective service providers will be contacted to discuss the proposed project and transaction and to communicate the need for the valuation of the medical practice. It is at this moment that the valuator first learns of the details of the transaction and begins to develop a set of facts surrounding the project. These facts will later be useful in submitting a proposal or engagement letter to the attorney, physician, hospital administrator, or other user to secure the valuation engagement.

At this point, the preplanning stages of the engagement are beginning to unfold. The purchaser of the service, whether a physician, attorney, or hospital administrator, has communicated to the valuator the need for the valuation. The valuator has begun to categorize the information from conversations with the prospective client and develop a list of questions to begin the process.

One of the first steps in the preplanning process is engagement acceptance. The practicing certified public accountant (CPA) as a valuator is obligated to assess whether the engagement should be accepted before proceeding with the project. The engagement acceptance steps should include an evaluation of the client and the practice to determine the integrity and competence of the client and management of the practice being valued. This is akin to engagement acceptance procedures conducted before accepting an audit engagement. To the accountant, this process is essential to identifying potential risk areas that might prevent the valuator from rendering an objective opinion of value. This may also help in assessing the risk that the report may be challenged or that the information gathered from the practice lacks credibility.

Independence is likely the most important consideration in the engagement acceptance process. A valuation report that is considered to be biased because of a perceived lack of independence can often be disregarded in court proceedings and can be disastrous to the reputation of the valuator. Of critical importance is a thorough check for conflicts of interest. Whenever the valuator is engaged in connection with an event or transaction involving external use of the report by parties other than the practice being valued, perceived conflicts of interest, whether or not real, can ruin the credibility of the valuator and the valuation conclusions. Therefore, care should be taken to identify any and all possible perceived conflicts of interest and notify the parties involved in the event or transaction.

The objective assessment of the competence and integrity of management should include verbal inquiry designed to highlight any previous problems that signal possible trouble. This would include gaining an understanding of the experience of the individuals in management, discussing the results of any previous valuation engagements, and learning of any conflicts in dealings with previous valuators. As support of management's decision to accept or reject the engagement, the valuator should retain written documentation of these inquiries.

The next phase is to assess the overall risk of the engagement. In nearly all valuation engagements, risk varies depending upon the intended use of the valuation, the expected users of the report, and the nature of the transaction. For example, under increased scrutiny by the Internal Revenue Service and the U.S. Department of Justice, the valuation of a physician's practice for acquisition by a tax-exempt hospital carries with it the risk that federal authorities may scrutinize the transaction and the accompanying valuation report. On the other hand, the valuation may be required as part of divorce proceedings and the valuator may be called upon to serve as an expert witness and testify in support of her conclusions.

Regardless of the needs of the users of the report and the purpose for which the report is written, there will be some element of risk involved. An assessment of the risk should be given a great deal of consideration during this process. A firm lacking experience in the valuation of medical practices may think long and hard before accepting an engagement in which expert testimony will be required or in which IRS or Office of Inspector General (OIG) scrutiny of the report is even remotely possible. As with the acceptance of many types of engagements performed by accounting firms, the CPA must rely on informed judgment before accepting any valuation engagement, especially those involving a greater degree of risk.

After assessment of the risk and needs associated with the prospective valuation engagement, a determination should be made as to the scope of the engagement, the standard of value, the interest being valued, and the nature and intended use of the report.

At this point, questions should be addressed between the valuator and users of the report regarding the overall scope of the engagement. For example, the valuator should inquire as to whether a full-scope engagement will be permitted, or whether the scope of the valuation project will be limited, either in the availability of data for analysis, or in a limitation on the assets being valued. Specific information about any scope limitations should be set forth in detail, and communicated in writing to confirm the terms of the engagement.

Of particular importance when defining the scope of the engagement is the identification of the interest being valued, the standard of value, and the valuation date. Each of these issues should be discussed and confirmed with the client.

What is the interest and property being valued? The valuator must know whether the valuation will involve the determination of value for specific assets or an equity interest. In certain circumstances, only certain assets are to be included in a transaction. For example, we were recently engaged to value specific assets of a medical practice to be sold to a hospital. In this case, the physician was leaving the area, and was simply interested in selling the patient accounts receivable, office and medical equipment, and patient medical records. As a result, the scope of our work was limited to those specific assets, and did not include an opinion of the business enterprise value of the practice.

Is the engagement related to the valuation of a 100 percent interest in the subject practice, or will a smaller, perhaps minority, interest be valued? In this case, the valuator will be computing the value of the applicable interest being valued and, in the case of a minority interest, making a determination of a possible minority interest discount.

What is the applicable standard of value? In a hospital acquisition of a medical practice, fair market value is the standard of value. In divorce and corporate dissolution proceedings in some states, fair value is the standard of value. The valuator must identify the applicable standard of value for the specific proposed transaction or event, given the relevant statutory or judicial precedent, and again confirm in writing.

What is the valuation date? In certain cases, the parties to the proposed transaction or event may establish the date at which the value conclusion is given; however, state law often dictates the applicable date in dissolution and divorce matters.

What is the intended use of the report? Who are the intended users? Which report format will be necessary to convey the facts of the project, along with the assumptions and conclusions of the valuator? In one particular case, we assisted a physician group in identifying the value of the practice for buy/sell purposes. The purpose of the engagement was to advise the physicians on the value of the practice, which would be used as a starting point for negotiating the terms of a buy/sell agreement among themselves. Therefore, a full format report was not required, and our engagement was limited to a preliminary indication of value and a letter report was all that was necessary to communicate the facts, assumptions, and conclusions.

For these reasons, it is imperative that the valuator communicate with the prospective users of the report to determine the scope of the work and the nature of the report. These facts should be solidified prior to the start of work to avoid misunderstanding and wasted effort.

Now we have reached the point at which the terms of the engagement are documented and confirmed by the client. During these preplanning stages of the engagement, the valuator will make an assessment based on the knowledge gained during the interview of the prospective client and will make decisions on valuation methodologies and research required to form an opinion of value. It is in this portion of the engagement that a specific assessment is made of the nature of the practice, including preliminary investigation into the information available to support the engagement and planning for reporting on the value of the practice. Preliminary time and fee budgeting will also be accomplished during the engagement acceptance process, as well as staffing requirements given the nature and timing of the report. During this stage of the engagement, dates will be established for site work and specific tasks assigned to staff members. In Appendix A, we have enclosed a sample time, fee, and expense budget used in the valuation process. It is important to note that from both a legal and ethical standpoint, fees cannot be determined on a contingency basis.

The Engagement Letter

The engagement letter represents written confirmation of the understanding of the terms of the arrangements for conducting the valuation. The engagement letter is prepared by the valuator and includes such information as the nature of the valuation work to be performed, the scope of the services to be provided, staffing, timeframe, and expected fee for completing the project. Often, the engagement letter asks the intended client to sign the letter as documentation of acceptance of these terms. On several occasions, the engagement letter has served to clarify the understanding of the engagement when a misunderstanding has occurred. For example, a client once complained about the fee charged for a valuation engagement, but with a quick reference to the engagement letter, we proved the client's acceptance of the terms of the engagement in which the questioned fee was clearly identified. More serious engagement terms may often be misconstrued and subsequently clarified by the terms of the engagement letter. In an example of a standard of value misunderstanding, the executed engagement letter served as proof of the agreement between the valuator and his client over the use of fair value, rather than fair market value, and preserved what might have been a bitter ending to a valuator/client relationship.

The engagement letter should be addressed to the client or prospective client, to the attention of the highest level of management responsible for oversight and direction of the process. A principal in the valuator should sign the letter. To solidify the terms of the engagement, it is critical that the engagement letter be executed and approved by client management at the earliest possible point in the engagement, so as to set into place the specific terms of the engagement and reduce the likelihood of misunderstanding.

It is extremely important that an engagement letter contain as many specific references as possible to avoid misunderstanding, including specific details about the standard of value, the nature and use of the valuation report, and the assets being valued (i.e., equity interest, business enterprise value, or specific assets). Expected delivery dates are often included in the timing section of the engagement letter, and it is often wise to link the due date of the final product to the date at which the requested information is received. This shifts the risk of delays caused by management of the practice in gathering the information or in scheduling the site visit.

Appendix B provides a sample outline of the terms and conditions to be considered when drafting an engagement letter. Of course, the format of the engagement letter should be based on the specific terms of the engagement and the needs of the client.

REQUESTING PERTINENT DATA

To effectively control the flow of information between the target medical practice and valuator, a listing should be prepared of the information necessary to conduct the engagement. This information should be submitted in as much detail as possible to avoid miscommunication and to provide the target medical practice with a complete list of information that will be needed for the project. To go back to the physician's practice and request additional information long after the process has begun can cast a shadow on the credibility of the valuator. Furthermore, one of the worst possible things to do in a valuation engagement is to request too little information and render an opinion of value based on limited data made available to the valuator. It is for this reason that great care should be taken when developing the information request form. The list should be as complete as possible, yet concise so as to avoid overwhelming the practice with unnecessary "fluff."

In many cases, the information request process may be the first contact between the valuator and the medical practice being valued. In some cases, the attorney, hospital administrator or PPMC management member may serve as a liaison in the process of gathering the information. In other cases, the information request may be sent directly to the physician or administrator of the practice. This is often the most desirable, if circumstances permit, because it allows for direct interaction between the valuator and the staff at the medical practice. Be very careful, however, to avoid disclosing information about a prospective transaction that may be unknown to the staff.

It goes without saying that the information request is a very important phase in the planning process. The valuator should be careful to include as much detail as possible to avoid sending subsequent requests for data. The information requested should be relevant to the valuation and should be readily accessible by the medical practice. Information that is not pertinent to the valuation or that would require several weeks to obtain would certainly delay the process and may not serve the needs of the client. Again, professional judgment should guide the valuator in decisions about the relative pertinence of requested information.

For an example of an information request form, consider the list provided in Appendix C. This is a example of the information request form that we use in most medical practice valuations and includes information that is both pertinent and timely to the operation of the medical practice and to the valuation engagement.

Here are some tips for providing a complete and concise information request:

- Keep the list as concise as possible, while requesting the information that is vitally necessary to perform a thorough valuation.

- Your information request form should include space for the respondent to provide you with detailed information about the practice, including the history of the practice, the ownership, the organizational structure, and data processing systems.

- To provide as much advance notice of the information needed for the valuation, it is not inappropriate to send the information request form along with the engagement letter. Under this scenario, once the engagement is approved, the medical practice may begin the process of pulling together the information requested. It also allows the medical practice to get an understanding of the types of information, which will be required prior to accepting the engagement.

To further explain the process, let's look in greater detail at some of the more common areas of information requested from a medical practice. While not all of this information may be available in the typical medical practice, it is important to consider this data for all practices you encounter. The following information is not intended to be all-inclusive; however, it does provide an explanation of the more common items requested from medical practices in a valuation project.

Articles of Incorporation and By-Laws

Legal documents related to the formation of the medical practice are useful to the valuator in identifying details about the practice. These include the exact name of the medical practice, the date of formation, and the individuals responsible for the formation and governance of the organization. In a corporate setting, the articles of incorporation and the by-laws are commonly requested. In the case of a partnership, the partnership agreement will spell out a number of important details about the medical practice, including partner compensation and formative/dissolution provisions. This document will also provide the date the partnership was created and the partners who were present at that time. In the case of a limited liability company, the limited liability company operating agreement will provide similar information as to that found in partnership agreements and corporate by-laws. This is important in understanding how physicians are compensated and the structure of the entity. This information will also provide specific information about the terms and conditions that are applicable in the event of dissolution of a limited liability company. If the medical practice is a sole proprietorship, there will likely be very little in the form of documentation relative to the formation of the practice. In this case, the documents referred to in this section are generally inapplicable to the practice. Information regarding the formation and history of the practice should be addressed with the physician-owner.

Copies of Other Offers to Buy the Stock or Assets of the Practice

If applicable, obtaining a copy of this data is important to assessing any previous offers to buy the assets or the stock of the practice and will help in testing the conclusion of value. This does not mean that previous offers were representative of fair market value, but it serves as a guideline to follow in consideration of the methodology and the conclusions.

Copies of Corporate Minutes

Corporate minutes are necessary to document the activities of a corporate practice, though not always done properly. Consider the existence of corporate minutes and read them to identify issues about the past, present, or future of the practice and the effects on the valuation.

Lease Agreements

Several types of leases often exist in the physician's practice, including leases for equipment and the rental of clinic space. Requests should be made to obtain copies of all lease agreements currently in effect, including equipment leases, real estate leases, and subleases. The terms of these leases should be summarized for analysis by the valuator to assist in analyzing rent expense or capital expenditures in the financial statements of the practice. The valuator should be familiar with disclosure requirements of leases, to ascertain whether a given lease should be reported as an operating or capital lease. In the case of an operating lease, payments are ordinarily classified as an expense in the financial statements. A capital lease, however, is treated similarly to financing with debt. As is often the case in equipment leasing, the lease agreement may contain a bargain purchase option, which may necessitate classification as a capital lease.

The valuator must be aware of the specific terms of the various lease agreements to allow testing of the proper classification of the leases, and to permit any necessary economic adjustments to properly reflect those leases in the historical and projected financial statements. The valuator should also be aware of the terms upon which the lease is canceled or terminated. Termination of leases should be considered in the prospective financial statements included in the valuation; therefore, the timing of the termination is critical to the assumptions made by the valuator. Often, termination of a lease signals the possibility that a replacement piece must be leased or that working capital will be required to purchase similar equipment at the conclusion of the lease term.

A careful study should also be made of the real estate lease agreements in place in the practice. Escalation clauses in the lease agreements, as well as termination dates, are important to the projection of financial information. The valuator should also consider the space requirements of the practice and evaluate the possibility that additional rent expense may be required at some future date.

Financial Statements and Tax Returns of the Practice

Obtaining financial statements of the practice is one of the most critical phases of the information gathering process. The financial statements of the practice give summary financial information about the income and expenses of the practice and five years of statements should be requested for every medical practice valuation engagement. In Revenue Ruling 59-60, the Internal Revenue Service recommends obtaining five years of financial statements for review during the valuation. As will be discussed in the data entry section of this chapter, financial statements can be found in all types of forms and sizes ranging from highly summarized to overly detailed financial information. It is the job of the valuator to condense this information into a format that is readily available for analysis. It is important that the parties to the valuation become familiar with financial statements of a medical practice and have the ability to analyze the results of operations of the medical practice. An understanding of the specific specialty of the practice and how that specialty impacts the financial statements of the practice is also extremely important.

Consider, for example, the primary care practice that includes a significant amount of equipment and furnishings, including lab and X-ray equipment. This is in stark contrast to the anesthesiology practice in which minimal office facilities are maintained and virtually only office equipment is maintained in the practice. Likewise, an understanding of the expenses of the practice and the expected revenue levels of the physicians in various specialties is also important in properly analyzing the financial statements. Some practices may choose to outsource lab work and may incur significant contract lab fees, whereas other specialties with an in-house lab will have lab supply and depreciation expense. Therefore, it is important to understand the specialty and the nature of the practice to properly analyze the financial statements.

It is also important to obtain five years of tax returns from the practice. This provides several items of information that may be critical to the valuation process. First, the tax return serves as an independent verification of the items of information found in the financial statements, because the accounting firm may expend more resources in verification of items on the practice's tax return. Also, the risk of an IRS audit often results in the exercise of greater care than when internal statements are prepared. It is important to reconcile the tax return information to the financial statement information and inquire about any significant differences between items presented in these pieces of data.

Charges, Collections, and Adjustments

Almost as important to the valuation process as financial statements of the medical practice are the reports on charges, collections, and contractual adjustments during the historical analysis period. Again, it is important to have five years of information on charges, collections, and adjustments. This data facilitates an analysis of physician productivity and the collectibility of patient charges. The information taken from these reports should be analyzed thoroughly to identify trends in the practice, including any changes in individual physician productivity or the rate of collection of patient charges, as well as to identify significant or unusual contractual adjustments.

When analyzing productivity data, a summary should be made of the amounts of charges, collections, and contractual adjustments by individual physicians and this information compared to specialty norms. Specialty data on patient charges can be found in several resources commonly available, including the Medical Group Management Association (MGMA), *Physician Compensation and Production Survey*, and the American Medical Group Association (AMGA) *Medical Group Compensation and Productivity Survey*.

Aged Accounts Receivable Reports

It is the responsibility of the valuator to analyze patient accounts receivable within the practice. Most often in the process, a review of the aged accounts receivable, separated by payer classification, is necessary. Aged accounts receivable reports provide totals or subtotals of patient account balances, separated into aging "buckets" generally consisting of 30-day periods. Exhibit 3.1 shows an example of an aged accounts receivable report, with subtotals by payer.

This data provides significant information about the ability of the practice to effectively manage patient accounts receivable, and is necessary to separately assign value to this asset of the practice.

For example, significant older balances of accounts receivable

Exhibit 3.1

Aged accounts receivable report

Payer Class	Current	30 to 60 Days	60 to 90 Days	Over 90 Days
Medicare	$10,000	$12,000	$11,000	$35,000
Self-Pay	15,000	13,000	14,000	48,000
Commercial	8,000	7,000	9,000	39,000

signal the resistance of the practice to write off older account balances as they become uncollectible. An aging report that includes negative (credit) balances could signal the existence of misposted payments and charges and inaccurate balances in accounts receivable. The accounts receivable aging report also documents management ineffectiveness in the collection of accounts receivable by identifying those areas in which account balances have grown over time.

Also signaled by an accounts receivable aging report is the failure of the practice to properly record contractual adjustments. For example, Medicare accounts receivable balances likely include significant portions of unrecognized contractual adjustments. As payments are received, contractual adjustments should be recorded for the discount. Without proper recording of these contractual adjustments, the Medicare accounts receivable balance will continue to escalate.

There are also advantages to reporting accounts receivable information by physician. Because payer and patient mix and accounts receivable management styles may vary by physician, the characteristics of the aged accounts receivable balances could vary significantly between physicians in the same practice, especially in a multispecialty practice.

In many cases, it may be necessary for the valuator to separately value accounts receivable. This is likely because the engagement terms may require a separate identification of tangible and intangible assets or simply because the engagement may call for a separate valuation of accounts receivable. In either case, the valuator will directly input the aged accounts receivable balances and apply certain procedures to these balances to determine the net realizable or estimated fair market value of this asset.

Aged Accounts Payable Listing

Accounts payable of the practice include those expenses incurred but not yet paid by the practice, and may signal cash flow difficulties or possible liabilities to the purchaser. The valuator should obtain as much information about accounts payable as possible, including an aging of these liabilities as of the valuation date. Although many smaller practices do not operate a computerized accounts payable system, a hand-prepared list may be sufficient to identify possible areas for concern. Once this information is obtained, a review of the data for unusual entries should be made, with follow-up inquiries to identify the nature of the liability.

Supply Inventories

In a medical practice, supply inventories often include inventories of medications and administrative and medical supplies used in the practice. It is a good idea to request a copy of any inventory listings prepared by the practice to evaluate for completeness and accuracy. As with other tangible assets, the valuator may be called upon to specifically value the inventories in the practice. In the case of a valuation of inventories, it may be considered appropriate to simply estimate the value of inventories based on the inventory expense of the practice over a given period of time. For example, the typical practice retains approximately two months' worth of inventories on hand; therefore, an estimate of value of inventories could be obtained by computing the average monthly expense and multiplying by two.

Appraisals of Assets

As with offers to acquire the practice, copies of any appraisals of assets previously made on behalf of the medical practice should be requested. Again, this is a commonsense approach to analyzing other independent appraisals of practice assets, which may not necessarily affect the opinion of the valuator but could provide sufficient information to allow a test of reasonableness.

Budget or Projections

The valuator should seek to obtain copies of budgets or projections for analysis in connection with the projection of financial statements into future periods. These budgets and projections should be reviewed to determine the accuracy with which they are prepared and the similarity between budgeted and actual results. If sound principles are applied in practice projections, the valuator may choose to incorporate this data into her own projections.

Note Agreements

Similar to leases, a review of debt financing agreements is critical to a proper assessment of the value of the practice. Copies of all note agreements should be requested and retained for analysis of the effect of those notes on the current and future operations of the practice. As with leases, the end of the agreement often signals additional cash flow available to the practice or the possible need for additional financing.

Debt is often a complex issue in the valuation of any business. The valuator must understand the differences between debt-free and net-of-debt values and the appropriate standard for the particular situation. For example, in a contemplated asset transaction where debt will be retired by the seller rather than assumed by the purchaser, debt of the practice will have little impact on value. In a divorce, dissolution, or stock sale, debt often has a direct impact on the value of the equity interest being valued.

Tax Bills

Real estate and personal property tax bills can also be a useful tool for the valuator in assessing the reasonableness of value. The appraised value of tangible assets by the taxing authority may represent an independent third-party determination of value and should be requested.

Strategic Plan

In the event that a strategic plan has been developed for the practice, it is imperative to obtain a copy and analyze the contents. By referring to the strategic plan, the reader may learn of the consideration of employment of additional physicians or staff or a change in the over-all direction of the practice. This information may also contain external market analyses and information on internal conflicts within practice.

Fee Schedule

The practice fee schedule represents a listing of the fees charged by the providers for the procedures and services performed in the clinic, hospital, or other facilities, such as nursing homes. The information presented in the fee schedule is usually by Physicians' Current Procedural Terminology (CPT) code, published annually by the American Medical Association. The relative similarity of the practice's fee schedule to the market signals whether the practice is charging a market rate for the services provided to patients, and whether a prudent manager of the practice would make any future changes to patient fees. An unusually high fee schedule also signals the potential for low collection rates and a significant devaluation of accounts receivable through contractual adjustments and bad debts.

Fixed Asset Detail

Fixed asset information requested from the practice should include a description of the equipment owned by the practice, along with the date of acquisition and purchase price. In many cases, a depreciation schedule will suffice for most of the information. Inquiries should be conducted into the useful life of the equipment and whether any equipment has become obsolete or unusable, and consideration given to the possibility that the practice might dispose of or replace certain assets in the equipment listing in the near future. Inquiries should also be made about any nonoperating or personal assets included in the depreciation schedule and adjustments made to remove those assets if necessary.

Quite often, the engagement will call for a value for the practice that includes separate identification of the tangible and intangible assets. In this case, a review should be made of the fixed asset listing and consider a calculation of the values of the fixed assets included in the practice. This will help to determine the tangible value of the practice and will establish a value for IRS disclosure. Consideration should be given as to whether an asset appraiser should conduct this portion of the engagement. Depending upon the nature of the assets and the relative significance to the overall value of the practice, the valuator may elect to outsource this segment of the project to an outside firm specializing in equipment valuation.

Physician Compensation

Another essential item to be requested is the compensation of the physicians in the practice. Physician compensation is one of the key indices in the evaluation of profitability. Physician compensation consists of two components. First, the salary of the physician is considered compensation for the services that the physician renders in the practice, including administrative and patient-related services. The second component of physician compensation is a return on physician's investment in the practice, or a dividend. These components of compensation are usually not separately identified, but are both essential to the value conclusion. Physicians usually base their compensation on the cash available. In the situation of a C corporation, the physicians may often take out enough salary to deplete the net income of the practice so as to avoid paying tax at personal service corporation tax rates. It is for this reason that the compensation paid to a physician is not always reflective of the true value of the physician from an economic standpoint. In many cases, the dividends or return on investment that is paid to the physician is often a considerable amount and can sometimes be as much as the salary compensation itself. Consider the physician who ordinarily would make about $150,000 per year according to published survey reports but because of increased productivity and tremendous goodwill in the practice is compensated at approximately $250,000 per year. The $100,000 difference theoretically represents a return on the physician's investment in the practice, rather than salary compensation.

It is important to analyze the total compensation paid to each physician in each of the years presented in the historical analysis. This analysis will show trends in compensation over time and assist in projecting future physician compensation. This information is also extremely important in comparing physician compensation to published survey reports, which should be compared to each period presented. Comparative reports included in the valuation report that show a comparison of the actual physician compensation to norm levels are very important in communicating to the user of the report how the physician is compensated in relation to norms for that specialty.

Production Reports

Computerized reports on the productivity of physicians in the practice are effective in analyzing the relative output of the physicians in relation to peers in the same specialty. Productivity reports showing the frequency of procedures performed, as well as the charges generated from these services, provide a wealth of information to the valuator. First, the type and dollar volume of procedures and services most often performed by the physician are easily identified and may show trends in the practice that help in assessing future productivity. Second, patient encounter and charge data can be compared to published surveys to identify the productivity of the physician relative to others in the same specialty.

Managed Care Contracts

As more managed care contracts and capitated reimbursement penetrate the practice, the ability of the practice to secure profitable contracts is essential to future successes. The responsibility of the valuator is to obtain information about the contracts held by the practice and determine which significant managed care organizations are not contracting with the practice. Both from the standpoint of risk assessment and the identification of future trends in practice revenues, information is necessary about the length of the contractual relationship and the volume of covered lives. It is also prudent to inquire as to reasons for not contracting with any managed care payers not currently contracted with the practice.

Under capitated contracts, the practice is paid on a per-member-per-month (PMPM) basis. Under each significant contract, inquiries should be made as to the number of members and the PMPM rate. This is especially useful in the projection of future capitated revenues for financial statement purposes.

Referring Physicians

Particularly in specialty practices, relationships with referring physicians are important to the continued stream of patients into the practice. In the case of a surgery practice, for example, referrals from primary care physicians represent the mainstay of patient additions. To have an understanding of the referral patterns into the practice gives insight into the relative risk of operating the specialty practice. Significant changes in the patterns of referring physicians can alter the risk assessment and the projection of future revenues for the practice.

Prior Valuations

The valuator should seek to obtain copies of any previous valuations of the practice to determine the methodology and the values derived and presented in that report. This information can be especially useful in analyzing the methodology planned for the current valuation project. This will also serve as a guide in the projection of future earnings for the practice by review of the projections used in the previous valuation. Other details about the practice can be gleaned from the valuation report of a previous valuator, such as the history and ownership of the practice, as well as changes in physicians and staffing since the previous report. The current valuation engagement should not be expected to involve identical methodology and result in an identical value conclusion. However, it is certainly necessary to understand the differences between the past and current engagements and to be able to communicate those differences to the users of the reports.

Competition

To assess competition risk, the valuator must have an understanding of the current marketplace. To do this, a listing should be requested of the competing doctors in the area or researched with the local medical society or chamber of commerce. This gives some perspective on the competition that is experienced by the practice. Inquiries as to plans for additional physicians in the area are important to understanding whether the practice can continue to produce the same revenues in the future, or whether any marketplace changes will result in the loss of patients.

Employee Listing

The valuator should give substantive attention to the staffing in the practice being valued. This includes requesting a list of the names and positions of each staff member along with the pay rate in which that staff member is compensated. In addition to this, the latest year's annual compensation should be taken from the W-2's issued by the practice. This information will give insight into the reasonableness of staff compensation in the historical financial statements and assist in preparing projected financial statements. It is often appropriate to include in the report the names and positions of the employees, as well as full-time equivalent (FTE) status. This list could include a table listing the individual names and positions and full-time equivalent status of the individual employees, although listing compensation rates in the valuation report is not always common. Staff survey models may be employed in computing the reasonableness of staff compensation and in analyzing the reasonableness of pay rates, with adjustments made to restate staff compensation for any perceived additional FTEs required or any pay rates that are unusual in relation to the market.

As is often the case in many medical practices, physician family members may be employed in the practice. In this case, it is often necessary either to eliminate the payroll of that employee from the financial statements or to adjust the payroll amounts to reflect the current market pay for unrelated individuals in those positions.

Curriculum Vitae

Much can be learned about the educational background and experience of the physicians by reviewing resumes, or curriculum vitae. Our reports typically include details about the education and experience of the physicians, which we believe are important facts in understanding the capabilities of the providers.

Practice Information Questionnaire

In conjunction with the information request form, a questionnaire should also be submitted to the practice for information about the history, background, and other specifics of the practice. Questionnaires used in our valuation practice include detailed questions about the background, operations, service area, management, accounting, and future expectations of the practice. Reproduced in Appendix D is a copy of the typical questionnaire we use in the valuation of a medical practice. Many of the points covered in this questionnaire are important in nearly every medical practice valuation.

For example, we often seek detailed responses from management on the legal structure of the practice. In the event that management is unable to produce copies of legal documents such as by-laws or partnership agreements, answers to our questions about the legal name, date of formation, and the type of entity can provide us with the information we need to better understand the entity. Also important is a thorough historical summary, including the dates and events that are important in the history of the practice. Previous ownership changes or the existence of intellectual property or noncompete covenants are also discussed.

Also asked are questions about nonoperating assets in the practice or any items of obsolete or unusable equipment. It is also important to ask management to describe any items for which management believes the value of the equipment is significantly different than the perceived estimated useful life of the equipment. Other questions to be asked include description of any outstanding litigation in the practice or pending or unasserted claims against the practice. Information about the structure of management in the practice is always important and should be discussed, along with management's plans for physical plant expansion or any change expected in the nature of the practice.

Our form also includes questions concerning the accounting and billing systems in the practice, including whether the practice utilizes computer software and hardware for accounting and billing and what software products are utilized in the practice. Questions related to electronic claims filing are also included in the questionnaire.

Physician perquisites are extremely important in the valuation of the practice, because they identify discretionary expenses and other fringe benefits paid by the practice on behalf of the physicians in addition to their cash compensation. Our questionnaire includes an entire page devoted to the identification of physician perquisites and fringe benefits, as well as unusual and nonrecurring expenses in the practice. Management should be asked to provide detailed information about all such expenses, so that adjustments can be made if appropriate. Often in our valuation of medical practices, we have noticed that physicians are hesitant to identify fringe benefits and other items paid on their behalf. What should be communicated in this case is that the information given to us in the form of perquisites and unusual expenses is in fact not related to operations and should not be included in overhead. Therefore, all such information disclosed in these areas should be considered for adjustment out of overhead, resulting in greater profitability and often a greater value assigned to the practice.

ENGAGEMENT PLANNING

Planning the valuation engagement is a combination of the skills and judgment of the valuator in determining the specific methodology to be employed in determining the conclusion of value and beginning the process of determining the content of the report. Each time a valuation engagement is undertaken, the valuator will critically review the information gathered during the information request process. This will aid in evaluating the adequacy of the information provided and determine the extent to which analysis and judgment may be applied to the financial information to arrive at a conclusion of value. For example, the valuator may receive five years of financial statements from the medical practice. The valuator will critically analyze the financial statements, looking for unusual or nonrecurring expenses or such expenses that may relate to physician fringe benefits or perquisites. The valuator will also compare financial statements and tax returns for obvious discrepancies between methods of accounting for financial and tax purposes. At the same time, analytical reports on the operation of the practice, including reports on charges, adjustments, and collections, will also be analyzed to determine the adequacy of the information presented and to assess whether this information can be summarized in a useful format.

As a specific example, consider the accounts receivable aging report submitted by the practice being valued. In this scenario, we will assume that insurance balances are adequately summarized by payer classification and aged appropriately into aging buckets of current, 30-days, 60-days, 90-days, and so on. Let us assume further that the information on self-pay accounts receivable is not so clearly identified as to the aging of those account balances. In this situation, you should consider the lack of information relative to the aging of self-pay accounts receivable. This requires a decision whether to employ alternative procedures during the site visit to collect more detailed information on self-pay accounts receivable or to utilize some other method of determining the appropriate age of this component of patient accounts receivable.

Or consider another scenario in which the posting of accounts receivable is inadequate and does not provide sufficient detail to conduct the valuation of accounts receivable. In this case, accounts are aged based upon the date of last activity, rather than the date of service. For example, a patient is charged for an office visit in February and does not make a payment on this balance until May. In this scenario, the account balance should be considered 120 days old in June, but because the posting of the payment is considered to be the date upon which the age is calculated, the account reflects a 30-day-old balance. In this scenario, you are presented with the problem of identifying the true aged balance of accounts receivable to sufficiently assess the value of the accounts receivable.

It is during these planning stages of the engagement that the valuator must critically analyze the significant components of financial and operational information presented by the practice being valued and determine the reasonableness, accuracy, and sufficiency of the data presented. Without this analysis, the valuation conclusion could be significantly misstated, yielding disastrous results.

Valuation Working Papers

Because some element of risk is always present in the valuation of a medical practice, clear and concise documentation in support of the assumptions and conclusions reached during the engagement should be maintained in the engagement files. It is critical that the documentation included in the file sufficiently reflect the information presented by the target medical practice and the valuation working papers. These working papers include support for engagement acceptance, research, assumptions made, and conclusions drawn, as well as the detailed calculations supporting the value. It is not uncommon to see multisided files or three-ring binders used to accumulate data for the engagement files. Regardless of filing methods, organization is key to a clear trail of the planning, analysis, and conclusive decisions made during the engagement. Listed below is a sample table of contents for a valuation engagement file.

- Engagement letter
- Correspondence with the client and/or the medical practice
- Research materials
- Information request form
- Financial, tax, and statistical reports
- Legal and organizational documents in the practice
- Detailed working papers supporting the assumptions and calculations made
- The final report
- Planning, working, and reporting checklist

Because of the potential risk for litigation in the valuation of the medical practice, it is important to keep the files as complete as possible while making certain that rough drafts and reviewer's notes are destroyed.

Data Entry

An important first step to the analysis of financial and operational data about the medical practice lies in the process of entering the data supplied by the medical practice. In these early stages of the engagement, the information provided by the medical practice is organized, assimilated, and entered into a format that can be used by the valuator to make the necessary calculations to arrive at the conclusion of value. This includes entry of financial statement information, statistical data about the practice, and other operational information that has been provided by management.

Because spreadsheet programs have become increasingly powerful and capable of performing a significant number of calculations otherwise done manually, we believe tremendous benefit exists from the use of these spreadsheets. Alternatively, a number of programs are available on the market that allow the user to analyze data and prepare reports in an automated and accurate format. There are benefits and disadvantages in the use of either vehicle for entering data and making calculations. For example, spreadsheets are only as good as the formulas entered by the user. An error in a formula can result in incorrect mathematics in the calculations and could yield significantly different results. Spreadsheets are, however, extremely flexible and can be customized to the specific demands of the practice and the individual preferences of the valuator. Prepackaged programs, however, are limited in the format of reports and the use of methodology to those presented in the program. Essentially, what you gain in flexibility, you lose in the additional risk of inaccuracy. Those individuals or firms with substantial spreadsheet experience and controls in place to discover spreadsheet errors are most likely to consider the use of spreadsheets in the valuation process, simply because of the flexibility available. In our practice, a multilayered spreadsheet model is used in all medical practice valuations. The first sheet is used as the input section, into which all basic financial and statistical information of the practice is entered directly. Using formulas to link this input sheet to the other sheets in the spreadsheet program, information is taken from the input screen and disseminated into the various sheets that make up the workbook. A single spreadsheet workbook is used for the entire valuation project, with separate sheets for such methods as discounted cash flow, excess earnings, comparable sales, and so on. This allows the structure of having a single source at which to enter information and likewise allows for flexiblity in specifically customizing the model to the medical practice valuation engagement.

To allow for as much consistency as possible in the data entry section of the spreadsheet, blank spreadsheet templates are often created and used on all engagements. In our practice, we relieve the data entry staff of as much judgment as possible by using a financial statement format that is similar to the MGMA financial statement chart of accounts. This allows the data entry staff member to group medical practice financial statements according to a standardized chart of accounts and to make accurate comparisons of the practice data to statistics taken from survey reports. It is important that the data entry include not only the income and expenses of the practice but the balance sheet information as well. This information should be summarized for all of the financial statement years presented, and should preferably include five years of activity.

Also critical to the input process is the statistical and operational data on the production, collections, and physician compensation taken from the practice. This information is accumulated for as many years as practical, and entered into a summary format that allows analysis of the productivity of the physician and a comparison of productivity and compensation of the physician against established norms.

After entering financial statements and production and compensation information for the practice, it is also necessary to enter such other financial information as office and medical equipment details and aged accounts receivable data. In our practice, we use the input section of the spreadsheet to also enter statistical information from published studies, which can be utilized throughout the report for comparative purposes.

The data entry portion of the valuation project can generally be done by an individual with sufficient spreadsheet skills to navigate successfully through the spreadsheet to the predetermined points at which data is entered. This individual should also have a basic familiarity with financial statement format and have sufficient knowledge to utilize definitions of specific account captions and group information from medical practice financial statements into the format to be used in the valuation calculations and report. For example, in using the MGMA cost report for expense item captions, the data entry staff person should have the ability to refer to the survey questionnaire in the back of the MGMA report to determine the definitions of the specific expense captions and utilize those definitions in grouping the medical practice financial statements.

Likewise, the data entry staff member should have sufficient knowledge of financial statements of medical practices so as to notify the supervisor of problems encountered during the data entry phase. The data entry staff member should also be sufficiently knowledgeable of physician practice statistical reports. Of course, information from computer systems used in medical practices varies widely from one practice to the next, requiring that the staff member possess the skills necessary to disseminate and enter information into the spreadsheet from the format presented by the medical practice.

Upon completion of the data entry phase, the supervising valuator should review the data entry and reconcile to the source documentation. For example, the supervisor should be able to recalculate financial statement net income from the data entry sheets. This review helps ensure that data has been correctly entered and thus serves as a solid foundation from which assumptions and calculations are made by the valuator.

SUMMARY

From first learning of the need for a valuation, the users of the valuation and the prospective service provider are engaged in a process of communication about the practice, the nature of the valuation, and the scope of the project. Preplanning includes determining the standard of value, the date of the valuation, and the property and interest being valued. It is your job as valuator to establish in writing the crucial terms to which you and your client will be bound.

The importance of requesting the right information the first time cannot be underestimated. Because of the risk associated with the valuation engagement and the sheer volume of information to be considered in the process, the information requested should be suffi-cient to allow you to render an opinion of value, but not place undue burdens on the practice to gather the data.

Determining how the data will be accumulated and electroni-cally summarized is the key to efficiency in your valuation practice. The use of the right staff, with the right software or spreadsheet, im-proves the chances for creating a profitable valuation practice.

The Capitalization Rate

If any issue alone can have such a far-reaching impact on a valuation as to totally control the ultimate value conclusion, risk is that issue. Risk is so important, in fact, that a very small change in risk can potentially have a very large impact on value. So critical is the assessment of risk in a valuation that the entire value conclusion potentially hangs in the balance, and the valuator who misses this point and discounts the assessment of risk is in jeopardy of lost credibility, or worse.

The science of valuation is all about investment. What is the investment required to achieve the desired level of future economic benefit? Will the investment result in an acceptable payback period? What is the reasonable expectation of return on investment by a prudent investor?

Because investments come with varying types and amounts of risk, risk often plays a paramount role in the investor's decision-making, and some investments are simply avoided or are in high demand because of their relative risk. This includes the risk that part or all of the invested corpus may be lost or that the investment yield may be inadequate.

Investors demand compensation for assuming risk. The greater the risk, the greater the investor's demand for compensation. This is clearly evident in some of the most common investments found in today's market. For example, consider the person who has $10,000 in surplus funds for investment. This individual investor weighs the various investment options available, including money market accounts, certificates of deposit, mutual funds, and stocks, just to name a few. In the case of the bank money market account, which is highly liquid and secured by the Federal Deposit Insurance Corporation, the investor considers the risk of lost principal to be virtually impossible. Therefore, the demand for investment returns is low; likewise, the interest rate is low.

On the other end of the spectrum in our example is the individual stock investment, which bears the risk that the investor may lose all, or more likely part, of his investment due to market fluctuations. In this case, the investor demands more compensation for the investment in stocks, thus the higher return generally expected by investors in the stock market, whether in the form of dividends or in the appreciation of stock value.

In light of these and many more examples, there is an important correlation between risk and return. The higher the risk assumed by the investor, the greater the expectation for return. Therefore, before making an investment decision, the prudent investor makes an assessment of the risk associated with the potential investment vehicle. From this assessment of risk, the investor develops an expectation of the rate of return.

The assessment of risk in a medical practice valuation is derived directly from this principle, but its application is somewhat different. This chapter will take a close look at the analysis of risk in the development of the capitalization rate and address how the capitalization rate so critically affects the value conclusion.

CAPITALIZATION AND DISCOUNT RATES

In the above example, the investor analyzes the selected investment vehicle and develops an opinion of the risks associated with that investment. From that opinion, the investor determines, at least subconsciously, an expectation of return on the investment. In business valuation, the same formula applies; however, it is applied in reverse.

You as the valuator are charged with determining the value of a medical practice. The central focus of the entire valuation process, regardless of regulatory issues, patient demographics, or financial statement analyses, is to answer the following question: What would be the amount of capital required in an alternative investment, given like risk, to yield the expected future economic benefits to the owner of the subject business? Thus exists the necessary conversion of economic benefits to a value conclusion, as follows:

Value = Economic Benefit ÷ Rate of Return

The capitalization rate represents the expected rate of return on the invested capital of the business. It can be defined simultaneously as both the "risk rate" of a specific investment and the "rate of return" required by a prudent investor, thus:

Value = Economic Benefit ÷ Capitalization Rate

While the capitalization rate is often applicable to a single level of historical, current, or anticipated future earnings, the discount rate involves a forward-looking approach. To add confusion, the term "capitalization rate" is often used synonymously with the term "discount rate." This is often due to a lack of understanding of the differences between these terms, and not because the terms are interchangeable. Consider the following relationship between these two rates:

Capitalization Rate = Discount Rate – Growth

In this calculation, growth relates to the perpetual growth rate expected in the practice, therefore providing the means of computing value based on a series of future earnings via the discount rate. Conversely, the capitalization rate is used to quantify value based on a single level of historical, current, or anticipated future economic benefits.

In applying the discount rate to a stream of expected future economic benefits, the time value of money is especially critical. Because the present-day value of the future stream of economic benefits is less than the total to be received over time, the use of a present value is necessary to convert the future benefits to a current value, thus:

Present Value = Economic Benefit ÷ $(1 + \text{Discount Rate})^{\text{Number of Years}}$

For example, consider the receipt of $100,000, two years from now, with a discount rate of 10 percent:

$$\$100,000 \div (1 + 0.1)^2 = \$82,645$$

This reflects the present value in today's dollars of a $100,000 economic benefit to be received two years from now. Of course, economic benefits from a medical practice are generally expected over a period of time, requiring the discounting of a series of future economic benefits. As the following example demonstrates, a series of future benefits can be discounted by summing the individual present values of each item in the series:

$$(\$50,000 \div (1 + 0.1)^1) + (\$50,000 \div (1 + 0.1)^2) = \$86,777$$

Thus, the same $100,000 economic benefit received equally over a two-year period results in an entirely different value than if received at one time after two years.

With every investment, there is risk. With every medical practice, there is an associated risk, and the risk will be different among even similar practices. Two medical practices next door to each other in the same professional building in the same specialty could have vastly different levels of risk. Therefore, the determination of risk must be specific to the investment being valued.

Who determines the risk associated with the ownership of the medical practice subject to the valuation engagement? In each case, it is the responsibility of the valuator to assess the risk of ownership of the practice, and to convert this assessment into a capitalization rate suitable for converting the expected economic benefit into a value conclusion.

It is very important that the risk rate relate to the specific investment target (i.e., the risk associated with the medical practice being valued, rather than the investor [the purchaser], unless the standard of value is investment value). Also critical to the success of the valuation is that the risk rate be matched to the stream of economic benefits used to measure value. For example, an after-tax capitalization rate would not be applied to a pre-tax earnings stream, nor would a discount rate be applied to historical earnings. Misuse of this matching principle is often the reason for failed valuations.

How then can risk be quantified, particularly given its inherent ambiguity? There are several methods for quantifying risk in the form of a capitalization or discount rate. The most common methods are the *build-up approach,* the *capital asset pricing model,* and the *weighted average cost of capital.* Each will be separately addressed in subsequent sections of this chapter.

Build-Up Approach

The build-up approach is generally preferred for medical practices, because there is relatively little publicly traded company data that is applicable to a closely held medical practice. This method of determining a risk rate is performed just as its name indicates.

Objective Risk Factors

The analysis begins with the determination of each of a series of risk factors used as building blocks to determine aggregate risk. The first of these components is the "risk-free" rate. This is the base from which other components of risk are added to arrive at total risk. Most often, the rate used in determining the risk free rate is the 20- or 30-year U.S. Treasury bond rate. These investments are broadly considered to have virtually no risk, because of backing by the full faith and credit of the U.S. government.

There is not a general consensus in the valuation community as to which one of these two Treasury bond rates is the most appropriate—the 20-year bond or the 30-year bond. The purchaser uses the long-term rate because it attempts to equate the investment with the expected holding period. The Internal Revenue Service, in its *Continuing Education Textbook,* recommends to its agents the use of the 30-year rate, based on the assumption that the relationship between the medical practice and the purchasing entity is anticipated to be a long-term relationship. However, both are widely accepted as appropriate in determining a risk rate under the build-up approach.

The effective date of the rate should be as of the date of the valuation. This is most likely as of the end of a month coinciding with the practice's most recent financial statements. The most available sources for T-bond rates are newspapers, banks, and on-line services.

The *Wall Street Journal* publishes these rates daily as of the prior business day. It often publishes rate trend charts as well.

The next component of risk to be added is the equity risk premium. It represents the difference between the rate of return for a risk-free investment and the rate of return from a long-term stock portfolio. The equity risk premium is published for several different sizes of companies based on annual revenues. Your role is to choose the rate most closely associated with the medical practice being valued. In many cases, the practice being valued will be significantly smaller in annual revenue than the smaller range of companies listed for comparable equity risk premiums.

In our practice and commonplace among valuation firms is the use of the publication *Stocks, Bonds, Bills and Inflation (SBBI)* by Ibbotson Associates to obtain this risk rate. The data reported on by Ibbotson includes the results of market studies of public companies since 1926. This data is updated annually and can be ordered directly from Ibbotson Associates in Chicago. Ibbotson's data is generally accepted in the business valuation industry as a reliable source for this data. Other industry resources, such as Practitioners' Publishing Company (PPC), Fort Worth, Texas, (800) 323-8724 regularly update this information in their publications. For the equity risk premium, we generally utilize the long-horizon expected equity risk premium published by Ibbotson in *SBBI*.

At this point in the build-up approach, you have added together two of the requisite building blocks in the determination of the risk associated with the "investment" in the medical practice. The total yielded thus far theoretically relates to the risk an investor would assume by purchasing large market capitalization stocks. Obviously, this does not equate to the risk of owning a medical practice, and further steps are necessary to continue the build-up process.

The third component to be added is a size risk premium. The size premium published by Ibbotson is based on companies with market capitalization of up to $3.2 billion. In our practice, we generally include the expected microcapitalization equity size premium, which includes companies with total market capitalization of less than $197 million. Of course, an obvious limitation should be considered when using this data: information taken from the size risk premium is applicable to companies with much greater total market capitalization than that of the typical medical practice being valued.

For this reason, the rate achieved at this point cannot reasonably be equated to the relative risk of most medical practices, requiring the consideration of additional risk premia to equate the risk of ownership of the medical practice.

The risk factors used thus far to build up the discount rate are all readily available through published materials. However, this is where the objective part ends and the more difficult, subjective part begins.

Subjective Risk Factors

The additional components of risk that are considered upon reaching this point in the build-up approach are based on the professional judgment and experience of the valuator. These risk components consider the risks of the health care industry and the specific practice being valued. These additional components of risk are ordinarily summarized in a risk category known as Subjective Risk or Specific √ Company Risk. There is no mathematical equation for quantitatively calculating the subjective risk, which is based entirely on the judgment of the valuator.

The consideration of risk in a specific entity requires that a virtually unlimited number of factors be considered in the determination of the subjective risk premium. For just a few of the many factors that are part of the overall subjective risk assumption, consider the following, grouped by major emphasis:

Economic and Industry Risk

- Economic conditions in general and specific to health care
- Health care industry factors

Market Risk

- Competing physicians in the local market
- Referral patterns of referring physicians

Practice Risk

- Accounting and billing systems in place
- Ages and socioeconomic levels of the patients
- Ages of the physicians

- Experience of office management
- Experience and reputation of the physicians
- Internal controls over accounting and billing
- Length of time in practice at the current location
- Overhead of the practice
- Specialties of the physicians

Reimbursement Risk

- Payer mix and expected changes

For each of these and other factors, you should make a determination of the risk associated with each factor, and weigh those factors based on the relative importance of each to the total risk. To guide you in your consideration of the risk factors noted above, consider the following synopses of issues as they relate to medical practices.

Economic and Industry Risk

- Economic conditions in general and specific to health care

The economy plays a major role in the past, present, and future successes of the practice. In understanding the practice and the relationship of the economy to the practice, a great deal of research and inquiry may be necessary. A number of economic factors, including local, regional, and national, impact the practice.

Consider the practice in a small city with a single large industrial employer. Let us assume the employer is a supplier to the automotive industry. Then let us assume that the single largest client of this employer makes a decision to produce these parts in a company-owned factory location, rather than outsourcing the work. Or, because of changes in the Japanese yen, import competition has forced the automaker to downsize production of a specific model. Both of these seriously impact the economic well being of the employer. Layoffs occur, and the practice loses patients as they move away.

Or consider the effects of unchecked growth in the national economy. Inflation ascends to levels not seen since the early 1980s. This represents a national economic situation that could seriously impact the practice in more ways than one. Inflation may put additional pressures on consumers, driving patients to put off elective procedures or routine checkups. These same inflationary factors may also drive the cost of drugs and medical supplies higher, along with labor costs, creating serious financial strains on the practice at the current levels of production.

Further possible would be new forms of regulatory constraints on the health care industry, such as a change by the federal government away from fee-for-service to a global case rate style of reimbursement, in which reimbursement is based on the episode of care, rather than specific services or procedures. A good example of a change from fee-for-service to allowing physicians to assume greater risk is in the Medicare-Plus-Choice program, in which Medicare risk products are offered as an alternative to the previous system.

These are just a few examples of how both local and national economic changes have potentially serious implications for the medical practice, whether or not those economic changes relate specifically to health care. You as the valuator should be ever watchful for marketplace changes that currently affect the practice or could impact the practice in the future.

- Health care industry factors

Industry risk involves those factors that are relevant to the specific industry of the business being valued, and in the case of the medical practice, industry-specific risk factors include the dynamics of managed care in the area before and after the date of valuation. You should ask questions about the likelihood of impact on the practice being valued. Is the practice currently contracting with the managed care companies it should be? If not, why? Are the contracts nearing renewal? Is the practice making a profit from its contracts? Has the practice been able to successfully negotiate its fee schedule or carve out procedures? Do the physicians belong to an independent practice association (IPA)?

Market Risk

- Competing physicians in the local market

Substantive discussion of competition was given in Chapter 2, and you should refer to that section when planning your analysis of subjective risk. Obviously, current or expected competition for the practice will impact your analysis of subjective risk, and should be given your thorough attention during your risk assessment.

• Referral patterns of referring physicians

Specialty practices often rely on referrals from other physicians in generating patient encounters. A specialty practice experiencing changes in referral patterns from physicians will likely be at greater risk than a practice with a stable referral base. Furthermore, the specialty practice (e.g., general surgery practice) that relies on referrals will generally be riskier in this area than a primary care practice with longstanding patient relationships that generate repeat encounters and referrals by patients to family and friends.

Practice Risk. The valuator should give substantive attention to determining the risk associated with the medical practice being valued. What are the significant factors about the practice being valued that an investor would want to know to make an informed decision about the purchase of the practice? These factors may be both positive and negative. Keep in mind that if the purpose of the valuation is to estimate the fair market value of the practice, influences of the purchaser should not be considered.

• Accounting and billing systems in place

Your analysis of subjective risk should include consideration of the accounting and billing systems in place, including both electronic and manual systems. Practices with electronic systems for claims submission generally experience better turnaround time of claims reimbursement and are generally better able to track patient account balances for follow-up collection efforts. Many manual systems (still in place in some practices even today) do not allow for efficient follow-up work on outstanding claims or patient balances.

Your focus should be on how up-to-date the practice is in its technology related to billing and accounting. Of course, in a sale or purchase, the prudent buyer of the practice may institute changes to improve the current performance of the practice in this area; however, your concerns about the inability of current management to implement necessary systems (rather than the possibility of changes by new owners) should weigh in your judgment of the risk relative to this practice.

- Ages and socioeconomic levels of the patients

How old is the patient base? Does the practice cater to middle-class patients or to Medicare patients? These questions tell you a lot about the demographics of the practice and are effective in answering questions about the longevity of the patient base and the potential exposure of the practice to changes in reimbursement. Of course, in a primary care practice, a longstanding patient base is favorable to the continued success of the practice; however, an aging patient base may signal a need to market the practice to younger patients.

- Ages of the physicians

Ages of the physicians also tell us much about the going concern of the practice. For example, consider the practice of the physician nearing retirement. In a proposed sale of a family practice to a nearby hospital, you are advised of the age of the physician. Through inquiry, you determine that the physician plans to retire soon after selling the practice. Your risk assessment should include consideration of the length of time in which the physician will remain with the practice and whether the doctor will remain to assist in the transition of the practice to the successor physician. Not only will this assist you in the assessment of risk, but the inquiries you make in this area will guide you in your projections of future economic benefits of the practice.

- Experience of office management

How well does the office manager perform his or her duties? Is an effective system in place for hiring competent staff and providing adequate training of all disciplines within the office? Is the administrator experienced in managing a medical practice? All of these questions impact your assessment of management competence. Given the current compliance environment in health care, an inexperienced management and office staff team might not prevent billing errors or fraudulent activity.

- Experience and reputation of the physicians

Experience of the physicians in both service to patients and management of the medical practice can represent a strong indicator of the potential for continued success of the existing practice. On the other hand, new physicians may lack the practical experience of building a practice and a business, which may increase the risk that the practice may not successfully continue in the coming years. Of course, it is prudent to obtain and review a copy of each physician's curriculum vita (CV) for experience in medicine and in the current practice. It is also advisable to interview the physicians on their qualifications to gain an understanding about any special areas of expertise, technologically advanced procedures and equipment, or participation in clinical trials or drug studies.

Reputation is also important. One example of this is a physician that goes off-site one-half day per week to treat indigent patients for free. From an investor's perspective, this physician clearly has an opportunity to increase revenue by charging these patients or discontinuing this activity and replacing it with regular in-office treatment of patients covered by insurance. However, in assessing the risk of the practice, a large part of the risk is directly associated with the physician. In this case, it may be that the physician has a very respectable reputation in the community because of her generosity with her professional time, and is not only well-respected within the medical community, but in the public eye as well.

- Internal controls over accounting and billing

As with the electronic accounting and billing systems, a comprehensive set of internal controls over the billing, cash receipts, and cash disbursements functions demonstrate the ability of management to successfully operate the practice with a lessened risk of impropriety and material errors. In contrast, a small practice with very little segregation of these duties is at greater risk for abusive activity or mistakes. A thorough inquiry of management into the control systems in place will help answer your questions about how well the practice controls the flow of claims and payments.

- Length of time in practice at the current location

The longstanding presence of the practice in the area is a good indicator of stability. Patients who have been coming to the practice in the same location for a number of years are more likely to continue. This translates into a stable patient base and greater stability for the practice than for one undergoing changes in its physicians and locations.

• Overhead of the practice

The ability of the practice to manage its overhead is also an indicator of the relative risk that an investor might assume in this practice. Again related to the experience and effectiveness of management, overhead control is essential to success in periods of declining reimbursement. The practice manager who can effectively control overhead not only brings value to the practice through maximizing cash flows, but lowers the risk of investing in the practice by demonstrating good cost control management skills.

• Specialties of the physicians

As we have discussed in Chapter 2 and in the above comments related to the subjective risk premium, the specialty of the practice plays an important role in the assessment of risk. Primary care practices are generally less risky in terms of patient referrals and reimbursement risk, although usually less capable of generating significant economic benefit equal to most specialty practices. Your consideration of the specialty of the physicians in the practice should always include a comparison against published norms to assess the relative success of the practice in terms of productivity, cost control, and physician compensation.

Reimbursement Risk. This risk can be considered as part of managed care risk and practice management risk, but when assessing value based on a practice's future income, you must closely look at the practice's ability to create revenue within its own parameters. Does the practice have a large percentage of its patient base covered by one payer? What are the current reimbursement situations with the practice's top payers?

• Payer mix and expected changes

As a subset of patient demographics, payer mix plays an important role in the assessment of risk in a medical practice. A high Medicare- or Medicaid-based practice is often subjected to the risk of declining reimbursement. A patient base with higher commercial focus may have enjoyed full fee-for-service reimbursement for years, but is now faced with increasing capitated contracts or losing patients to health plans with which the practice is not contracting. Chapter 2 discusses payer mix and reimbursement in detail, and should be referred to when analyzing payer mix and any changes the practice may be expecting.

For an example of how reimbursement risk affects your subjective risk assessment, consider federal legislation that changes reimbursement for specialists. Consider the Balanced Budget Act of 1997, in which the *Resource Based Relative Value Scale (RBRVS)* is changed by Congress, resulting in a shift of billions of health care dollars away from specialists and to primary care physicians. When valuing a specialty practice, your consideration of subjective risk should include the risk that specialists with a significant Medicare patient base will be negatively affected by this change and others like it.

Concluding the Build-Up Approach

Regardless of the factors you choose to consider in your subjective risk assessment, your assumptions should be supported by such data as financial analysis, comparisons to industry standards, physician and management representations, managed care penetration, and so on. We have seen examples in which valuators create a spreadsheet or use software to develop the subjective risk premium. In these cases, several factors are given a value, say between 1 and 10, and a weight assigned to each. Sometimes, these are included in the valuator's report. If you decide to use an electronic aid for assessing the subjective risk premium, our suggestion is to make certain that factors specific to the risk of a medical practice are addressed, such as several of the factors mentioned above.

The result of combining the objective and subjective building blocks of this approach yields a discount rate for the practice. Exhibit 4.1 is an example of the use of this approach. According to the IRS,

Exhibit 4.1

Medical practice discount rate

Risk-free rate	6.2
Equity risk premium	7.5
Small stock risk premium	3.5
Subjective risk premium	2.0
Total (Discount Rate)	19.2

the average discount rates used in medical practice valuations that were reviewed during 1994 and 1995 were between 16 percent and 21 percent.

CAPM Approach

The capital asset pricing model (CAPM) approach is similar to the build-up approach with one significant difference: the use of a beta value. This approach employs the use of a build-up approach, with equity risk adjusted by the beta factor to determine the investment's risk, thus:

Discount Rate = Risk Free Rate + (Equity Risk Premium × Beta) + Size Risk Premium + Subjective Risk Premium

Beta values are published and can be found in such publications as *ValueLine* and *Compustat.* A beta value of 1.0 is equivalent to market risk and generally yields the same result as the build-up approach example noted above. A beta value less than 1.0 means that the investment is less risky than the prevailing market, whereas a beta value of more than 1.0 translates to a riskier investment than market risk. According to the Internal Revenue Service's *Continuing Education Textbook,* medical practice valuations that were reviewed during 1994 and 1995 had typically included beta factors that ranged from 1.1 to 1.4. The IRS recommends that when using the CAPM approach in a medical practice valuation, a lack of marketability discount should be used. This is because medical practices are less marketable than many other investments and should be valued lower than a publicly traded company. The discount for lack of marketability will be further discussed in Chapter 7.

Weighted Average Cost of Capital

The weighted average cost of capital (WACC) is one of the methods used to determine the discount rate when using the discounted cash flow method. This method relies on the combination of two methods to arrive at the WACC. These two calculations represent the equity and debt portions of WACC. Consider the following example of a WACC calculation:

$$\textbf{WACC = (Cost of Debt} \times \textbf{Debt Proportion) + (Cost of Equity} \times \textbf{Equity Proportion)}$$

The cost of debt portion equals the borrowing rate generally applicable to the practice. The cost of equity portion of the WACC method equals risk-free rate, plus market equity and small stock risk premiums, plus the subjective risk factor. The tax rate used should be the federal, state, and local rates applicable to the practice.

For an example of the application of the above formula, consider the facts in Exhibit 4.2. The cost of debt (borrowing) is 9 percent, the cost of equity is 19.2 percent from the build-up example referred to above, equity and debt make up 75 and 25 percent, respectively, of the market capital structure, and the tax rate is 40 percent. In this case, the sum of the weighted debt and equity costs are added together, yielding a WACC of 15.75 percent.

The equity and debt portions of this calculation should generally represent market weights, as opposed to the actual debt structure of the practice, particularly if a controlling interest is being valued. It is recommended that the multiple iterations of the calculation be performed until the weights are representative of prevailing market. Alternatively, published market data generally representative of the medical practice market may be used as a source for assessing the market debt structure. One source of specific industry medians for debt and equity of medical practices is published in the *Cost Survey* by the Medical Group Management

Exhibit 4.2
Market Capital Structure and Tax Rate

Debt		Equity	
9.0	Cost of debt	19.2	Cost of equity
× .60	1 minus tax rate		
5.40	After tax debt cost		
.25	Debt proportion	.75	Equity proportion
1.35	Weighted cost	14.40	Weighted cost

Association (MGMA). This survey report includes data for several of the most common medical specialties and is compiled and published annually.

If the interest being valued is a minority interest, the practice's debt structure should be used under the theory that the minority owner does not possess the power to significantly influence the debt structure. If investment value is the goal, the practice's debt structure is irrelevant and the investor's debt/equity structure should be used.

SUMMARY

In summary, if fair market value is being estimated, the approaches referred to above are generally the most appropriate for determining the applicable risk or discount rate. If investment value is being estimated, typically the WACC method is most appropriate. Also, it is appropriate to use specific risk characteristics of the investor's required rate of return.

As you perform the valuation, you will gather the necessary information with which to assess risk. This is typically one of the last tasks performed during the valuation process because it requires going through the entire mental process before an assessment of risk can be made. Additionally, this process allows you to put into perspective the importance of each aspect leading to risk. Sometimes, factors that may seem very significant at the beginning of a valuation may become less so as the process continues. It may be that there are reasonable explanations for factors singled out in the early stages of the project. And sometimes, just the opposite occurs. Facts and circumstances tentatively identified as red flags at first should be highlighted pending further explanation. As the valuation process unfolds, these factors act as "pieces of the puzzle" to assist in developing an opinion of value based on your assessment of the practice as a safe or risky investment.

Valuation Methods

In determining the value of a medical practice, we have already discussed several important aspects of the process. First, the definition of value must be determined by taking into consideration the purpose of the valuation. Then, information and data must be gathered for use in making judgments that help determine the value. In gathering much of the information, the valuator must understand the different methods of valuing the practice in order to obtain the right kind of information.

Depending on the purpose of the valuation, there may be one method or more than one method used to determine the value. Typically, the valuation will need to be performed using more than one method. The valuation determination will be considered under three different approaches. These three approaches are the *income approach*, *market approach*, and *cost (or asset) approach*. Each of these three should be considered. And if one or more of these approaches is not used the valuator should document the reasons.

The valuation community has a number of sources for use as guidelines in performing valuations. One of the oldest and most prevalent is Revenue Ruling 59-60. The original purpose of this ruling in 1959 was to provide guidance in the valuation of closely held corporations for estate and gift tax purposes. It is also to be used as a guideline in the valuation of closely held businesses for which there is little or no market comparison data. Revenue Ruling 59-60 laid the foundation by which valuations are performed today.

Since medical practices are typically closely held, many practices are incorporated, and market comparison data for medical practice transactions is very limited, the valuation community relies on this ruling for guidance. Familiarity with this ruling is one of the first things to which a valuator is introduced in the educational curriculum offered in the study of business valuation services. If you are interviewing valuators to engage their valuation services, inquire as to their understanding of Revenue Ruling 59-60 as a means of testing their depth of valuation expertise.

Revenue Ruling 59-60 advises the valuator to consider the following eight factors in the valuation of closely held corporations for their effect on the value.

1. Nature and history of the business

2. Economic and industry outlook of the business

3. Book value and financial condition

4. Earning capacity

5. Dividend-paying capacity

6. Goodwill and intangible value

7. Stock sales and size of stock to be valued

8. Market comparison price of similar stock

A copy of Revenue Ruling 59-60 has been included in Appendix E.

THREE APPROACHES TO VALUATION

Income Approach

Simply stated, the income approach measures the practice's ability to generate income. By using this method, if the practice cannot generate a bottom line, it has no value. This being the case, the only value would be that of the practice's tangible assets (i.e., furniture, fixtures, equipment, supplies, and accounts receivable).

There are two methods of obtaining value under the income approach. One is by discounting the future income and the other is by capitalizing the income. The two methods used under the income approach are, appropriately named, the *discounted cash flow (or net earnings) method* and the *capitalization of earnings method*.

Additionally, depending on the literature you may read, the *excess earnings method* may be categorized as an income approach method or a cost (asset) approach method. Arguably, it is an income approach method because it measures the value of income (albeit historical income). The argument for this method being an asset approach method is defined by the fact that it is a measurement of the fair market value of tangible assets plus the earnings capacity to retain earnings as of the effective date of the valuation. This method is discussed below under the cost (asset) approach section.

Market Approach

This approach measures the value of a practice by comparing it to the value of similar practices. This is accomplished by using comparative transaction data much like the manner in which real estate is valued. It is based on the "going prices" for similar investments. Also used are financial and other comparable statistics with which to compare the subject practice.

Most medical practice valuations will be performed on closely held practices. When using public company data as a comparison basis, the assumption is that the practice being valued is a "marketable" business, in other words, actively sought and traded on the market. In this case, adjustments to the valuation of the closely held practice may be necessary for "lack of marketability." The risk associated with purchasing a less marketable investment is higher. Refer to Chapter 4 for discussion of risk rates.

Cost (or Asset) Approach

The cost approach (asset approach) relies on the practice's current balance sheet as of a specific point in time (the valuation date). The limitation with this approach is that it does not directly take into account the long-term history of the practice or the practice's outlook for generating a future profit.

This method would be effective if the practice was a startup practice or if the practice had no stable history of earnings. This method would suffice for a business that has little or no intangible asset value. Therefore, this method may not be the most appropriate for valuing a medical practice. Many medical practice valuations result in significant portions of the value being intangible asset value.

There are two main methods for estimating value under the cost approach. One is a balance sheet method that takes into account each item on the balance sheet and assigns each a value. The other is the *excess earnings method,* which takes into account the practice's historical earnings to determine a value for intangible assets. This intangible value is added to the tangible asset value to arrive at a total value for the practice.

COMMON VALUATION METHODS

Income Approach

Discounted Cash Flow Method

The discounted cash flow (DCF) method values the practice based on the available income after operating expenses and owner compensation with adjustments made to determine the practice's future available net cash. A variation of discounted cash flow is the discounted net earnings method, which determines value based on the practice's future net earnings capacity after operating expenses and owner compensation. Both variations are calculated in the same manner. For purposes of this discussion, we will present details on performing the discounted cash flow method. We will then discuss the differences of performing the discounted net earnings method.

The mechanics of the discounted cash flow method are to analyze the practice's previous financial statements, current market and industry forces, patients, operations, and management, and apply assumptions with which to calculate a go-forward financial picture for a number of years to determine net available cash. A present value factor is then applied to the available cash to bring it back to today's value. The sum of this "discounted available cash" is the value of the practice.

The steps to calculating the value of a medical practice using the discounted cash flow method are described below. Keep in mind from previous chapters that the valuator has at this point already gathered the required data, conducted an on-site inspection and assessment, and conducted interviews with the subject practice's physicians and key personnel.

Step 1. Normalizing the Financial Statements. The discounted cash flow method is based on the practice's most current tax year or most current twelve months of activity. This period serves as a "base year" from which the future years are projected. However, before future projections are made, it may be necessary to make certain adjustments to the Base Year's financial statements to "bring them into line" of representing a "normal" year for the practice. This is why this process is called "normalizing the financials."

As well, the financial statements should be normalized so that the subject practice can be fairly compared to the operations and earnings of similar practices, both closely held and publicly traded.

In normalizing the practice's financial statements, adjustments would need to be made for nonrecurring, unusual, and extraordinary revenue and expense items. Examples of these would be physician perquisites such as automobile lease payments and above-average education and travel expenditures. Another example is an adjustment to convert depreciation from "book basis" to "tax basis."

Included in the normalization would also be items that are not assumed to transfer to another party through the transaction. Examples of such revenue items would be medical directorship income, diagnostic test reading fees, and rental and interest income unrelated to the operations of the practice. Examples of such expense items would be health insurance coverage for dependents, physicians' life and disability insurance, salaries of family members, country club and health club dues, charitable contributions, cellular phones, and Internet connections.

Below are listed the typical revenue and expense items that should be considered when normalizing the financial statements for purposes of building the Base Year of the DCF model.

Revenue Items

- Capitation Withhold Bonuses
- Change in Major Payers' Fee Structures
- Medical Directorships
- Unrelated Rental Income
- Unrelated Interest Income
- Honorariums

Expense Items

- Rent
- Malpractice
- Staff Salaries and Bonuses
- Depreciation and Amortization
- Taxes and Penalties
- Business Gifts
- Interest
- Physician Compensation
- Physician Benefits
  - Retirement Plan
  - Automobiles
  - Cellular Phones
  - Health Insurance
  - Life and Disability Insurance
  - Continuing Medical Education
  - Travel, Meals, and Entertainment

Once this step is completed, the valuator can then begin to project the financial picture from the Base Year. The valuator should set up a grid or spreadsheet format to itemize and calculate the revenue and expenses for future years. Typically, the DCF is calculated for the next five years followed by a terminal value calculation.

An example of normalized financial statements has been included with the Sample Report located in Chapter 8.

Step 2. Projections of Revenue Items. This step is one of the most critical steps in the DCF process. It is imperative that the practice's sources of revenue (past, present, and future) are analyzed to best determine what the practice can expect over the next few years. Of course, no one has a crystal ball. However, by taking into consideration all the relevant facts as of the valuation date, realistic expectations should be projected.

The practice's managed care contracts, patient demographics, patient payer categories, physician and provider productivity, and managed care and economic market should be analyzed to determine their impact on the future revenue stream of the practice.

It is recommended that separate line items be projected for the practice's top managed care plans and payer categories such as private pay patients, Medicare, and Medicaid.

Other influences that the valuator must consider is the inflation rate in the subject practice's geographic area. Also, the valuator must consider changes that have occurred in the practice that may have a significant impact on the revenue projections such as new or terminated managed care contracts, substantial changes to fees, additions or terminations of providers, and scheduling changes of provider office hours.

One side issue to Step 2 is the appropriate handling of accounts receivable (A/R). In the DCF model, it is assumed that the purchaser or the newly formed entity is assuming the practice's accounts receivable as part of the deal. The DCF model lays out future revenues and a portion of those revenues is the collection of accounts receivable that are already on the books. This assumes the cash basis method of accounting for the practice.

However, if the case is such that the accounts receivable will not be transferred to another rightful owner as part of the deal, then its value should be taken out of the equation. The manner in which this should be done is under the same philosophy as stated above. If it is included in the revenues projected, then subtract the value of accounts receivable from projected revenues.

By subtracting the value of accounts receivable from projected revenues, this assumes that the seller will continue to collect that amount after the transaction. In essence, the new entity (purchaser) will be starting over at ground zero in providing services. The accounts receivable balance of the new entity will begin at zero, as well.

Also, subtracting the value of the accounts receivable from the revenue items does not penalize the seller's value by "charging" him with the income tax associated with it. The seller is going to pay tax on the accounts receivable when he collects it anyway. An example of this situation is presented in Exhibits 5.1A and 5.1B.

What we typically see in this situation is that the value of accounts receivable is subtracted from the total value of the practice. This application is incorrect and penalizes the seller who is not selling his accounts receivable.

Step 3. Projections of Expense Items. In projecting the practice's future operating expenses, two types must be kept in mind: "fixed" and "variable." Fixed costs can be projected with minimal effort. Variable costs must be projected by taking into account fluctuations in revenue projections. It is also important to take into consideration those expenses that will increase annually with inflation, such as medical and office supplies. Additionally, consider annual salary increases for employees and also their effect on payroll taxes, bonus incentives, and retirement plan contributions.

Step 4. Calculation of Taxable Income. Subtract Operating Expenses and Physician Compensation arrived at in Step 3 from Revenues determined in Step 2 to determine Taxable Income.

Step 5. Applying Income Tax. The tax rate used should include the federal and all applicable state and local tax rates to which the practice is subject. When determining the federal rate, a corporate tax rate is typically used under the IRS's assumption that the purchaser, for purposes of fair market value, is a corporation. The IRS highly recommends that a DCF calculation be supported on an after-tax basis. This applies even if the practice or the other party to the transaction is a nontaxable entity.

Step 6. Calculating Net Earnings. Subtract the income tax calculated in Step 5 from taxable income calculated in Step 4.

Exhibit 5.1A
Discounted Cash Flow Methods
Valuation as of December 31, 1998

	Base Year 1998	1999	2000	2001	2002	2003	Terminal Year
Professional Revenue:							
Patient Fees	$253,870	$260,000	$266,500	$271,830	277,267	$280,039	
Capitation Contracts:							
Payer 1	14,146	14,146	14,146	14,853	14,853	14,853	
Payer 2	23,990	23,990	23,990	25,190	25,190	25,190	
Payer 3	164,669	164,669	164,669	172,902	172,902	172,902	
Payer 4	50,875	50,875	50,875	53,419	53,419	53,419	
Projected Net Professional Revenue	**$507,550**	**$513,680**	**$520,180**	**$538,194**	**$543,631**	**$546,403**	
Year-End Capitated Bonuses:							
Payer 3	6,303	6,303	6,303	6,303	6,303	6,303	
Payer 4	44,988	17,625	0	0	0	0	
Patient Refunds	(3,161)	(3,199)	(3,240)	(3,352)	(3,386)	(3,403)	
Projected Net Professional Revenue	**$555,680**	**$534,409**	**$523,243**	**$541,145**	**$546,548**	**$549,303**	
Operating Expenses:							
Salaries-Staff	121,834	121,640	125,289	129,048	132,919	136,907	
Payroll Taxes-Staff	10,369	9,305	9,585	9,872	10,168	10,473	
Insurance	6,352	6,543	6,739	6,941	7,150	7,364	
Medical Drugs and Supplies	2,864	3,125	2,935	3,037	3,068	3,083	
Laboratory Fees	545	595	559	578	584	587	
Office Supplies and Postage	18,118	18,337	18,569	19,212	19,406	19,505	

Exhibit 5.1A
(Continued)

	Base Year 1998	1999	2000	2001	2002	2003	Terminal Year
Rent	18,570	18,570	18,570	18,570	18,570	18,570	
Depreciation & Amortization	4,188	1,696	0	0	0	0	
Depreciation (future expense)	0	5,000	0	0	0	0	
Other Operating Expenses	24,871	25,617	26,386	27,177	27,992	28,832	
Total Operating Expenses	**$207,711**	**$210,428**	**$208,631**	**$214,435**	**$219,857**	**$225,322**	
Earnings before Physician's Compensation/Benefits and Income Taxes	$347,969	$323,981	$314,612	$326,710	$326,691	$323,982	
Owner's Compensation and Benefits:							
Owner Salary:							
R. S. Wheeler, M.D.	160,000	160,000	160,000	160,000	160,000	160,000	
Payroll Taxes	7,470	6,548	6,548	6,548	6,548	6,548	
Professional Liability Insurance	5,048	5,048	5,048	5,048	5,048	5,048	
Total Owner's Compensation	**172,518**	**171,596**	**171,596**	**171,596**	**171,596**	**171,596**	
Projected Earnings before Income Taxes	175,451	152,384	143,016	155,113	155,094	152,385	
Effective Income Tax Rate 38.9%	(68,250)	(59,277)	(55,633)	(60,339)	(60,332)	(59,278)	
Projected Net Income	**$107,201**	**$ 93,107**	**$ 87,383**	**$ 94,774**	**$ 94,763**	**$ 93,107**	
Add Non-Cash Expense: Depreciation	4,188	6,696	0	0	0	0	
Less: Capital Expenditure	0	(5,000)	0	0	0	0	
Cash Flow available for distribution	**$111,389**	**$ 94,803**	**$ 87,383**	**$ 94,774**	**$ 94,763**	**$ 93,107**	

Discount Rate %	20						
		0.83333	0.69444	0.5787	0.48225	0.40187	0.33489
Present value—cash flow		**$ 79,002**	**$ 60,682**	**$ 54,846**	**$ 45,699**	**$ 37,417**	

Estimated value calculation:

Sum of present values (Years 1997–2001)	$277,646	
Terminal Value:		
Cash Flow—beginning of terminal year	$93,107	
Present value factor—terminal year	0.33489	
No. of years	5	
Terminal Value	155,904	
Total Estimated Value	$433,550	
Total Estimated Value (Rounded)	**$433,500**	
Allocation of Value (Form 8594)		
Less Fair Market Value of:		
Fixed Assets	**(90,000)**	
Accounts Receivable	**(79,600)**	
Supplies	**(1,600)**	
Intangible Assets	**$262,300**	

Exhibit 5.1B

Discounted Cash Flow Method

Valuation as of December 31, 1998

	Base Year 1998	1999	2000	2001	2002	2003	Terminal Year
Professional Revenue:							
Patient Fees	$253,870	$260,000	$266,500	$271,830	277,267	$280,039	
Capitation Contracts:							
Payer 1	14,146	14,146	14,146	14,853	14,853	14,853	
Payer 2	23,990	23,990	23,990	25,190	25,190	25,190	
Payer 3	164,669	164,669	164,669	172,902	172,902	172,902	
Payer 4	50,875	50,875	50,875	53,419	53,419	53,419	
Projected Net Professional Revenue	**$507,550**	**$513,680**	**$520,180**	**$538,194**	**$543,631**	**$546,403**	
Year-End Capitated Bonuses:							
Payer 3	6,303	6,303	6,303	6,303	6,303	6,303	
Payer 4	44,988	17,625	0	0	0	0	
Patient Refunds	(3,161)	(3,199)	(3,240)	(3,352)	(3,386)	(3,403)	
Less: FMV Accounts Receivable		$ (79,600)					
Projected Net Professional Revenue	**$555,680**	**$454,809**	**$523,243**	**$541,145**	**$546,548**	**$549,303**	
Operating Expenses:							
Salaries-Staff	121,834	121,640	125,289	129,048	132,919	136,907	
Payroll Taxes-Staff	10,369	9,305	9,585	9,872	10,168	10,473	
Insurance	6,352	6,543	6,739	6,941	7,150	7,364	

Medical Drugs and Supplies	2,864	3,125	2,935	3,037	3,068	3,083
Laboratory Fees	545	595	559	578	584	587
Office Supplies and Postage	18,118	18,337	18,569	19,212	19,406	19,505
Rent	18,570	18,570	18,570	18,570	18,570	18,570
Depreciation & Amortization	4,188	1,696	0	0	0	0
Depreciation (future expense)	0	5,000	0	0	0	0
Other Operating Expenses	24,871	25,617	26,386	27,177	27,992	28,832
Total Operating Expenses	**$207,711**	**$210,428**	**$208,631**	**$214,435**	**$219,857**	**$225,322**
Earnings before Physician's Compensation/Benefits and Income Taxes	$347,969	$244,381	$314,612	$326,710	$326,691	$323,982
Owner's Compensation and Benefits:						
Owner Salary:						
R. S. Wheeler, M.D.	160,000	160,000	160,000	160,000	160,000	160,000
Payroll Taxes	7,470	6,548	6,548	6,548	6,548	6,548
Professional Liability Insurance	5,048	5,048	5,048	5,048	5,048	5,048
Total Owner's Compensation	**172,518**	**171,596**	**171,596**	**171,596**	**171,596**	**171,596**
Projected Earnings before Income Taxes	**175,451**	**72,784**	**143,016**	**155,113**	**155,094**	**152,385**
Effective Income Tax Rate 38.9%	(68,250)	(28,313)	(55,633)	(60,339)	(60,332)	(59,278)
Projected Net Income	**$107,201**	**$ 44,471**	**$ 87,383**	**$ 94,774**	**$ 94,763**	**$ 93,107**
Add Non-Cash Expense: Depreciation	4,188	6,696	0	0	0	0
Less: Capital Expenditure	0	(5,000)	0	0	0	0

Exhibit 5.1B
(Continued)

	Base Year 1998	1999	2000	2001	2002	2003	Terminal Year
Cash Flow available for distribution	**$111,389**	**$ 46,167**	**$ 87,383**	**$ 94,774**	**$ 94,763**	**$ 93,107**	
Discount Rate %	20	0.83333	0.69444	0.5787	0.48225	0.40187	0.33489
Present value—cash flow		**$ 38,472**	**$ 60,682**	**$ 54,846**	**$ 45,699**	**$ 37,417**	
Estimated value calculation:							
Sum of present values (Years 1997–2001)	$237,117						
Terminal Value:							
Cash Flow—beginning of terminal year $93,107							
Present value factor— terminal year 0.33489							
No. of years 5							
Terminal Value	155,904						
Total Estimated Value	$393,020						
Total Estimated Value (Rounded)	**$393,000**						
Allocation of Value (Form 8594)							
Less Fair Market Value of:							
Fixed Assets	**(90,000)**						
Supplies	**(1,600)**						
Intangible Assets	**$301,400**						

118

Step 7. Making Adjustments Necessary to Reflect Cash Flow. In this step, adjustments must be made to bring the Net Earnings to a Net Cash Flow status. Because the value is to be calculated on an after-tax basis, it is necessary to include or exclude items for tax purposes. Once Net Earnings have been determined, items that are non-cash or non–tax deductible should be adjusted.

Non-cash expenses such as depreciation and amortization should be added to Net Earnings because they are "non-cash." The practice has paid for these assets with real cash through other means. Additionally, items that are not tax-deductible and other cash outlays should be subtracted from Net Earnings. These items would be such expenses as the principal portion of debt, additional capital expenditures that are reasonably expected to be made in the immediate future (i.e., computer system upgrade), and additional working capital cash requirements to support the growth of productivity projected for the practice.

Step 8. Calculating Net Cash Flow Available for Distribution to Owners. Subtract Step 7 from the Net Earnings calculated in Step 6.

Step 9. Determining Present Value Factors. Information and data that is used to calculate the risk rate is gathered by the valuator throughout every aspect of the valuation process. By the time this decision is made, all other analysis of the subject practice has been completed. The present value factors can be taken from a published present value annuity table for the risk rate determined. Refer to Chapter 4 for a complete discussion of determining the risk rate.

One point that should be understood by all users of the valuation is the behavior of the risk rate and its direct impact on the calculated value. Leaving all other variables constant, the higher the rate, the lower will be the value, and vice versa.

Step 10. Calculating the Present Value of Net Cash Flow. This step determines today's value of the projected future cash flows. Multiply each year's Net Cash Flow determined in Step 8 by its respective present value factors to determine the Present Value of Net Cash Flow.

Step 11. Calculating the Terminal Value. The next step in the DCF is to calculate a terminal value. This is also called a residual value or a perpetuity value. The terminal value places a value on the stability of the practice's future years. The year following the projection's last year is the terminal year. The assumption is that the practice has reached a stable level of operations at the end of the last year of the DCF projection. A value is then calculated on this level of activity to represent the practice's value of future return on investment.

This is calculated by multiplying the Net Earnings of the projection's last year by the terminal year's present value factor, and then multiplying by the number of additional years. The number of additional years typically used in the terminal year calculation is five. However, it is the valuator's judgment as to how many years will be used in the terminal value calculation. The valuator's judgment is based on circumstances of the subject practice.

Step 12. Calculating the Business Enterprise Value. To arrive at the total Business Enterprise Value (BEV) add the results from Step 10 and Step 11. This sum represents the total value of the medical practice. This sum is then allocated among the tangible and intangible assets. For example, let us say the total BEV from a DCF calculation is $500,000. Let us also say the tangible assets are valued as follows: fixed assets, $50,000; supplies on hand, $2,000; and accounts receivable $100,000. The practice's intangible asset value is the remainder, if any, of the value left after allocating tangible assets. In this case, the practice's intangible asset value is $348,000 ($500,000 less $50,000, $2,000, and $100,000).

Revenue Ruling 65-193 supports the allocation of the BEV among tangible and intangible asset values. It makes the following statements:

> In some instances it may not be possible to make a separate appraisal of the tangible and intangible assets of the business. The enterprise has a value as an entity. Whatever intangible value there is, which is supportable by the facts, may be measured by the amount by which the appraised value of the tangible assets exceeds the net book value of such assets.

See Exhibits 5.1A and 5.1B for examples of a discounted cash flow calculation of value.

The discounted net earnings method is calculated in the same manner as the discounted cash flow method with the difference being that items that are included are income statement items whereas the DCF addresses all items that affect cash.

Valuation Assumptions. After the DCF is calculated, the valuator should test the reasonableness of the valuation assumptions. Assumptions that are made about the future profit potential of the practice should make logical sense given the specific circumstances of the practice. For example, the valuator should evaluate rates of growth for productivity in relation to the practice's managed care contracting, reimbursement, and reimbursement structures. Factors such as patient volume and demographics should be evaluated in relation to projected changes such as the "graying of America" and changes in industrial employers that affect injuries and worker-related illnesses.

It is worth noting again the critically important point that the valuator must test the practicality of the assumptions made. A final "sanity check" will assess for the value's reasonableness and appropriateness in using the practice's history, industry standards, market data, and all of the first-hand information gathered about the practice as of the valuation effective date.

As further guidance offered to the valuator, the IRS's *Exempt Organizations Continuing Professional Education Technical Instruction Program Textbook* offers the following guidance to its field agents in their review of medical practice valuations. The following factors should be evaluated for their validity in supporting the DCF projections:

- *Who owns the patient base—payer or physician?* In a managed care arrangement, the patient goes where the payer directs, affecting the base upon which revenues are projected.

- *What is the mix of managed care and fee for service?* The larger the percentage of income generated by managed care, the greater the guarantee of revenues. Thus, the mix of managed care and fee for service arrangements is an important factor in revenue projections, as are the length of managed care contracts and the probability of their renewal.

- *A description of the physician practice.* This should include a description of the medical community environment (primary service area of the practice and local medical competition, including number of practitioners in the specialty of the subject practice and other specialties). It should also thoroughly analyze the patient base. This may include a discussion of the volume and quality of patient charts, patient age mix and demographics, and payer source. The age of physicians and number of years in practice should be stated.

- *Are necessary adjustments made to the income stream?* Future cash flows/income may need to be adjusted for
  - Diagnostic Related Groups (DRGs), which are now being applied to certain physician services under Medicare.
  - The incorporations of pre- and postsurgical care into global surgical fees that incorporate presurgical and postsurgical care along with surgery. In a surgical specialty, only the portion of payments reflecting the surgical component should be included in revenue projections.
  - Increases or decreases in fees or capitation because of competition and government regulations. These might include, for example, expected decreases in physician referrals resulting from changes in federal antikickback laws.
  - Effects of tightening of federal antireferral restrictions (Stark I and II).
  - Does the cash flow analysis include under expenses or salary the higher salaries for the additional nonphysician staff with the requisite training needs (i.e., gate keepers)?

Capitalization of Excess Earnings Method

To calculate the value of a practice using the capitalization of excess earnings method, a capitalization rate is applied to the practice's normalized net earnings or net cash flow.

In using this method, the valuator must take into consideration the IRS Revenue Ruling 68-609, which states that this method should be used basically as a last resort, when no other valuation method would be appropriate.

The capitalization of excess earnings method is an appropriate means of valuing a practice if the practice's current operations and earnings levels are expected to remain at the same levels into the next several years. Also, this method is appropriate when the subject practice has little value assignable to tangible assets.

In applying the capitalization of excess earnings method to estimate the intangible value, the following steps would be performed.

Step 1. Compile income statements from the past few years' performance of the practice (preferably at least five years) including the current year-to-date statements. Place this data in a columnar comparative format on a ledger sheet or in a spreadsheet.

Note: Five years' income statements are typically sufficient. However, there may be certain circumstances that may make a particular year unfair to use in this calculation. For example, one of the physicians may have been out of the practice for six months due to an illness or injury. Therefore, the financial picture for the year during her absence would not be representative of a typical year for the practice and its operations. It may also be necessary to ignore unusual or abnormal years that do not represent past or future performance.

Step 2. Make adjustments for revenue and expense items that are nonrecurring, extraordinary, and discretionary. Items such as this would be advertising and charitable contributions because they are considered to be discretionary. That is, these expenses were not required as part of the ongoing operational costs of the practice yet there were available funds to spend on these items. They are considered "excess earnings." Other items would be automobile expenses incurred by the physicians such as lease payments and insurance. These items are considered to be compensatory benefits to the physicians that they would otherwise be paying out of their salaries. It may be necessary to make adjustments to such revenue items because they are unrelated to the practice's operational earnings capacity (such as unrelated rental income and interest). The purpose of these adjustments is to determine the actual costs of the practice's operations versus the earnings available for owners' compensation, discretionary spending, and retained earnings.

Step 3. Subtract the adjusted expenses from the adjusted revenues to determine the earnings available for retained earnings and distribution to the owners.

Step 4. Subtract the owners' compensation or a "reasonable" compensation from the earnings available calculated in Step 3. In many cases, the owners' compensation is likely to be above the level of "reasonable" compensation for this group of physicians. The valuator should compare the actual compensation to a peer comparison set of compensation data to determine the "excess earnings" available to an investor. These "excess earnings" represent the practice's capacity to generate additional earnings above and beyond a reasonable level of salaries and benefits for the owner physicians.

Step 5. Subtract the practice's average return from tangible assets from the results in Step 4. This represents "excess earnings" attributable to intangible assets.

Step 6. Apply a multiple or a capitalization factor to the result calculated in Step 4 to determine the amount that will represent the intangible value of the practice, usually referred to under this method as goodwill. The multiple or capitalization factor used in this step can be arrived at by various methods. One of the most common methods is to use a capitalization factor comparable to a risk rate and dividing it into the "excess earnings" calculated in Step 5. Another method is to use a subjective weighting process for say, 1 to 10, to assess the practice in such areas as operations, staffing, financial stability, managed care market, physician productivity, and management to determine an arbitrary factor that is then multiplied by the "excess earnings" calculated in Step 4.

Step 7. Add the calculated "intangible value" from Step 5 to the estimated value of the practice's tangible assets to arrive at the practice's total value using the excess earnings method.

Rule of Thumb

"Rule of thumb" is not a valuation method, per se, although various articles and literature that you read about the valuation of medical practices may lead you to believe otherwise. Typical rules of thumb that have been applied to medical practice valuations are a multiple of annual revenue, net revenue, or net earnings. For example, a purchaser that offers a purchase price of "three times earnings" is willing to pay, say, $600,000 for practice that has had $200,000 net earnings before physician compensation during its most current fiscal year or previous twelve months. A valuator can use rule of thumb to help gauge the reasonableness of the value attained through other methods.

Market Approach

The market approach values a practice by comparing it to other practices with similar operations. The market approach is the method most often relied upon in real estate valuations.

In valuing medical practices, the market approach uses actual transactions as a means of comparison. Until recently, this data has been limited because many of these transactions have not been reported. Transactions are typically not reported because they are considered to be personal and private in nature by the parties involved, particularly the sellers. In recent years, there are more sources that are actively collecting transaction and comparable data for closely held businesses including medical practices. If you are a valuator who performs a large number of valuations, you should record your own data from your internal records to establish an "experience database" to use as an additional source in this approach.

When comparing recent market transactions under this approach, the following factors should be considered when relying on a specific set of comparable data:

Financial ratios: Review such financial ratios as revenue, operating expenses, and physician compensation for a fair comparison to the subject practice.

Profit margins: Analyzing the profit margin for equitable comparison can be difficult unless there is sufficient information with regard to physician compensation including benefits and retirement plan contributions.

Number of physicians/providers: It is very important when making a market comparison to obtain the number of providers in the comparable practices. It is additionally important to obtain, if possible, the number of full-time equivalencies (FTEs) of providers. Many large practices employ part-time physicians and mid-level providers.

Geographic markets: Obtain as much information as possible about the geographic location of the comparable practices. From a valuation standpoint, vast differences can exist in practices that are located in the same city or region. Such factors that can affect the value are the economic condition with regard to unemployment and inflation; area industry with regard to types of injuries, diseases, and illnesses; and population with regard to median age and associated illnesses as well as areas that are over- or underserved as to number of physicians. However, in much comparable data, this type of information is extremely limited.

Managed care payers: Information about the major payers affecting comparable practices and their values is important to use in this approach, again, if possible to obtain. Typically, the comparable data will not provide comparable gross charges along with the other data. Payers in some markets offer a much deeper discount on payment for services than others. Therefore, reviewing a net revenue figure alone can be misleading. By having both the gross charges and net revenue, the valuator can make a more accurate assessment of the comparable data and adjust it, if necessary, to compare fairly and equitably.

Managed care penetration: The valuator should take into consideration the level of managed care and its maturity in the markets of the comparable practices. It is important to address its effect on an equitable comparison to the subject practice.

The following are available sources for comparable market data. However, specific and detailed information for medical practice transactions is still very limited.

- BizComps

- Pratt's Stats

- Done Deals

- *Mergerstat Review*

- Robert Morris & Associates

- Institute of Business Appraisers

- The Center for Health Care Industry Performance Studies and Findley, Davies, and Company

- Goodwill Registry

It is recommended that the valuator obtain a copy of the survey questionnaire that is used by the companies that collect transaction data. Remember that the comparable market data is only as good as the information reported. If the respondents did not comply with the definitions of line items that were provided by the survey, then there is a margin of error in the data. Or, if the survey does not ask for specific breakdowns of particular revenue and expense items, again, there may be a margin of error.

This point is stressed here because there are so many different methods of recording revenues and expenses that are being practiced in medical practice accounting. For the most part, most practices' financial statements are based on the cash-basis of accounting and typically they reflect what the physician wants to see. This may include revenues and expenses that are not true practice-related items but are reflected in the financials as a means of communicating information to the physician, the reader.

In using comparable information from publicly traded companies' medical practice data, consider applying the public companies' price-to-earnings ratio to the subject practice's equity structure to weigh the support of the market approach.

The group of available buyers of larger practices, especially multispecialty practices, is a much smaller group than the group of buyers of small practices. Likewise, when using market data in valuing larger practices, there may be little or no current transaction data with which to compare.

Cost (or Asset) Approach

The cost approach (or asset approach) is basically the difference between the fair market value of the practice's assets less the fair market value of its liabilities. Additionally, the value may or may not include a value for intangible assets.

A practice's net book value is the difference between the assets and liabilities as they are on the practice's balance sheet as of a specific date. The cost approach revalues these items to fair market value. The valuation of these items can be done under various methods such as replacement cost, reproduction cost, and book value.

Replacement Cost in Use

This method estimates the value based on the cost of replacing existing assets, facilities, equipment, and staff. This can be calculated by subtracting the portion of "estimated past usage" of the property from its replacement cost. The result is the "replacement cost in use" of the asset. Estimating the asset's past usage is done by estimating the remaining working life of an asset (which is not usually the same as the depreciated life) and subtracting it from its original life. The entire practice's replacement cost in use can be estimated by estimating the costs of setting up the same situation (i.e., the current value of asset prices, salary ranges, leases, etc.). The replacement cost method is the recommended method for practices that sell or merge and continue to operate "as is." It is the value of a turnkey operation.

No matter what the method of estimating value, the valuator must consider the functional obsolescence of equipment, as well as the condition and the ability of the assets to continue to be serviced with parts, upgrades, and so forth.

Reproduction Cost

This method estimates the value of reproducing the practice from scratch. This would include building, purchasing, or renting a facility, hiring a staff, installing a computer system, purchasing or leasing medical and office equipment, furniture and fixtures, stocking supplies, and so on. This would also include the cost of hiring outside services to assist in such things as recruitment, newspaper placement ads, training, and installation and setup.

Book Value

This is based on the depreciated cost of the assets. It is calculated by subtracting an asset's accumulated depreciation as of the valuation date from its original cost. Typically there is more life left to the asset after it is fully depreciated. Therefore, this will usually be the lowest of values when compared to the replacement cost in use and reproduction cost methods.

METHODOLOGY ISSUES

Discounted Cash Flow

This method takes into account the working capital, capital expenditures, and so on that are needed to generate a profit. This method is an appropriate one for valuing startup practices or a practice where future earnings are expected to differ from historical earnings. However, it is important for the valuator to obtain sufficient information and data with which to project the practice's future earnings. It is very important in using this method that the valuator (if an independent valuator with no internal knowledge of the subject practice) obtain physician and/or key management representation regarding the earnings outlook for the practice.

Issue: Base Year

When projecting the future years' financial statements in the DCF calculation, it is very important that these projections begin with the most appropriate Base Year data. This may be the most current tax year or it may be the most recent twelve months of data that crosses over two fiscal years. However, if the determination of the Base Year requires splitting fiscal year 's data, the valuator should pay particular attention to items that may be sensitive to fluctuations of the calendar year, such as payroll taxes. Whichever may be the case, the Base Year should represent the most current and accurate information available, including normalization. It is upon this data that the following years in the DCF will be based.

Issue: Variable Expenses

When projecting the practice's operating expenses for future years, the valuator should consider the behavior of variable expenses with the projected fluctuations in revenue. For example, the more patients a practice will treat, the more clinical supplies will be used; the more billing and collection resources will be used; and so on.

Issue: Depreciation

When projecting the depreciation for future years, it is important that the valuator consider the actual accumulated depreciation on the books of the seller and project from the valuation effective date. When calculating depreciation for the anticipated capital expenditures of the practice, it is also appropriate to apply the IRC Section 179 deduction.

Issue: Anticipated Capital Expenditures

For purposes of the valuation, future capital expenditures should be projected for the period of time projected in the valuation. These should be the capital expenditures that the practice anticipates making regardless of whether a transaction takes place. They should represent the expenditures to be made by the practice only, not by the purchaser after acquisition.

Issue: Leases

Many lease agreements, especially those for building and occupancy, have graduated lease payment schedules. These agreements should be reviewed to ensure the accuracy of projected lease payments.

Issue: Risk Rate

The discount rate components that are obtained from published data already assume the historical inflation rate. Therefore, projected cash flows include a factor for inflation. If the valuator does not wish to reflect inflation in the value, it should be extracted from the discount rate. As of the publication of this book, the average inflation rate is around 2.8 percent. Inflation rates can be obtained from several published sources. It is recommended that the valuator research this figure for appropriate application to the valuation at hand. Also, it is recommended that the valuator consult local chambers of commerce, libraries, and so on for valuations of practices that are in unusual or remote economic areas where averages may not be sufficient.

Issue: Growth Rate

This is one of the most important areas of the valuation. The valuator should consider every aspect of the information and data obtained during the valuation process and apply them to this projection. In particular, special focus should be given to the physicians' history, office hours, facility and capacity, number of patients, market demographics and population, management, fee schedule, and managed care contracts.

Issue: Working Capital

It is important that the DCF recognize any additional working capital that would be required for the practice to operate at the projected levels. Working capital is the amount of funds that are made available from operations and are needed to invest back into the practice to continue meeting operating expenses, such as payroll, supplies, rent, and so forth. Calculated, the practice's current available working capital is the difference between its current assets and its current liabilities.

As the practice's productivity is projected to increase, the accounts receivable will increase as well. As this occurs, it will take time for the increase in cash receipts from billing A/R to catch up to the volume of increased productivity. Until it does, the practice will need these funds to be available from other sources. Therefore, the need for these funds must be projected in the future operations of the practice.

One method of projecting future working capital needs in the DCF is to calculate the Base Year's working capital as a percentage of gross charges. Then, apply this percentage to the projected productivity in gross charges for every year represented in the DCF.

Again, working Capital is calculated by subtracting Current Liabilities from Current Assets. The result represents the amount of additional funds required to invest back into the operations of the business to maintain a certain level.

To project working capital needs for a DCF valuation, begin by calculating the Base Year's working capital and project over the next five years based on the Base Year's working capital as a percentage of gross charges. Depending on whether the DCF assumes debt repayment and interest, these liabilities will need to be treated accordingly when calculating working capital from the balance sheet items.

Issue: Terminal Year

Although determining which year in the projection will represent the terminal year is the valuator's judgment, the Internal Revenue Service's field guide endorses Year 6 as the Terminal Year. It is acceptable for the valuator to use a different year than Year 6. However, if you are the valuator and you deviate from what has been considered typical for a going-concern practice, there should be sound and documented reasoning for the deviation. An example of such a case that may warrant deviation would be a solo physician that plans to practice for no more than the next three years with no plans for filling the void left from his departure. In this case, it would be feasible for the projections to cover a much shorter period of time in which to gain a return from a future revenue stream. It would be the responsibility of the purchaser to fill the void and maintain the practice's patient base and income stream. Consequently, the price paid for this practice would be lower than if the physician planned to hire his own replacement and assist in the transition of his patients, staff, and practice to the new physician.

Issue: What's Included in the Value?

In calculating the value by using the DCF method, the result is the total. It is called Business Enterprise Value (BEV). There is nothing that should be added to this figure to determine the value.

Included in the BEV is the value of tangibles and intangibles. The BEV should be allocated among the tangible assets' value such as for furniture, fixtures, equipment, supplies, and accounts receivable (if transferred to the purchaser). The excess portion of the BEV that is not allocable to tangible assets represents intangible assets. The seller should also understand that if the purchaser is not assuming liabilities, the BEV includes the funds that the seller has available to apply to the practice's outstanding debt.

Issue: Real Estate

Most medical practice valuations do not include real estate. This is for two main reasons. One is that the purchaser usually does not purchase the medical office building. The other is that it is rare that the real estate is included in the tangible assets of the practice entity. In instances where the physician(s) own the building, it is typically owned through another entity separate from the practice. Consequently, the practice pays the physicians' building entity for rent. The issue here is that the valuator should ensure that the rent payments represent fair market value. If they don't, adjustments should be made on the DCF to reflect fair market value rent.

Also, it is important for the purchaser and seller to understand that if there is to be a real estate valuation as part of the medical practice transaction, a business valuator is typically not qualified to perform real estate valuations. Real estate valuations require an additional set of knowledge and criteria that separate them entirely from business valuations. It is advised that the party engaging valuation services hire a real estate valuator. This can also be done by engaging the business valuator to subcontract a real estate valuator to determine the value of the medical building. It is not uncommon for business valuators to be acquainted and work with real estate valuators.

Issue: Range of Values

It may be necessary to calculate the DCF using different variables that represent different scenarios. A typical situation to which this would apply is in the case of a group of physicians that have above-average compensation levels but are willing to accept lower compensation and varying benefits. The DCF can be revised to calculate the value under various compensation scenarios. This is not to be confused with the hypothetical projections made by the purchaser (investor). The physician compensation levels directly impact the value, and vice versa. Another example is aiding in the physician's decision to sell or keep accounts receivable. Calculating the DCF with and without accounts receivable will illustrate the impact on value. The physicians can then compare this difference to their own expectations of collectable A/R and their costs of collections.

The Ten Most Common Mistakes Made in the Discounted Cash Flow Method

In our experience, there is a common thread among many of the valuations we have seen in practice over the last few years in the health care industry. Listed below are what we have determined are the top 10 mistakes made in the discounted cash flow method of valuation.

1. Using inappropriate growth rates

2. Including the value of accounts receivable (A/R) in the Business Enterprise Value (BEV) when the accounts receivable will not be transferred to the purchaser

3. Adding the fair market value of accounts receivable to the BEV

4. Incorrectly projecting payroll tax expense for physicians and highly paid individuals

5. Using an inappropriate federal and state income tax expense

6. Using an inappropriate discount rate

7. Using assumptions that are inappropriate for the definition of value being estimated

8. Assuming historical owners' compensation will continue status quo

9. Improperly accounting for principal and interest payments

10. Improperly accounting for future depreciation and capital expenditures

The following are some examples of actual situations that we have seen or experienced with regard to the discounted cash flow method.

Mistake # 1: Using Inappropriate Growth Rates

Common mistakes made by valuers in estimating growth rates using the discounted cash flow method usually happen because not enough qualitative thought has been given to the practicality of what is being projected. In order for a practice to experience growth, several things must occur. To name a few, the practice must have capacity to absorb additional patients, the practice must be able to sustain its current managed care payers' reimbursement structures, and the practice must be able to withstand competitive changes occurring in its market area.

Although the valuator should use the practice's history as an indication of what the practice has been capable of accomplishing thus far, the historical growth rates do not automatically transfer to assumed future growth. It is not reasonable to use an average or even a weighted average of prior years' growth without a detailed analysis of the other factors that affect a practice's revenue stream, especially given the industry's volatility and unpredictability with regard to managed care.

Projecting the Same Growth Rate for Every Year. Some discounted cash flow valuations are projected using the same growth rate for every year shown in the projection. Although there are certainly instances where this may be the case, it is unlikely that most practices will experience an accelerated pattern of growth annually without the addition of providers, staff, locations, and so on. One exception would be a startup practice or a practice with a new physician on staff. In this case, early years of practice would typically exemplify accelerated growth, but even so it is unlikely that each year would grow at the same rate. Remember that when estimating the practice's value it is to be based on the practice's ability to generate future income as of the valuation date.

Many of the valuations we have seen have been projected with flat assumptions of a 4 percent or a 5 percent growth rate annually for the next five years. Clearly, this is unlikely given the facts and circumstances that surround the managed care challenges faced by medical practices today.

Projecting an Overly Aggressive Growth Rate. In the recent years of medical practice acquisitions there has been a frenzied bidding war. For the most part, the nonprofit purchasers have been competing with the for-profits for the same practices. The nonprofits have been compelled to get the price as high as possible in order to negotiate with the physicians. Sometimes, that goal has been reached beyond reason with overly aggressive growth rates. And, some of these valuations have been determined with a blend of investment value initiatives (mixing the definitions of value between FMV and investment value).

One situation we have seen was in the case of an acquisition of several practices at one time by a hospital health system. Each practice being acquired was projected at the same growth rate regardless of the practice's specialty, physicians' age, patient demographics, and so on.

Ignoring the Impact of Revenue Stream by Payer. It is increasingly important that the valuator review the practice's history and utilization, current managed care contracts' terms and reimbursement structures, and the current market area and competitive forces. These factors should be analyzed separately for each of the practice's major payers to project their impact on the practice's future revenue stream.

For example, say you are valuing the future revenue stream of an internal medicine practice with approximately 65 percent of its patient base covered by Medicare. Effective January 1, 1998, the Medicare reimbursement rate changed significantly compared to prior years. During 1997, the Medicare reimbursement rate was

$35.7671 per Resource Based Relative Value Scale (RBRVS) for primary care services, $40.9603 for surgical services, and $33.85 for non-primary care services. So on January 1, 1998, the three-category rate structure collapsed into one. The rate for 1998 is $36.6873 regardless of the type of service performed.

So, in the case of this internal medicine practice, it automatically received an increase of approximately 2.57 percent in reimbursement for primary care services performed for Medicare patients. In this practice's case, this accounted for the bulk of services provided. In valuing the practice's future revenue stream, this change should be taken into account along with expected utilization.

If surgeries accounted for a significant portion of the practice's business, the impact of Medicare's rate change is a decrease of approximately 10.44 percent. As you can see, the Medicare rate change would have the opposite effect on practices with a large volume of surgeries.

Mistake #2: Including Accounts Receivable in the BEV When A/R Will Not Be Transferred to the Purchaser

In many acquisitions, the purchaser intends to buy the accounts receivable of the practice in addition to other tangible assets such as medical equipment, furniture and fixtures, office equipment, and supply inventory. In this case, when using the discounted cash flow method to estimate the BEV of the practice, the value of accounts receivable is included as part of the total BEV. Since most medical practices account for their business using the cash basis of accounting, the assumption here is that the projected cash receipts include the amount of collectible accounts receivable as of the valuation date. Consequently, accounts receivable collected subsequent to the valuation date will belong to the purchaser.

On the contrary, if the purchaser does not intend to purchase the accounts receivable from the practice, then it is assumed that the seller will continue to collect the balance subsequent to the sale. Therefore, when calculating the discounted cash flow method, it is appropriate to assume that the projected cash receipts to the purchaser should not include the value of the practice's accounts receivable as of the valuation date. The value of accounts receivable should be subtracted from the first year's projected receipts. This accounts for the assumption that the seller will collect it within the next twelve months.

Whether the intention of the purchaser is to buy accounts receivable or not, it must still be valued for proper treatment in the discounted cash flow method.

Many valuators subtract the value of accounts receivable from the total BEV arrived at through the DCF calculation. There are several conceptual problems with this approach. On one hand, the seller should not calculate net cash flow under the assumption that there is cash that would not be received in the period shown on the DCF. Additionally, the value is overstated because projected receipts include accounts receivable to be collected immediately after purchase (less operating expenses, physician compensation, income tax expense, etc.), which likely results in a positive cash flow. This, in turn, is discounted to present value and is part of the BEV. Alternatively, when the fair market value of accounts receivable is subtracted from Year 1 receipts, the result will most likely be a negative cash flow. This point illustrates the overstatement of value.

On the other hand, the seller is being penalized by the purchase price from a tax standpoint because it includes a cash flow that is overstated whereby the seller's value is taxed on that amount within the DCF model. As well, the seller will also be taxed on the professional receipts collected from the accounts receivable balance that was not transferred.

Exhibit 5.1 illustrates the difference in value resulting from these two scenarios. As can be seen, the difference in purchase price can be quite significant to the purchaser and the seller. It is very important for the valuator and all the parties involved with the transaction to understand the impact of various calculations.

Mistake #3: Incorrectly Projecting Payroll Tax Expense for Physicians and Highly Paid Individuals

This is an expense item where there is a high frequency of errors made by valuators. The primary reason is that many valuators are not tax accountants or do have financial backgrounds but are simply unaware of the rules. This underscores the importance of the fact that valuators must study their discipline and understand all facets of their duties.

Employer-paid payroll taxes (or FICA) are currently paid to the federal government at 7.65 percent of each employee's gross salary as reported on Form W-2. This tax is made up of two parts: 6.2 percent equals Social Security tax and 1.45 percent equals Medicare tax. Payroll taxes are collected and reported on a calendar-year basis. During the calendar year, the employer pays both the Social Security portion and the Medicare portion. However, the Social Security portion is paid only up to a specified limit. When the limit is reached during the calendar year, the remainder of the year's salary is not subject to this portion of the tax (6.2%). For calendar year 1998, this limit is $68,400 and is adjusted annually for inflation. Once an individual's calendar year wages reach this limit, only the Medicare portion (1.45%) is paid. So, for individuals with salaries greater than $68,400 in 1998, their net pay is larger for the remainder of the calendar year after reaching the Social Security limit. Likewise, the employer-paid payroll tax expense is less during the remainder of the calendar year.

For example, Dr. Wheeler's salary for 1998 is $160,000. Her payroll tax expense for the year is calculated as follows:

Social Security	($68,400 × 6.2%)	$4,240.80
Medicare	($150,000 × 1.45%)	$2,175.00
Total Liability for 1998		**$6,415.80**

Until the Revenue Reconciliation Act of 1993 (RRA93) all of FICA (Social Security and Medicare) was capped at the annual salary limit. After RRA93, the Medicare portion of the payroll tax is collected throughout the year regardless of the amount of annual salary.

Payroll tax errors made by valuators are caused by not having sufficient knowledge of the FICA laws. Common mistakes often made include (1) annualizing year-to-date payroll tax expense, (2) using prior year payroll tax expenses and applying a cost-of-living adjustment, (3) ignoring highly-paid employees other than physicians such as physician assistants, nurse practitioners, and practice administrators, (4) ignoring differences due to a fiscal year-end other than calendar year, and (5) ignoring the impact of significant changes due to personnel terminations and additions.

Capitalization of Excess Earnings Method

Issue: Appropriate Use

This method should be used when the earnings of the practice can be reasonably projected to represent its past earnings. Revenue Ruling 68-609 refers to this method as the "formula" approach and states that "the 'formula' approach may be used in determining the fair market value of intangible assets of a business only if there is no better basis available for making the determination."

Market Comparison Approach

Issue: Reliability of Data

This method may only be appropriate if enough comparable data can be found. And even then, once found, can this data be reasonably compared to the practice being valued? In many cases, the answer is no. As described above, the valuator should analyze a set of criteria. However, the data to support this criteria for comparable guideline companies and market transaction data is just not there.

Cost (or Asset) Approach

Issue: Appropriateness to Medical Practice Valuations

This approach is typically an appropriate method for the valuation of medical practices. It is a method that is most appropriate in measuring significant values of tangible assets. In professional practices, including medical practices, the significant value is typically in the intangible value. The value of a medical practice's fixed assets, supplies, and accounts receivable is usually not a large percentage when compared to the total value.

Issue: Advantages/Disadvantages

This approach does have some advantages over the income approach and the market approach. One is that is it relatively easy to delete items from the value since all assets and liabilities would be itemized as a result of using this method. Another advantage is that it avoids the valuator's subjectivity with regard to growth assumptions, risk rates, and the like. A disadvantage is that this method measures the value of a practice at a specific point in time with no regard for the future potential of the practice as a going-concern.

One particular nuance with which the valuator must be familiar is the manner in which most physician practices keep their books, which is according to the cash basis of accounting. Practices that use the cash basis are usually on a modified cash basis in that the accrual item, Depreciation, is also utilized. And, unless the practice is owned by a health system that utilizes the accrual basis of accounting or the practice is one that purchases and resells inventory for sale to its patients such as optometry or audiology services, it is very likely that the financial statements are on the cash basis of accounting. This is important because in using a valuation method based on the balance sheet, the valuator must make adjustments for items that will not be reflected, such as accounts receivable and certain liabilities.

VALUATION OF OTHER ASSETS

Tangible Assets

Fixed Assets

Fixed assets may be valued by applying one of the methods discussed under the cost (asset) approach methods or by some variation that takes into account the assets' accumulated depreciation to determine their worth as a going-concern. One method of assessing value this way is to add back a percentage of the accumulated depreciation as of the valuation date to the assets' book value. The percentage added back is a subjective measurement made by the valuator by taking into consideration qualitative factors such as condition and obsolescence.

However, it may be necessary to engage the services of a "Machinery and Equipment" appraiser. On occasion the physicians may request this. In many instances, it may be the most appropriate depending on the purpose of the valuation. Clearly, if the purchase involves only tangible assets, then it is highly recommended that the valuation of fixed assets is performed by an expert in medical practice fixed assets, especially clinical and ancillary equipment and supplies. In the case of a discounted cash flow valuation, the total value will not change no matter what the value of the fixed assets. Remember that, in the case of the DCF method, the fixed assets are valued as a means of assigning a portion of the value to fixed assets.

Accounts Receivable

Accounts receivable should be valued to determine the most accurate assessment of collectibility. The quality of data that can be obtained from the subject practice makes the determination for the level of accuracy that can be assessed. Ultimately, the valuator should review and analyze the practice's historical collection efforts, aged accounts receivable balances, payer classes, and patient responsibility accounts. If possible, the large categories of receivables should be analyzed separately to determine their collectibility.

Methods of calculating the value range from individual assessments of dollar amounts and summing them to determine the value to applying a historical collection rate to a category of receivables to determine the value.

Supplies

Supplies are typically valued as an average of routine purchases over a period of twelve months. Depending upon the practice's specialty and its purchasing habits, this may range from two weeks' inventory to three months' inventory. It is recommended that an actual supply inventory be taken on the closing date of the transaction. Also, the purchaser may require an exclusion of such items as practice stationery and other preprinted materials that will not be used after the transaction.

Intangible Assets

The remaining life of the intangible asset must be projected when placing a value on the specific intangible assets. For example, when placing a value on a favorable lease agreement, the number of remaining years should be considered. The lease agreement may be valued by determining the present value of remaining payments obligated under the current contract. Other agreements that can be valued in this manner are management service agreements, noncompete agreements, and employment agreements.

Valuing some intangibles is a rather subjective process. The goal of the valuator is to determine the most rational basis in assigning a dollar amount to a particular intangible. Any type of reasonable measurement should be considered as a means of valuing the asset such as remaining life, as discussed above, projected decrease in revenue due to loss of intangible, projected cost to replace intangible, and projected costs of reproduction of the asset and providing related training.

The following is a list of intangibles that are considered when valuing a medical practice.

- Software and technical manuals
- Referral relationships
- Contracts and agreements
- Licenses
- Certificates of need
- Affiliation agreements
- Noncompete agreements
- Databases
- Trained and assembled workforce; know-how
- Employee agreements
- Trademarks, logos, trade names
- Leases, leasehold options
- Going concern, turnkey operation value
- Professional library
- Location and phone number
- Procedures/training manuals
- Regulatory approvals

- Managed care contracts and enrollments

- Medical records

DISCUSSION OF VALUATION SOFTWARE

Beware of relying on valuation software without a complete under-standing of the valuation process. Software should be used only as a tool in assisting the valuer in his or her analysis and decision mak-ing. While it is certainly acceptable to use such software to calculate financial ratios and various valuation methods—it is absolutely im-perative that the valuator understands and verifies the components of input into these models (not just what the outcome means).

On-Site Inspection/ Owner Interview

There is a misconception rampant in much of the valuation world that the on-site portion of the valuation process is "optional." Depending on the definition of value and the purpose of the valuation, an on-site visit may be required. Also, many of the valuation societies and organizations have standards that place additional requirements on the valuator in the name of competence. And, from a defense standpoint, how can the valuator defend his estimate of value when he hasn't even verified the validity of a "store front"?

An on-site visit is highly recommended when the purpose of the valuation is for an acquisition or merger; not only will the valuator be estimating a numerical value, he will also be rendering an opinion on the practice's operations and management as they affect the value.

There are several objectives of the valuator's site visit. First, the valuator verifies the existence of the practice and its facility as a bona fide business. The valuator also verifies the practice's fixed assets (i.e., furniture, fixtures, clinical equipment, business equipment, etc.). The valuator is also charged with the responsibility of gaining an understanding of the practice's operations and management. And finally, the valuator should interview the owner/physicians or the managing physician to gain their perspective on factors that have an effect on value.

APPOINTMENT SCHEDULING

The valuator should review several factors with regard to appointment scheduling. Those factors are such things as the practice's office hours, frequency and length of appointments and various visit types, computerized scheduling, protocols for working in last-minute appointments, and handling of referral patients.

The valuator should evaluate these factors for efficiency and effectiveness regarding the operations of the practice and consequently the practice's value. Especially in instances where the practice will continue as a going concern, operational issues are an important component of which all parties to the transaction should be aware. They may also contribute to assumptions used in the final estimate of value.

For example, we valued a three-physician internal medicine practice in which, at the time of our site visit, the physicians had recently changed their individual office hours. In the normal course of a site visit, a valuator would review past appointment schedules to determine factors such as visits per day and capacity for additional patient visits. In this case, the valuator would have determined that the two senior physicians' schedules were filled to a maximum capacity for the office hours for which they were routinely scheduled. However, those hours only equated to $3\frac{1}{2}$ days per week and even then were only between the hours of 10:00 A.M. and 4:00 P.M. In the valuator's opinion when assessing the practice's assumptions related to growth, these two physicians have no additional growth potential. However, the physicians' recent changes in scheduling were (1) adding an additional half day per week to the schedule and (2) adding an hour per day by scheduling the first patient at 9:00 A.M. instead of 10:00 A.M. From this standpoint, the physicians added capacity for growth and consequently they added value to their practice.

The most important point to be understood from this is that there will be circumstances that make each valuation unique. For that reason, it should also be understood that valuations are not merely formulas by which we calculate a value. There are many facets of research that go into the mathematical equation before it comes out on the other side as a numerical value.

The valuator is charged with the responsibility of performing adequate due diligence in order to determine the most accurate estimate of value. However, if you are the physician or the administrator of a practice being valued, you should communicate to the valuator changes that have occurred that may have an impact on the practice value.

COMPUTER SYSTEM

The valuator should summarily evaluate the practice's computer information system during the site visit. By this time, the valuator should have examples of computerized performance reports from the practice's system and will have familiarity with the types of reports that the practice uses to make management decisions.

Often it is discovered that the practice's computer system is obsolete, homegrown, antiquated, in dire need of an upgrade, very slow and seemingly bogged down with unpurged data, and the list goes on. The practice's computer system is one of the most important and most expensive assets of the practice. Not only is it vital to the efficiency of data collection but it is also vital to survival under managed care. The pressure is extreme for practices to upgrade their computer systems for the ability to track data needed to make decisions in a managed-care world. They need such data as the number of patients treated for a particular plan, the frequency of procedures for a particular plan's enrollees, the current reimbursements by a particular payer for the most frequent procedures, patient demographic information, and so forth.

And often it is discovered that the practice staff has not been adequately trained in operating the computer system. An additional problem that is frequently encountered is a lack of technical support afforded a practice, even if they are paying for an annual maintenance and service agreement with the system's vendor. Due to this, a practice may have a system with many more capabilities than are being utilized. In our experience, this is one of the most common discoveries. And unfortunately, from a valuation standpoint, this can limit the information and data obtained for purposes of assessing a value. From a going-concern standpoint, this is an issue that will need to be addressed by the practice and the other parties to the transaction. If the practice is to continue to use and maintain its current computer system, it may be necessary to invest additional capital in upgrading the existing system as well as investing in qualified training for the staff.

MEDICAL RECORDS

There are several factors that the valuator is looking for with regard to medical records. First, if there is a value to be placed on the medical records, the valuator must obtain a count of active medical charts. This may entail a physical count or at least an approximation. Additionally, the valuator may use a sampling of records to obtain a representation of the practice's patient demographics such as major employers in the area, major payer classes, types of illnesses treated, age and sex, and geographic locales.

From a due-diligence standpoint, the valuator is reviewing the records for completeness and, in some cases, content of clinical documentation. It is important that each record contain the appropriate patient and insurance information. It is also important that the practice's documentation in the records is legible, whether it is in the form of telephone notes, vital statistics readings, or progress notes for diagnosis and treatment. The record should be orderly and all information should be securely attached. Obviously, the more legible, organized, and complete the records are, the less the chance for legal liability due to their neglect.

The valuator should inquire as to the whereabouts of all medical records. Many times, records that are considered to be inactive are stored off-site in a storage facility, the physician's attic, and so on.

TELEPHONE SYSTEM

The primary purpose of the practice's telephone system is to allow patients to call for appointments. If the patient cannot accomplish this effectively, then the practice does not have an effective telephone system. The valuator should summarily evaluate the telephone system and how it works or doesn't work for the practice. Many times it is found that there simply are not enough telephone lines. In that case, lines can be busy to outside callers because of such business-related things as electronic transmission of insurance claims and faxes used to obtain preauthorizations and referral information.

Additionally, the valuator should inquire as to what the patient hears when the practice line picks up—is it a live receptionist, an automated menu, an answering service during the lunch period, voice mail? And, whatever the case may be, does it seem to be effective? This is one of those cases in which staff should be questioned. Not surprisingly, they are very willing to share with the valuator their obstacles to and/or their praises for the user-friendliness of the system. The same point goes for the computer system (ask the users—they will tell you).

In this system review, the valuator should also assess whether an additional capital expenditure might potentially be needed as part of the ongoing maintenance and business of the practice.

ACCOUNTING SYSTEM

Not only do practices' accounting software packages vary, but so do the accounting processes and procedures used by practices. Primarily, because medical practices are what we refer to as a "cottage industry" businesses, accounting is not one of those areas that have traditionally been given great concern. Before the world of accounting software, a practice's accounting system was usually a shoebox delivered to the accountant once a month or every quarter. Today, many practices use a financial accounting software system that enables the recording of receipts and expenses internally. However, there are varying levels of sophistication—not only of the software but of the practice staff assigned to this task as well. And there are still medical practices that perform the entire accounting function manually.

Like the computer system, the practice's accounting system may or may not give the practice the type of data it needs in order to make informed decisions. The site visit gives the valuator the opportunity to question staff members in the accounts receivable cycle for clarification of computer-reported data, aged accounts receivable matters, billing and collection procedures, and electronic claims processing. The valuator should inquire of the status of claims filing as to whether it is current. The valuator should also review samples of correspondence used in billing and collections such as statements, follow-up letters, letters regarding turnover of accounts to collection agencies, and payment plan forms. The valuator should review the rejected claims history for reasons for rejection and the process by which the practice handles rejected claims. This will typically be one of the areas of due diligence that will be the most time-consuming. But it is important for the valuation in that the gross charge levels of the practice may constitute one value but the poor billing and collection habits of the practice may constitute another.

More than likely, the valuator will need to converse with the practice's outside accountant to obtain the level of detail necessary to complete the valuation. However, the valuator should gain an understanding of the adequacies and efficiencies of and procedures used in the practice's current accounting system. The valuator should also review the practice's internal control system throughout the accounting process to ensure an adequate segregation of duties. No one person should have the element of control over the practice's cash cycle.

One caveat that physicians should understand with regard to the value of their practice is in the case of spouses and/or family members performing financial duties of the practice. This is especially important in such common examples as in the case of a practice entertaining a buy-in by another physician. The physician that is buying in may not be particularly comfortable with the fact that the other physician's spouse handles all the financial matters. This is a scenario that we have seen numerous times. From a valuation standpoint, certain questions should be addressed. For example, (1) Is the spouse an employee of the practice? (2) Is the spouse being paid, and if so, how much and on what basis? (3) Should it be recommended that the practice hire a replacement or shift this responsibility to a business manager that has the capacity? These kinds of issues should be addressed and resolved by all parties prior to a transaction.

PERSONNEL

With regard to the practice's staff, the valuator should review the resumes of the practice's existing staff, especially those staff members in key positions. The valuator should assess the levels of training available at the practice from orientation to cross training. Also, the responsibilities of the administrator or business manager should be reviewed for their level of sophistication in handling the requirements of a managed care practice. As painful as this may be for physicians and management alike, it is a very important aspect of the future well-being of a medical practice today. In many cases it may be recommended, as fallout of the valuation process, that management obtain additional training in key areas or that the practice seek alternatives for obtaining the level of management required, especially if the practice is a fairly large or growing group practice.

The valuator should also evaluate the prudence of the practice related to the maintenance of personnel records, frequency of Operational Safety and Health Administration (OSHA) and other training required by regulatory authorities, time reporting and approval process, staff scheduling, and salary and benefit structure.

FIXED ASSETS

The valuator should verify the existence of the practice's fixed assets: furniture, fixtures, medical equipment, business equipment, automobiles, and other assets that may be included on the practice's balance sheet. Some or all of these assets may not be transferred depending on the purpose of the valuation and the intent of the parties to the transaction. Assets to be transferred will be valued.

The valuator may or may not be the one assigned to value fixed assets. However, in the course of the valuator's due diligence, she should, nevertheless, confirm the existence of major assets and note any significant facts related to condition, use, obsolescence, maintenance, and so on. We have seen many instances where the practice owns a piece of medical equipment such as an EKG machine or an autoclave but the equipment is no longer in working order. The equipment is typically sitting idle in a closet or storage room. However, the asset is still on the books of the practice and the assumption is that it is in operation. These assets need to either be deleted from transferable assets or be valued based on current use, which may be as residual or scrap only.

The valuator should also inquire of lease arrangements with regard to fixed assets. Sometimes, unfortunately, the practice's accountant overlooks lease arrangements. This results in an asset being capitalized on the practice's balance sheet as if it belonged to the practice when indeed it may not. It may be a leased asset with no purchase arrangement whatsoever. Consequently, the seller does not have this asset to sell. We have seen this situation several times in our valuation experience.

If you are a physician, whether you are valuing your practice or not it is recommended that you always forward all documentation regarding fixed assets to your accountant for the appropriate treatment. It is easy to fall into a pattern of just letting the accountant know what it is you bought and how much you paid for it. But, it is important that the proper accounting treatment be given to your financial statements. If not, you may have significant costs involved with the amendment of your tax returns related to depreciation deductions taken on assets that you never owned. Your costs will not only be related to your accountant's fees and retroactive taxes, but you will more than likely also incur penalties as well as risk having your return automatically flagged for future audits.

INVENTORY OF SUPPLIES

The valuator should assess the practice's supply inventory on hand. This will include office and administrative supplies, exam room and clinical supplies, and durable medical equipment. An approximation should be made for the amount of inventory on hand for purposes of estimating a value. However, it is recommended that a supply inventory be taken on or near the closing date of the transaction. This date is typically several months following the effective date of a valuation.

Additionally, at the same time the valuator reviews the accounting procedures, he should evaluate the purchasing and ordering authority of supplies as well as the security of the merchandise in the practice. Again, no one staff member should have control over the purchase *and* disbursement of supplies. The valuator may make an observation of what appears to be high expense ratios with regard to supply inventories but he may observe low levels on hand as well as receive information from staff that they typically do not "keep much on hand." Then potentially the practice has an embezzlement issue. Internal control should be evaluated for every type of cash transaction.

MARKETING

The valuator should review the practice's marketing strategy, if any, for its impact on the future revenue stream of the practice. Many practices actively market through advertising in the Yellow Pages, high school and college football programs and yearbooks, and local newsprint publications. Some practices have contracts, which may be exclusive, with area employers to provide physicals for executives, Departments of Transportation, Workers' Compensation injuries, and preemployment drug screen testing.

It may be that the practice has no marketing plan. And this is not necessarily to be viewed as a negative. Many practices do not need to make the investment of time or money in marketing because, quite simply, they do very well without it. It usually depends on the market competition for patients and the managed care penetration whether a practice has invested in a marketing strategy. And the valuator must assess the viability of marketing for the subject practice.

FACILITY

The first question the valuator will answer with regard to the facility will be whether she would want to visit the subject practice as a patient. If her answer is no, then more than likely it would be no for other patients as well. The facility's condition and curb appeal do have an impact on the value as well as on the requirements for future capital expenditures. Other questions that the valuator should address are with regard to the accessibility of the practice. Practices that are (a) difficult to locate and (b) difficult to transport in and out of are not going to be the practices of choice for the patient. Even though managed care dictates the selection of physicians, the patient will usually have more than one choice.

Another factor that the valuator should consider is the patient flow of the practice. The practice should allow for unrestricted traffic flow in and out of clinical areas and to and from the patient lobby. It should also allow for patient privacy in clinical areas and the business office where it is sometimes necessary to conduct financial counseling. It is also important that staff have ample space in which to operate. Practices that have overcrowded work spaces, poor lighting, and high noise levels contribute to poor morale among the staff, and that usually translates into poor customer service to the patient.

As part of the review of the facility, the valuator should assess the feasibility of excess capacity to treat additional patient volume. For example, if the practice facility only allows for two exam rooms each for two physicians and the appointment schedules are booked to capacity, then it is not a reasonable assumption that this practice's revenue stream would grow significantly without revisions to existing space or moving to another location.

PHYSICIAN AND MANAGEMENT ISSUES

Last but not least, and this may be the most important aspect of the site visit, the valuator should schedule time to meet with key physicians and management in order to gain necessary information required to form a valuation opinion. Information that should be discussed with these individuals includes, but is not limited to, the following:

- Projections of the practice's growth and direction
- Staffing issues
- Malpractice cases and contingent liabilities

- Financial issues

- Planned capital expenditures

- Physician credentials

- Perceptions of market forces and competition

- Managed care information

- Call coverage

- Clinical studies and research activities

- Related-party transactions

- History of practice

- Tenure of previous providers and reasons for leaving

- Clarification of employment agreement, buy/sell agreements, and so on

- Prior IRS audits and outcomes/liabilities

- Citations by regulatory authorities

- Building ownership/lease arrangements

- Staff turnover issues

- Use of outside labor

This kind of qualitative information will assist the valuator in forming opinions and assumptions about the ability of the practice to continue to generate an income stream.

It is especially important for the valuator to inquire of the owners as to their perception of the practice's future growth. The owner/physicians should have involvement in making sure that the valuator understands their practice. If you are the owner/physician, and again depending on the purpose and depth of the valuation, you should communicate to the valuator things about your practice that would impact the value. If you are the valuator, you should inquire of the owners and management as to any outstanding issues that may have an impact on the value of the practice.

SUMMARY

The valuator must take logic and common sense into consideration when valuing medical practices. Following a site visit to the subject practice and the interview process conducted while on-site, the valuator should have a much greater understanding of the practice as a business. The valuator can then apply the qualitative information obtained through the on-site proceedings to quantitative measurements to determine an estimated value. As the valuator goes through the valuation process and, in particular, the on-site portion, he or she will assess those factors and characteristics of the practice that contribute to its intangible value.

The valuator should record his or her observations and interviews with clear, concise documentation in the valuation workpapers. This documentation serves as the valuator's support for his or her opinions of value.

Ultimately, the valuator should use the on-site visit time as efficiently and effectively as possible. It is recommended that the valuator request and obtain as much information and data as possible prior to scheduling the site visit. Granted, this is much easier said than done for 9 valuations out of 10. However, the valuator should explain to the practice the purpose and flow of the process. Typically, once the practice understands the process, they are willing to do what it takes to speed the process along. This will allow the valuator to do his or her homework and sufficiently prepare for the site visit. The up-front preparation will assist the valuator in identifying which areas will require additional focus while on-site. We have found from experience that this greatly simplifies the entire process for the valuator and all parties involved.

An example of a typical valuator's on-site checklist is provided in Exhibit 6.1. This may be used as a guide to tailor a checklist for a specific valuation engagement.

Exhibit 6.1

Example of an on-site checklist

Section 1: APPOINTMENT SCHEDULING

Review appointment schedules to obtain an average number of patients per day or week treated by each physician/provider. Also, review for number of new versus established patient visits.

What are routine office hours:_____

Morning and afternoon appointments begin and end at:_____

Description of visit type, length of visit for routine visits, follow-ups, physicals, etc.

Does the practice participate in Medicare assignment?

Does the practice accept Medicaid patients?

Does the practice confirm appointments prior to day of visit?

How are work-ins, urgent care visits, and walk-ins handled?

How are referrals organized and handled?

Does the practice have a patient recall system? If so, for what conditions and visit types is it used, in what form is it used (mailing reminders, phone calls, etc.) and how often?

Section 2: COMPUTER INFORMATION SYSTEMS

Is the computer system owned or leased? If leased, describe arrangements.

Describe hardware and software.

When was the last time the system was upgraded?

Monthly service and maintenance contract? With whom and at what costs?

Describe any immediate plans for upgrade or replacement and expected costs.

Exhibit 6.1

(Continued)

Section 3: MEDICAL RECORDS

Describe the general content and condition of patient charts:

How does the practice maintain filing order? (alphabetic, numeric, etc.)

What information is provided on the chart labels?
>   Patient name
>   Account number
>   Allergies
>   Primary insurance
>   Date of birth
>   Phone number

Is the information properly secured in the charts?

Are the notes dictated by physicians? Describe dictation and transcription methods and related costs.

Do the physicians sign the chart notes?

When was the last time inactive charts were removed from the active files?

What is the approximate count of active charts and what time period do they cover (number of years, etc.)?

Review records for patient demographic sample if information is not available from practice's computer system:
>   Date of birth/age
>   Sex
>   Zip code
>   Diagnosis/illness
>   Primary insurance

Section 4: TELEPHONE SYSTEM

Is the system owned or leased? If leased, obtain copy of lease arrangement.

Describe capabilities and function of telephone system.

What is the type/make/model of the telephone system?

How many lines does the system allow and how many does the practice use? Describe their use (private, hospital, fax/modem, internet, etc.).

Exhibit 6.1
(*Continued*)

Section 5: ACCOUNTING

What software is used for accounts payable?

Who performs the accounts payable function? Describe process.

Who performs the payroll function? Describe process and time reporting procedures

Describe the accounts receivable process.

Describe billing procedures including electronic claims filing and handling of claim rejections.

What is the practice's patient billing cycle?

Describe follow-up collections system.

Obtain copies of routine billing and collections correspondence used by the practice (statements, payment plan authorizations, etc.).

Does the practice use a collection agency? If so, what are the practice's policies for turning over accounts?

Are office visit charges posted on the day of service?

How long following hospital dates of service are hospital charges posted?

Section 6: PERSONNEL

Review personnel records for appropriate documentation.

Evaluate confidential security of personnel and payroll records.

Review staff resumes and job descriptions to determine appropriateness of matched skill sets and competencies.

Inquire as to training programs offered for staff such as seminars, workshops, paid tuition for college, correspondence courses, etc.

Exhibit 6.1
(*Continued*)

Section 7: FIXED ASSETS

Obtain an inventory listing of major assets owned by the practice, also noting relevant features such as condition, age, functional obsolescence, service and maintenance contracts, and lease arrangements.

Compare for reasonableness against the practice's fixed asset depreciation schedule. Note: Be aware that laboratory equipment and laboratory computer hardware and printers are usually owned by outside lab companies.

Section 8: SUPPLIES

General comment on the purchasing methods, authorization channels, and amount of clinical and administrative supplies routinely kept on hand.

Section 9: MARKETING

Describe the practice's current marketing activities.

Does the practice advertise? If so, where? (i.e., Yellow Pages, athletic programs, small town newspaper; wall frame flyers in hallways/elevators, etc.)

Describe any contractual relationship with area employers/organizations for occupational/industrial medicine services (i.e., physicals [DOT, executive], drug screenings, etc.).

Section 10: FACILITY

Describe outside appearance and general condition of facility.

Is it accessible to handicapped and disabled patients and employees?

What is the general location of the practice within the community and what is its geographic proximity to hospital(s)?

What are the typical traffic flow patterns in front of or near the practice? Is it easy to locate and easily accessible?

Does the practice have signs that are visible and legible from the roadway or driveway?

Describe the inside appearance, layout, and general condition of facility. (Obtain copy of facility floor plan from fire escape route plan, if available.)

Is patient flow restricted and does it allow for the appropriate level of privacy?

Exhibit 6.1

(*Continued*)

What is the number of: Exam rooms _____

Procedure rooms _____

Lab areas _____

Radiology areas _____

Nurses' stations _____

Other clinical areas _____

Physician offices _____

Front office work stations _____

Business management offices _____

Restrooms _____

Lounge/kitchen areas _____

Other employee areas _____

What services are offered by the practice?

Laboratory

Radiology

OB

Ultrasound/Sonograms

Mammograms

MRI

Stress testing

EKG

EEG

EMG

Pharmacy

Drug screening

DOT physicals

Executive physicals

Physical therapy

Occupational therapy

Speech therapy

Audiology

Mobile units

Other services

Exhibit 6.1

(Continued)

Section 11: PHYSICIAN AND MANAGEMENT ISSUES

Gather information that may not have been available on physician's curriculum vitae such as education, internship, residency, fellowship, and board certification.

Physician's other income sources: Activities and amount of annual income received from such services as teaching, expert witness testimony, reading diagnostic tests, U/R review, medical directorships, etc.

Are the revenues and expenses related to these activities accounted for in the practice financial statements?

Does the physician plan to continue these relationships/obligations if practice is purchased?

What hospital and long-term care facility affiliations does the physician have?

Is the practice affiliated with IPAs or other networks? If so, describe arrangements.

What is the physician's perception of competition and provider alliances in the area for similar practices and services provided?

What is the physician's perception of the practice's patient population (patient demographics such as age, sex, and cities/counties served)?

What are the major problems and illnesses treated by the practice?

What are the major managed care payers and what is their estimated percentage of the practice's patient base?

What is the physician's (and management's) perception of the practice's future revenue growth patterns? What factors are influencing growth or stagnation? What are the major payer influences and current trends in the practice's market area? What are the predominant contractual fee structures of the practice's managed care payers?

What other factors are affecting the practice such as market trends, internal problems, management, etc.?

What is the physician's (and management's) base salary, bonus structure, and other relevant facts pertaining to compensation plan?

Exhibit 6.1
(Continued)

What role does your administrator/business manager play in the management of the practice?

Does the physician have any fiduciary interest in other medical services outside the practice?

Ask for clarification that may be needed regarding practice debt/liabilities. Clarify ownership of building/facility space, rental payment arrangements, etc.

Why does the physician wish to sell/merge the practice?

How long does the physician intend to stay with the practice following acquisition/merger?

Will employees stay with the practice following acquisition/merger?

Will employee physician(s) and/or mid-level providers stay with the practice following acquisition/merger?

Does the physician have any pending malpractice cases? If so, provide brief description.

Completing the Valuation Process

In the preceding chapters, we have considered the various methods for calculating the value of a medical practice and have concentrated on the specific rules and techniques involved in computing value under each of several different methodologies. The conclusion of the engagement is no less important than the planning or engagement processes; therefore, great care should be taken when wrapping up the valuation. Despite competent work in planning the engagement and in carrying out the steps to properly execute the valuation methodology, the entire valuation can become worthless if the closing process is not performed in a skilled manner. As with any component of the engagement, the judgment of the valuator plays a critical role in completing the process and generating a meaningful and accurate conclusion.

One of the most significant steps in the closing process is the reconciliation of the amounts obtained during the execution of the valuation methodology. Despite the accurate application of various methods like the ones discussed previously in this book, the entire value conclusion may be incorrect if the reconciliation of these methods is inappropriately performed.

There are a number of other significant steps to be taken when completing the valuation process, including the consideration of premiums and discounts and reasonableness checks, without which the entire valuation may be discredited. This chapter will address the steps ordinarily considered in the wrap-up stages of the engagement to value a medical practice.

RECONCILING VALUATION METHODS

It has been made clear throughout this book that the valuation of a medical practice is not an exact science. The objective and independent judgment of the valuator is the key factor in determining the overall conclusion of value. It is vitally important to consider the fact that in the valuation of a medical practice, reliance on a single method can be a very risky proposition. No single method of valuation is an absolute in and of itself; therefore, the medical practice valuator should give consideration to as many methods as may be practically employed in the valuation to produce a sound conclusion of value.

When multiple valuation methods are utilized in calculating an estimate of value, the valuator is faced with the need to convert what is often a wide range of value estimates into a single value conclusion. This is generally accomplished in one of three methods: a simple average, an objective weighted average, or a subjective weighting.

The simple average of values obtained by various methods is accomplished in the following manner (shown in Exhibit 7.1). This is the least favorable approach and generally yields a number that is not representative of a subjective conclusion of value. Ordinarily, this approach should not be used in practice, and is presented here for illustrative purposes only.

The second method for converting various value calculations into a value conclusion is the objective weighted average, as illustrated in Exhibit 7.2.

Exhibit 7.1

Sample average of values

Discounted Cash Flow Method	$ 564,300
Capitalized Earnings Method	383,500
Comparable Sales Method	398,100
Average	**$ 448,633**

Exhibit 7.2

Objective weighted average

Method	Value	Weight	Weighted Value
Discounted Cash Flow Method	$ 564,300	3	$1,692,900
Capitalized Earnings Method	383,500	2	767,000
Comparable Sales Method	398,100	1	398,100
Total			2,858,000
Divided by Weights		6	6
Weighted Average			**$ 476,333**

The Internal Revenue Service speaks out against the use of a mathematical average approach such as in the exhibits provided above, advising that the valuator should *subjectively* arrive at the value conclusion. This subjective approach should be based upon the professional judgment of the valuator, applied to the individual facts and circumstances of the specific case. We generally prefer the use of the subjective approach over the average or objective average approaches. However, in valuation engagements without the risk of IRS involvement, you may choose to use an objective weighted average such as the one presented in Exhibit 7.2.

Each valuation approach has greater or lesser applicability to the specific practice being valued. In the valuation of a medical practice, earnings-based approaches are generally more applicable than asset-based methods, because so much of the value of the practice is dependent on the earnings generated by the physicians. On the other hand, asset values obtained for a manufacturing business may be more applicable, because of the significant investment in manufacturing equipment and processes. The valuator should also consider the relative availability of data in determining the subjective weight to be assigned to a specific method. For example, the comparable sales approach for a pediatric oncology practice may contain few references to actual sales of similar practices; therefore, the valuator would likely assign a very low relevance to the amount obtained through the use of this method.

Likewise, the specific nature of the valuation or the context in which the valuation is to be used should also impact the valuator's judgment of weights assigned to the various methods employed. For example, when the standard of value is investment value, the use of the discounted cash flow method may be most appropriate to demonstrate the value of the synergies between the buyer and seller, and would therefore be given a greater subjective weight.

In a purely subjective assessment of the value conclusion, the valuator might come to the conclusion based on judgment and experience that the value of the practice in the above exhibits is $520,000, as illustrated in Exhibit 7.3. Obviously, the overall conclusion of value may not necessarily equal any of the results achieved in the specific methods employed.

In Exhibit 7.3, the valuator has based the value conclusion on a greater weighting toward the discounted cash flow method, based on professional judgment and a detailed analysis of the practice during the valuation process. The valuator also has considered such factors as:

- Standard of value
- Uses of the valuation report
- Nature of the proposed transaction
- Availability of data
- Applicability to medical practices
- Medical practice specialty

Alternatively, the valuator may elect to exclusively select a particular method as being completely applicable to the value of the practice and assign no weight to the other methods. In the example presented in Exhibit 7.3, the valuator could arrive at a value conclusion of $564,300 by assigning the entire subjective weight to a single method, in this case, the discounted cash flow method. There are cer-

Exhibit 7.3
Subjective assessment of value

Discounted Cash Flow Method	$ 564,300
Capitalized Earnings Method	383,500
Comparable Sales Method	398,100
Value Conclusion	**520,000**

tain risks that accompany this selective use of valuation method. For example, a simple mathematical error or a dispute over matters of judgment in the valuation calculation could spell problems for the valuation conclusion as a whole.

Whenever converting several values into a single value conclusion, it is important to clearly document the process, including the judgment factors involved and the reasons for assigning greater weight to one or more specific methods. For example, the valuator should consider stating in the report that the overall conclusion of value is not strictly a mathematical process. The valuator should likewise show that professional judgment is important in determining the overall value conclusion for the practice. We do not believe that it is specifically necessary to disclose the weights assigned to each of the approaches when using a subjective approach, because that is a matter of judgment. Instead, the valuator should document that the value conclusion was obtained through the use of her independent and professional judgment.

TESTING FOR REASONABLENESS

In many services performed by accountants and other financial professionals, reasonableness checks are a routine part of the engagement. Whether in preparing tax returns or financial statements, the reasonableness of the numbers is often given priority in the wrap-up stages. The valuation of a medical practice is no different. At the conclusion of the engagement, it is wise for the valuator to step back and view the entire process from an independent vantage point, assessing whether the numbers derived from the valuation process are truly reasonable from an overall perspective. This means that you as the valuator should apply an analytical review to the value conclusion to satisfy yourself as to the reasonableness of the assumptions, calculations, and conclusions expressed in your report.

We often refer to this process as a "sanity check" or "gut check," and the process often involves the use of other methodology to test the reasonableness of the value conclusion. Obviously, each method used in the calculation of value can serve as a reasonableness check of the other methods that are used. In our example in Exhibit 7.3, our conclusion would be that the comparable sales and excess earnings methods would likely serve as reasonableness checks for each other, but not the discounted cash flow method. To satisfy ourselves on the reasonableness or "sanity" of that method, other checks should be employed.

Some valuation methods are considered so broad and undocumented as to be avoided when computing the value of a medical practice. Examples of these methods include the rule of thumb approach and the payback approach. Both, however, are excellent means for testing the reasonableness of values obtained through the use of more generally accepted methodology.

As a sanity check, the rule of thumb can often be effective in assessing the reasonableness of the value conclusion. Consider the following examples of fictitious derivatives of the rule of thumb approach:

- Family practice clinics sell for 35 to 100 percent of annual revenues.

- Goodwill in a primary care practice averages approximately one-third of annual revenues.

- Internal medicine practices generally sell for $130,000 per FTE physician.

Although these methods would obviously not be appropriate as a source for the calculation of value, in each of these cases, the overall value conclusion can be tested based on rule of thumb data available for the specific practice. Rules of thumb are readily available through many valuation publications.

The payback approach also yields an effective test of the reasonableness of value, under the theory that an investment should pay the owner sufficient return to "pay for itself" within a reasonable period of time. The most common approach for a medical practice involves the calculation of the payback of an investment assuming a five-year payback period and a market borrowing rate. Using a reasonable down payment, say 10 percent, will the practice generate sufficient return to allow payment of the financed purchase price within the five-year window? Consider the example in Exhibit 7.4. Using a present value formula, we find that the number of periods necessary to pay off the hypothetical loan to buy this practice is

Exhibit 7.4
Loan payback using present value formula

Practice value	$ 200,000
Market borrowing rate	10 percent
Down payment	$ 20,000
Annual projected return on investment	$ 30,000

4.9 years. Based on our expectation of 5 years, the payback is reasonable, and we therefore have a greater comfort level with the value conclusion.

The inclusion of reasonableness checks in the report is purely optional. We generally do not include this methodology in our reports, although other valuators do.

APPLYING PREMIUMS AND DISCOUNTS

At the outset of the valuation engagement, you identified the interest to be valued in the practice and the nature of the transaction or event triggering the need for the valuation. In the planning process, you used this information to establish the methodology for conducting the valuation and to identify the specific information about the engagement to be included in your report. Now that the calculations are complete and the value conclusion derived from the various methods employed, your focus once again turns to the interest being valued and the market for that interest.

Two important questions should be considered at this point in the project:

1. Is the interest being valued a controlling interest or a minority interest?

2. Is the interest being valued a marketable interest?

These questions are essential in determining whether you will be required to adjust your value conclusion, either upward or downward, to reflect the value of the specific interest subject to your valuation.

Elements of Control

In all valuation engagements related to medical practices, the degree of control exercised by the interest being valued is important to the overall value of that interest. Control can be defined as the ability of the owner of the interest being valued to adopt, change, or discontinue the specific operational aspects of the business. In other words, can the owner of the interest being valued exercise any control over the medical practice, by changing the legal structure of the business entity, sell the practice, set physician compensation, commit the practice to debt, or add new owners? If the owner of the interest being valued has the ability to exercise these and other elements of control, this owner is said to have a "controlling interest." In a solo practice, the physician-owner has complete control over these elements; therefore, control is a less critical issue in this structure. However, the relative degree of control exercised by one member of a group practice plays an important role in the valuation of that interest relative to the value of the practice.

Consider the role of a Dr. Emery Dewell, a single physician in a three-owner practice. Assuming the owners share equally in the ownership of the practice and in the division of profits, this physician basically has a one-third interest in the practice. Given this set of facts, is the value of the physician's one-third interest in the practice equal to one-third of the value of the practice taken as a whole? Generally, the answer is "no."

Suppose that this one-third owner has no greater or lesser influence on the operational aspects of the practice than do his co-owners. Would a hypothetical willing buyer pay exactly one-third of the value of the entire practice, when the one-third interest does not yield any majority control over the management of the practice? Likewise, would three unrelated purchasers pay as much in the aggregate for three one-third interests as a single purchaser would pay for the entire practice? The answers to these questions obviously vary depending upon the specific facts and circumstances of the practice being valued. Generally, however, it is most often the case that the whole is greater than the sum of its parts, meaning that complete control is more valuable than three-thirds' worth of control. The degree to which the interest owner can exercise control affects the difference between the value of that interest on a controlling or minority basis.

In order to quantify this phenomenon, we look to the discount for lack of marketability or the control premium. Whether the discount or the premium is employed depends upon the value yielded by the methodology employed in reaching our value conclusion. For example, many of the methods used in valuing a medical practice yield a value that is representative of a controlling interest. Some of those methods are described in Chapter 4. However, some methods that base the value conclusion on the results of comparisons to publicly traded companies reflect a minority-interest basis. For our purposes in valuing medical practices, we will limit our discussions to the valuation of a controlling interest, using the methods commonly applied in medical practice valuations.

When the value conclusion obtained for a medical practice results in a controlling-interest value, the underlying assumption is that the hypothetical purchaser is buying the rights to exercise complete control over the operational aspects of the practice, using the elements of control described above. When this controlling interest value is applied to an interest less than 100 percent, you must determine to what extent the value of that interest is lessened by the lack of complete control. This is quantified in the use of the minority interest discount. In our example of one-third owners above, and given a value of $300,000 for the practice as a whole, how much should the value of one physician's interest be discounted for this lack of control?

To determine this, your analysis should include specific facts about the elements of control exercised by the owner of the interest being valued. Can the owner exert such significant influence as to control the direction of the practice? Can he set policy and compensation amounts? Can he add a new owner? In some cases, a one-third owner has such influence over the practice that a minority interest discount is not appropriate or significant. In other cases, the control exercised by the owner is so small as to warrant a more significant discount. Furthermore, the simple ownership of an interest greater than 50 percent does not eliminate the need for a minority interest discount. Owners with a smaller interest may have a "swing vote," which could effectively reduce the control of the majority owner. And a 50/50 interest does not necessarily translate to equal control, which may result in a greater minority discount for one owner's interest.

Quantifying the minority interest discount requires judgment and a clear understanding of the elements of control exercised by the owner of the valued interest in the medical practice. Unfortunately, there exists no mathematical formula for determining the percentage discount to be applied to a given interest in any business, although published data is available that documents studies of publicly traded companies and the relative amounts of discounts for minority interests. As a rule, the typical minority interest discount often ranges between 20 and 30 percent, although wide variances from this range are commonly found. In valuing a minority interest in a medical practice, your calculation of the minority interest discount should include a thorough analysis of the data gathered during your interviews of the physicians regarding the elements of control, while considering the control afforded by the percentage of ownership interest in the practice. In majority ownership situations, the baseline discount is often in the 5 to 10 percent range, and higher for smaller ownership interests. Of course, the baseline rate should be adjusted for specific elements of control exerted by the owner.

Marketability

Assessing the relative market for a medical practice is also important to completing the valuation. In recent years, integration efforts by hospitals and merger and acquisition activity by group practices and PPMCs have created additional demand for physician practices, especially primary care practices. In considering the value of a practice, the valuator must be concerned with the existence or absence of a ready market for the practice, and the effect of these factors on value. For obvious reasons, a practice with a readily available market generally commands a higher value than a practice without a market. Furthermore, a partial ownership interest in a practice may be less marketable than the practice as a whole. The specialty of the medical practice is also an important consideration in the evaluation of marketability, especially given the activity surrounding primary care practices. Obviously, an understanding of the marketability of the practice and the application of an appropriate discount for lack of marketability is critical to an accurate representation of value.

Many of the approaches commonly used in valuing medical

practices today assume a readily available market for the medical practice. Published studies of medical practice transactions show dozens, of medical practice sales transactions for comparative purposes. But some practices, or fractional interests in medical practices, may require an adjustment to value to reflect a lack of marketability.

Again, no mathematical formula exists to apply to a specific practice to obtain a discount for lack of marketability. However, studies of initial public offerings are readily available that yield information on implied marketability discounts. Of course, no public market for physician practice interests exists, leaving the valuator to the use of judgment. In our experience, any necessary minority interest discount is usually small, usually less than 15 percent, because of the lack of significant impact on value resulting from the lack of a public market for physician practice interests.

Valuing Ownership Interests

Let us assume that you have been engaged to value Dr. Dewell's one-third interest in the example noted above, in which the value conclusion for the practice as a whole is determined to be $300,000. Through your analysis and inquiry, you have determined that a 25 percent minority interest discount and a 5 percent discount for lack of marketability should be applied. Exhibit 7.5 shows the steps to compute the value of Dr. Dewell's one-third interest. When using both minority and marketability discounts in the same calculation, it

Exhibit 7.5
Computing the value of one-third interest

Value conclusion for the practice	$300,000
Dr. Dewell's interest in the practice	× .33
Gross value of a one-third interest	100,000
Minority interest discount (1 minus 25 percent)	× .75
	75,000
Marketability discount (1 minus 5 percent)	× .95
Value of Dr. Dewell's interest	$ 71,250

is necessary to first apply the minority interest discount, then apply the marketability discount, as shown in the exhibit.

OBTAINING CLIENT REPRESENTATIONS

Without doubt, many of the resources used in the valuation are taken from information provided by the client or nonclient medical practice in the form of financial statements and other source documentation. Also included are other verbal or written representations made in response to the inquiries and investigation made by the valuator into the operation of the medical practice. As is common in engagements with which accountants use client representations to report on financial matters, a representation letter is most often necessary to supplement the working paper files. In a valuation, this letter should be addressed to the valuator and include statements that the information provided during the valuation process was accurate and complete, and that no pertinent information was withheld during the engagement. The letter should be signed by the persons responsible for providing this information to the valuator.

It should be the policy of the valuator to obtain a representation letter from the medical practice being valued, whether or not the medical practice is the actual client. For example, in a valuation performed for a hospital planning to acquire a medical practice, the operational and financial information is provided by the practice, regardless of the client relationship with the hospital. Therefore, the valuator should seek to obtain a representation letter from the physicians and certain office or administrative staff that were involved in supplying information for the valuation. This letter should be obtained before the final report is released.

REPORTING

The report is the culmination of the valuator's many hours of work in planning, analyzing, applying methodology and exercising judgment in the medical practice valuation. In fact, the valuator's report most often represents the only written external evidence of the work performed, and is generally the only deliverable product presented to the client. In the case of scrutiny by the IRS or other cognizant agency, the written report is the first line of defense of the valuation conclusion. Given the importance of the valuator's report, the development of a thorough and concise report should be the objective of everyone involved in the valuation of any business, and especially in the valuation of a medical practice.

Report writing does not often come naturally to financial professionals. Conveying the complex environment surrounding the health care industry and the challenging work of valuing a medical practice in a written form is often a difficult process, leaving the writer with the objective of converting complicated subject matter into an easily readable format. In addition to this obstacle, there are specific requirements applicable to valuation reports, as well as a variety of formats in which a report may be presented.

A valuation report may be presented in full format (long-form) or letter format written reports, or presented orally. The circumstances surrounding the event triggering the valuation or the intended users of the report often dictate which method is most appropriate. When the report is intended for general use, the report should always be presented in full format. In some cases, full format reports are also appropriate for limited use, especially when the potential for external scrutiny exists or when necessary to convey additional information about the engagement. Both full and letter format written reports as well as oral reports will be addressed below.

Professional Standards

When issuing a report, the valuator should be aware of standards applicable to the report. The Appraisal Foundation, a nonprofit organization developed to establish guidelines and professional standards for valuators, issues the *Uniform Standards of Professional Appraisal Practice (USPAP)* each year. Of particular importance are Standards 9 and 10, which specifically address the valuation of businesses and include professional and reporting standards applicable to business appraisal. These standards are reproduced in Appendix F. Other professional organizations, such as the American Society of Appraisers (ASA), the Institute of Business Appraisers (IBA), and the National Association of Certified Valuation Analysts (NACVA) issue their own standards for members performing business valuation services.

In the case of CPAs who conduct valuations, the American Institute of Certified Public Accountants (AICPA) has issued standards for conduct in connection with consulting engagements and reporting on historical and prospective financial statement presentations. Statements on Standards for Consulting Services and Statements on Standards for Accounting and Review Services establish specific standards often applicable to valuations, particularly when reports are made available for general use.

IRS Requirements

The Internal Revenue Service has long been considered one of the primary theoreticians in business valuation methodology. In Revenue Ruling 59-60, the IRS created some of the most often quoted standards for fair market value and factors to consider in the valuation of a closely held enterprise. Revenue Ruling 68-609 provides guidance for the excess earnings approach to valuing intangible assets. A copy of these Revenue Rulings are reproduced in Appendix E.

Presentation of Written Reports

There are generally two types of written reports on the valuation of a business: a full format (long-form) or a letter format report.

Full Format Reports

The most comprehensive written report is the full format report, which contains a complete analysis of the valuation of the business, including detailed information on the background of the business and its market environment, financial analyses, definitions and descriptions of the valuation methodology considered, and a complete set of exhibits supporting the business and the value conclusions. Because of the level of detail in the full format report, it is generally considered sufficiently comprehensive for most uses, including general use by outside parties. An example of a full format report is presented in Chapter 8, Exhibit 8.2.

Executive Summary. The first sections of the report contain the accountant's report and/or executive summary of the valuation. In this section, several items of information are presented in a very concise format, giving the user an overview of the process and the results of the valuation. This summarized information includes:

- Description of the medical practice and the interest being valued

- Date of the valuation and the report

- Standard of value

- Purpose of the valuation

- Reference to specific assumptions and limiting conditions

- Value conclusion

Definitions. Following the report letter and the executive summary are the pertinent definitions for the valuation engagement. In this section, detailed definitions are provided for the standard of value and the interest in the medical practice being valued. In general, these definitions are provided in sufficient detail to advise the reader of the meaning of the standard of value and the valuation processes employed in the analysis of a closely held business.

Description of the Clinic and Market. The description and market analysis section of the report is the first section in the report with detailed information about the subject medical practice. In this section, the history, ownership, and management of the practice is discussed in detail, followed by the market analysis.

The market analysis describes the nature of the practice; the competitive factors affecting the practice; and the national, regional, and local economic conditions. Because of the complexities associated with the health care industry, this section often contains very descriptive information about the practice of medicine and the outlook for the industry and the subject practice. Often important to this section is information about the physical location of the practice and the local health care community.

Financial Analysis.   Within this section of the report are the financial details of the practice, not only from a historical perspective, but also in a prospective format. Specific information about the financial history of the practice is given here, and references are made to any supporting exhibits that present historical financial statement information. Because normalizing adjustments are important to the understanding of the reader, this section should also include descriptions of the adjustments made to the historical financial statements during the valuation process.

Data and assumptions used in projecting the financial operations of the medical practice for use in such valuation approaches as the discounted cash flow method should also be discussed in this section as appropriate.

Valuation Process and Methodology.   As an essential ingredient in the usefulness of the written report, we generally include detailed background on the valuation process and definitions of the methodology considered in the valuation of the medical practice. The background of the valuation process includes definitions of the broad approaches considered, such as earnings-based, market-based, and asset-based approaches. Further definition of the process includes the definitions of the eight factors required by Revenue Ruling 59-60, as they apply to the current valuation.

Within each of the broad approaches considered, the report should contain a detailed description of the methodology employed within each approach. For example, the discounted cash flow method would be fully described within the definition of the earnings-based approach. The description of the methodology should normally include the theory behind the selection and use of the method, and the results obtained.

Also within this section are often descriptions of individual asset valuation methods, including a breakdown of the components of value separately identified in the scope of the engagement.

Conclusions.   This section contains the results of each approach and the overall value conclusion. Additional information presented in this part of the report would ordinarily include discounts for minority interests and for a lack of marketability.

Exhibits. The exhibits to the report are often at least as lengthy as the report text itself. Exhibit 7.6 is a partial list of exhibits normally included in the full format report.

The assumptions and limiting conditions provided in the report include those significant assumptions of fact related to the information presented in the valuation report, along with the specific limiting conditions related to the completeness and reliability of information provided during the engagement. Examples of common assumptions and limiting conditions are provided in the sample reports appearing in Chapter 8, Exhibits 8.1 and 8.2. The inclusion of a statement of assumptions and limiting conditions is required by US-PAP standards.

The certification by the valuator includes statements signed by the valuator certifying that the valuator is independent and unbiased and that the compensation for the valuation is not contingent on the results of the project. This is also required for USPAP reports. As a supplement, we also include the curriculum vitae of the valuators involved in the project for the benefit of the user of the report.

Because historical financial statements of the practice are essential to the user's understanding of the report, a summary of the financial statements is nearly always included in the exhibits to the report. Usually presented in comparative format, with common-sized ratio analyses, historical financial statements for at least five years are presented whenever available. Other statistical and operational data from the practice, including physician productivity and compensation, are also useful in supporting the assumptions and conclusions in the report.

The presentation of financial statements supporting the economic reality of the practice is another of the financial statement

Exhibit 7.6
Typical exhibits in a full format report

Assumptions and limiting conditions	Normalized financial statements
Valuator's certification	Prospective financial statements
Valuator's qualifications	Discount rate calculation
Historical financial statements	Schedules of valuation methods
Historical statistical data	

summaries often presented in valuation reports. In some cases, the normalizing adjustments themselves are also presented, showing the effect of the valuator's adjustment on the historical financial statements of the practice. Again, a comparative format is very helpful, along with common-sized data where appropriate.

If the data used in the discount rate analysis is too voluminous to include in the text of the report, it is often included as an exhibit to the report, accompanying the detailed calculations of value under the methodology selected. Each method selected for the subject practice is generally presented separately, with as many as possible of the assumptions clearly identified. When individual assets or classes of assets are separately valued, schedules supporting those calculations are also included.

Letter Reports

An example of a letter format report for a preliminary indication of value is included in Chapter 8, Exhibit 8.1. This format is useful for internal-use only reports, and generally includes less detail than the full format report. In the example shown in Chapter 8, Exhibit 8.1, a preliminary estimate of value was presented. This is generally an estimate of value limited to internal use only, and does not represent an opinion of value. Obviously, this report would be inappropriate for general use or for use between parties negotiating a transaction that could be subject to external scrutiny.

Background information is provided in a highly summarized format, giving the user information that is material to the understanding of the engagement. A financial analysis section is generally included which summarizes major details about the financial condition of the practice and significant economic adjustments made by the valuator. In the letter report, the valuation process and methodology is also explained, but in lesser detail than in the full format report. Likewise, an abbreviated section on the conclusions reached by the valuator is also provided.

The exhibits to the letter report are made up of the assumptions, limiting conditions, valuator certification, and valuator qualifications as presented in the full format report. However, the financial and statistical exhibits are limited to those most applicable to the calculation of value, including specific computations under the selected methodology, along with normalized financial statements and the discount rate assumptions.

Although less voluminous than the full format report, the letter report should never be mistaken by the user or the valuator as representative of an engagement that is smaller in scope or lesser in professional competence than the full format report. Except where the scope is specifically limited to a lesser engagement or a preliminary indication of value, the same planning, research, analysis, and judgment as used in preparing a full format report are required of the engagement resulting in the letter report. The letter report simply represents a more abbreviated disclosure of the same processes undertaken in any valuation.

Oral Reports

Oral reports are permitted by USPAP and other professional standard-setting bodies, and must conform to certain applicable standards. In practice, we often avoid the use of the oral report for a number of reasons, including the risk of misunderstanding or misinterpretation of orally presented data, the absence of a deliverable work product showing the detail of work involved in the valuation, and the client's need for written support of the valuation.

REVIEWS

Many firms use a checklist for performing valuation planning, engagement, and review procedures. These checklists range from internally prepared checklists to published checklists that are similar in format to audit program checklists. The use of checklists in a valuation project is strongly recommended to help ensure compliance with professional standards in conducting and reporting on the engagement, to guide staff in the completeness of documentation and work steps, and to support the judgment used in the engagement. Review checklists are also important to guiding the reviewer in evaluating the adequacy of documentation and the completeness of the report.

As with audit and accounting engagements, the steps to be

taken in an engagement vary from one project to the next. Therefore, you should consider customizing work and review programs to match the entity being valued. Because of the special nature of valuations of medical practices, we recommend programs tailored to the medical practice. Although some excellent examples of work and review programs are available in publications such as the *Guide to Business Valuations* by Practitioners Publishing Company (PPC), it is advisable to make certain that your programs are modified to specifically address the specific steps taken in the valuation of a medical practice. As an aid, PPC makes available the option of purchasing their programs in a format that can be changed by the user.

Whatever the method used to document the review of the working papers and report, a thorough review by an experienced valuator is essential to success in the engagement. Not only should the reviewer check the work performed by the staff and review the written reports issued, the reviewer should also check for compliance with applicable professional standards, as well as internal standards for preparing external reports.

OTHER ISSUES

Common Mistakes

Culled from our own practice and from reviewing the work of others, some of the more common errors noted in our work are presented below.

Mathematical Errors

With the increasing use of electronic spreadsheets in the valuation process, more and more errors are noted from faulty or misused formulas. Despite the relative simplicity of a math error, the implications of such a mistake can be devastating to the report. In one instance of a weighted average earnings calculation, one valuator incorrectly totaled the weighting amounts, resulting in an error of more than 20 percent of the value. Errors of this nature clearly prove the need for competent and thorough review prior to the issuance of the report.

Misapplication of Valuation Methods

One of the most commonly noted errors occurs in the misapplication of valuation theory, especially in the use of the discounted cash flow method. Probably the most common problem associated with this method is in the calculation of the terminal or residual value. We have also noted problems in the calculation of reasonable physician-owner compensation in this method and in the excess earnings method. Before undertaking a valuation, you should thoroughly analyze the calculation and formulas used in the process, and develop a complete understanding of each method to be employed.

Mismatching of the Discount Rate

Critical to the success of a valuation method is matching the discount rate to the proper earnings stream. If cash flows are used as the measure of economic benefit, the discount rate should be applicable to cash flows, not earnings. If a pre-tax benefit stream is used, the discount rate should likewise represent a pre-tax rate.

Again, proper training of the valuation consultants and a close review by an independent reviewer represents some of the most effective steps to preventing these types of errors. Similarly, a comprehensive work and review program checklist can serve as a good reminder of the rules associated with the various methodologies.

Valuing Tangible and Intangible Assets

In many cases, the valuator may be called upon to separate the value of tangible and intangible assets in the overall valuation of the medical practice. In these instances, it is common for the valuator to separately identify components of value between those tangible and intangible assets included in the scope of the engagement. For example, a medical practice valuation might yield an overall value conclusion of $1,000,000, which is composed of both tangible and intangible values. The responsibility for separating these into tangible and intangible components may fall upon the valuator.

Information concerning the specific valuation of components of tangible and intangible assets can be very useful to the users of the report, particularly in purchase or sales transactions. In these transactions, the Internal Revenue Service requires disclosure of the components of the purchase or selling price, including property and equipment, accounts receivable, inventories, goodwill, and other tangible and intangible assets. Therefore, the users of the report will often ask the valuator to separately identify these segments of value within the report.

The Internal Revenue Service also makes reference to the separate identification of tangible and intangible assets in its continuing education textbook. In this document, the IRS instructs its agents to use a discrete approach to the valuation of the practice as a means for testing the overall intangible value. As an example, the overall intangible asset that is defined as goodwill may be made up of several components, including patient medical records, trained and assembled workforce, professional goodwill, and computer systems and software. From the standpoint of tangible assets, the medical practice may include assets in the form of supply inventories, equipment, leasehold improvements, patient accounts receivable, and net working capital. A discrete presentation of these assets would involve a specific identification of the various components of value of the practice and separate identification of the amounts assigned to each component.

How do you separately identify values for these tangible and intangible assets? In many cases, you will have access to such information as patient accounts receivable, supply inventories, and equipment listings of the practice. You may use book value of these specific assets or apply methodology to arrive at a fair market value for these assets, if considerably different from book value. We address the valuation of separate asset classes in Chapters 5 and 6.

SUMMARY

Throughout this chapter, we have examined the process of completing the valuation, including reconciling the values and developing a value conclusion, applying appropriate discounts, and reporting on the engagement. Without competent judgment, the values obtained through the application of the various methods would be virtually useless. And without a completely self-contained report, the user may not correctly interpret the findings or the valuator's conclusion may be more easily challenged.

Many medical practice valuations are rendered inadequate by errors in judgment, poor documentation, or mathematical mistakes. Trained staff and competent review procedures help reduce the risk of issuing a bad report.

Proper reporting is a good means for demonstrating professionalism in the valuation. Most often, the only work product seen by the client is the written report; therefore, great care should be taken to prepare a comprehensive, attractive, and useful report that can be easily interpreted by the reader. One valuator said that a good report has only enough detail in the report to allow a knowledgeable user to arrive at generally the same conclusions and amounts as you have done. This means clearly stating your assumptions and showing sufficient detail to support your calculations, without clutter and useless data.

Sample reports are provided in Chapter 8. While these represent samples of actual medical practices and similar facilities, many amounts and all of the names have been changed to preserve confidentiality. These are intended to show examples of how reports may be presented, and do not represent authoritative sources for your own reports. A thorough understanding of the reporting processes and the applicable standards should always be your primary goal when undertaking the preparation of a report on the valuation of a medical practice.

Sample Reports

Exhibit 8.1
Letter Report
Estimate of Value

To provide the reader with an example of the letter report format, this exhibit demonstrates the use of the letter report with certain supplemental information.

General Surgeons, P.A.
PRACTICE VALUATION
March 31, 1998

TABLE OF CONTENTS

April 27, 1998

John Smith, D.M.D.
General Surgeons, P.A.
1234 Apple Street
Anytown, CA 00000

Dear Dr. Smith:

We have completed our engagement on the preliminary estimate of the fair market value of the owner's equity of General Surgeons, P.A. as of March 31, 1998. The preliminary estimate of value should only be used in connection with your evaluation of the stock purchase and income agreements with the Practice.

Overview of the Clinic and Market

General Surgeons, P.A. (the Practice), is a corporation organized under the laws of the State of California for the practice of general surgery. The corporation was formed in November, 1993 by Drs. Andrew Jones, William Doe and John Smith. The Practice is located in Anytown, California, which had a 1990 population of 65,585. Anytown is located in Havens County, which contains a 1990 population of 627,845. Anytown is located approximately 19 miles and 41 miles, respectively, from the larger cities of Hebron and Taylorsville, California.

Financial Analysis

Financial statement information for General Surgeons, P.A. for the years ended September 30, 1994 through 1997 is presented in Exhibit G. This information was summarized from the financial statements of the Practice, but was not audited by us.

In summarizing the accompanying financial statements, we made the following adjustments:

 Physician Compensation and Benefits: Significant discretionary expenses and perquisites are paid on behalf of the physicians by the Practice, including payroll taxes, profit sharing, health and life insurance and automobile expenses. These amounts have been reclassified from operating expenses and are combined with direct physician compensation to arrive at a total physician compensation and benefits amount.

Non-operating Income and Expenses: Income and expense items reported in the financial statements which are not related to the operation of the Practice have been separately identified after net income from operations. These include such items as interest income and expense, depreciation and gain or loss on the sale of assets.

For the years 1994 through 1997, revenues have fluctuated from year to year. In the fiscal year ended September 30, 1994, net patient revenues according to the Practice's financial statements was $1,017,300. In 1995, the amount increased to $1,117,900, or 9.89 percent over the prior year. In 1996, revenues dropped by 10.11 percent to $1,004,900, and in the fiscal year ended September 30, 1997, fell again to $984,900, for a decrease of 1.99 percent

Valuation Process and Methodology

We considered a number of applicable valuation methods and approaches in our engagement; however, because of the specific facts regarding this valuation engagement, we selected the discounted cash flow method.

This method is an income-based approach to the valuation of a business enterprise, and is founded on the theory that the value of a business enterprise is equivalent to the present value of a future stream of cash flows. The present value calculation is heavily dependent upon a discount rate, representing the valuator's opinion of risk associated with an ownership interest in the subject practice.

This assessment of risk is quantified through the Weighted Average Cost of Capital (WACC), which begins with the use of a build-up approach to assessing risk, then applying a calculation for the tax-affected cost of borrowed capital.

To determine an estimate of value under this method, the valuator summarizes the projections of debt-free, after-tax, future net cash flows for a projection period, then computes the present value of those streams of cash flows, and finally, adds the present value of the terminal period cash flows.

Exhibit D presents the computation of the discounted cash flow method. The development of the weighted average cost of capital rate is presented in Exhibit E. The projections used in the discounted cash flow method are reported in Exhibit F.

The value estimated with the discounted cash flow method is $262,601.

Conclusions

This preliminary estimate of value is limited in scope to calculation of value under certain methodology and does not result in an opinion of value. To render an opinion of value, we would be required to perform additional procedures and employ a variety of methods and approaches to value the Practice.

Based upon the specific procedures identified herein, the fair market value of the owner's equity in General Surgeons, P.A. at March 31, 1998 is estimated at approximately $260,000. We appreciate this opportunity to be of service. Should you have any questions or comments, please contact us.

Respectfully,

FIRM NAME

Robert Redd, CPA
Partner

Exhibit A
Assumptions and Limiting Conditions

Our report includes the following assumptions and limiting conditions:

1. This report may be used only for the purpose stated herein. No portion of this report may be provided to outside parties without our prior written consent.

2. You have confirmed in writing that the information provided to us was correct and complete to the best of your knowledge. Significant errors or omissions from this information could have a material effect on the estimate of value contained herein.

3. All property is assumed to be marketable and free and clear of liens, easements or encumbrances.

4. Complete compliance with applicable laws and regulations is assumed.

5. We do not assume any responsibility for changes in the operations of the subject medical practice or in market conditions.

6. We assume no obligation to amend this report to reflect events which occur subsequent to the valuation date.

7. Some assumptions in our report will not occur as anticipated, and other unexpected events may occur. Therefore, the actual results achieved during the projection period will likely vary from the projection, and the variations may be material.

8. We have not audited or reviewed the financial data presented herein and, accordingly, do not express an opinion or any other form of assurance on it. This financial data is presented in summary form only, and does not constitute a complete presentation in accordance with generally accepted accounting principles.

Exhibit B
Valuator's Certification

I certify that, to the best of my knowledge and belief:

1. The statements of fact in this report are true and correct.

2. The reported analyses, opinions, and conclusions are limited only by the reported assumptions and limiting conditions, and are my personal, unbiased professional analyses, opinions, and conclusions.

3. I have no present or prospective interest in the subject entity or bias with respect to the parties involved.

4. My compensation is not contingent on an action or event resulting from the findings in, or the use of, this report.

5. No one provided significant professional assistance to the person signing this report.

FIRM NAME

_____

Robert Redd, CPA
Partner

Exhibit C
Valuator's Qualifications

Robert Redd, CPA, Partner

Robert is a health care services manager with seven years of auditing, accounting and health care consulting experience. He has extensive experience in governmental and not-for-profit hospital auditing.

Robert received a bachelor's degree in accounting from Tennessee State University in 1992. Robert also holds a master's degree in health care administration. Robert is a Certified Public Accountant in the state of Tennessee.

Robert has supervised or managed many health care valuation engagements and has conducted audits of hospitals under Government Auditing Standards.

Exhibit D
General Surgeons, P.A.
Schedule of Discounted Future Cash Flows

	Base Year	Year 1	Year 2	Year 3	Year 4	Year 5	Terminal
Gross Revenue	$984,900	$979,404	$994,095	$1,013,977	$1,039,326	$1,065,309	
Physician Compensation and Benefits	369,900	357,011	357,904	361,483	365,098	368,749	
Operating Expenses	574,100	569,566	573,838	579,576	588,270	597,094	
Total Expenses	944,000	926,577	931,742	941,059	953,368	965,843	
Earnings Before Depreciation, Interest and Taxes (EBITDA)	40,900	52,827	62,353	72,918	85,958	99,466	
Less: Depreciation	(25,532)	(10,574)	(9,460)	(8,346)	(7,231)	(6,117)	
Earnings Before Taxes (EBT)	15,368	42,253	52,893	64,572	78,727	93,349	
Less: Effective Income Taxes (40 % of Earnings)	(6,247)	(16,901)	(21,157)	(25,829)	(31,491)	(37,340)	
Debt Free Net Income	$ 9,121	25,352	31,736	38,743	47,236	56,009	$ 56,569
Add: Depreciation		10,574	9,460	8,346	7,231	6,117	-
Less: Changes in Debt Free Net Working Capital		887	(2,204)	(2,982)	(3,802)	(3,897)	-
Less: Capital Expenditures	$350,000	(7,800)	(7,800)	(7,800)	(7,800)	(7,800)	-
Owner's Discretionary Cash Flow		29,013	31,192	36,307	42,865	50,429	56,569

Exhibit D
(Continued)

	Base Year	Year 1	Year 2	Year 3	Year 4	Year 5	Terminal
Weighting		1	1	1	1	1	1
Weighted Average Owner's Discretionary Cash Flow		29,013	31,192	36,307	42,865	50,429	56,569
Terminal Year Capitalization Multiple							5.5866
Terminal Value							316,028
Present Value Factor for Discount Rate on Net Cash Flow		0.9156	0.7674	0.6433	0.5392	0.4520	0.4520
Present Value—Owner's Discretionary Cash Flow		26,563	$ 23,938	$ 23,356	$ 23,113	$ 22,793	$142,838
Sum of Present Value—5 Years	$119,763						
Add: Present Value of Terminal Year	142,838						
Business Enterprise Value	**$262,601**						

Discount rate ~

198

Exhibit E
General Surgeons, P.A.
Risk Build Up Analysis

	Weighted Average Cost of Capital	
Risk Free Long Term Government Bond Rate	5.9%	
Common Stock Equity Risk Premium	7.5%	
Small Stock Equity Risk Premium	3.5%	
Subjective Risk Premium	7.0%	
Net Cash Flow Discount Rate	23.9%	No Debt
Weighted Average Cost of Capital (WACC):		With Debt
Equity Portion of Book Value	75.0%	
Equity Component of WACC		17.9%
Debt Portion of Book Value	25.0%	
Cost of Debt, After Tax	5.7%	
Debt Component of WACC		1.4%
Weighted Average Cost of Capital		**19.3%**
Increment of Net Cash Flow Rate over Discount Rate		–0.2%
Net Earnings Discount Rate		19.1%
Less: Average Growth Rate		1.0%
Net Earnings Capitalization Rate for Subsequent Year		18.1%
Divided by: One Plus Average Growth Rate		101.0%
Net Earnings Capitalization Rate for Current Year		**17.9%**

Exhibit F
General Surgeons, P.A.
Comparative Schedule of Projected Operating Income

	Base Year Amount	Base Year Percent to Total Revenue	Year 1 Amount	Year 1 Percent to Total Revenue	Year 2 Amount	Year 2 Percent to Total Revenue	Year 3 Amount	Year 3 Percent to Total Revenue	Year 4 Amount	Year 4 Percent to Total Revenue	Year 5 Amount	Year 5 Percent to Total Revenue
Net Revenues	$984,900	100.00%	979,404	100.00%	994,095	100.00%	1,013,977	100.00%	1,039,326	100.00%	1,065,309	100.00%
Physician Compensation and Benefits	369,900	37.56%	357,011	36.45%	357,904	36.00%	361,483	35.65%	365,098	35.13%	368,749	34.61%
Operating Expenses	574,100	58.29%	569,566	58.15%	573,838	57.72%	579,576	57.16%	588,270	56.60%	597,094	56.05%
Total Expenses	944,000	95.85%	926,577	94.60%	931,742	93.72%	941,059	92.81%	953,368	91.73%	965,843	90.66%
Net Operating Income	40,900	4.15%	$52,827	5.40%	$62,353	6.28%	$72,918	7.19%	$85,958	8.27%	$99,466	9.34%
Other Income (Expense):												
Interest Income	462	0.05%										
Interest Expense	(15,965)	–1.62%										
Depreciation	(25,532)	–2.59%										
Net Other Income (Expense)	(41,035)	–4.17%										
Net Income Before Taxes	$ (135)	–0.02%										

200

Exhibit G

General Surgeons, P.A.
Comparative Analysis of Historical Income Statements
Years Ended September 30, 1994 Through 1997

	Year Ended September 30, 1997			Year Ended September 30, 1996			Year Ended September 30, 1995			Year Ended September 30, 1994	
	Actual	Percent to Total Revenue	Percent Change	Actual	Percent to Total Revenue	Percent Change	Actual	Percent to Total Revenue	Percent Change	Actual	Percent to Total Revenue
Income											
Net Patient Revenue	$ 984,900	100.00%	-1.99%	$ 1,004,900	100.00%	-10.11%	$ 1,117,900	100.00%	9.89%	$ 1,017,300	100.00%
Expenses											
Physician Compensation and Benefits											
Physician Compensation	252,200	25.61%	22.90%	205,200	20.42%	-25.25%	274,500	24.56%	25.57%	218,600	21.49%
Physician Payroll Taxes	15,800	1.60%	8.25%	14,596	1.45%	-5.00%	15,364	1.37%	6.38%	14,442	1.42%
Physician Profit Sharing Contributions	—	0.00%	0.00%	—	0.00%	-100.00%	24,555	2.20%	148.83%	9,868	0.97%
Physician Discretionary Expenses	101,900	10.35%	-18.48%	125,000	12.44%	12.11%	111,500	9.97%	-12.07%	126,800	12.46%
Total Physician Compensation and Benefits	369,900	37.56%	7.28%	344,796	34.31%	-19.01%	425,919	38.10%	15.20%	369,710	36.34%
Operating Expenses	574,100	58.29%	-0.29%	575,760	57.30%	-6.68%	616,980	55.19%	5.43%	585,200	57.52%
Total Expenses	944,000	95.85%	2.55%	920,556	91.61%	-11.73%	1,042,899	93.29%	9.21%	954,910	93.87%
Net Operating Income	40,900	4.15%	-51.51%	84,344	8.39%	12.46%	75,001	6.71%	20.21%	62,390	6.13%
Other Income (Expenses)											
Interest Income	462	0.05%	-18.52%	567	0.06%	51.60%	374	0.03%	-59.61%	926	0.09%
Interest Expense	(15,965)	-1.62%	30.36%	(12,247)	-1.22%	-33.12%	(18,313)	-1.64%	4.83%	(17,469)	-1.72%
Depreciation	(25,532)	-2.59%	-45.77%	(47,080)	-4.69%	-18.17%	(57,537)	-5.15%	27.11%	(45,266)	-4.45%
Gain (Loss) on Sale of Assets	—	0.00%	-100.00%	(25,297)	-2.52%		—	0.00%		—	0.00%
Total Other Income (Expense)	(41,035)	-4.17%	-51.18%	(84,057)	-8.36%	11.37%	(75,476)	-6.75%	22.11%	(61,809)	-6.08%
Net Income	$ (135)	-0.02%	-156.45%	$ 287	0.03%	160.42%	$ (475)	-0.04%	-181.76%	$ 581	0.06%

Exhibit 8.2
Full Written Report

The accompanying exhibit provides an example of a full written report, including exhibits to the report.

Mary Wells, M.D., P.A.
MEDICAL PRACTICE VALUATION
As of August 31, 1997

TABLE OF CONTENTS

Exhibits:

INDEPENDENT ACCOUNTANT'S REPORT ON
MEDICAL PRACTICE VALUATION

Regional Medical Center
Sumrall, Texas

We have completed our engagement on the valuation of 100 percent of the tangible and intangible assets of Mary Wells, M.D., P.A. as of August 31, 1997. Based upon the information in the accompanying report, it is our opinion that as of August 31, 1997, the **fair market value** of this practice was approximately $820,000.

Our report, including the accompanying assumptions and limiting conditions, has been prepared for the purpose of determining the value of Mary Wells, M.D., P.A. in connection with the proposed purchase of the assets of the Practice by Regional Medical Center. It should not be used in any manner that is inconsistent with this purpose.

Sumrall, Texas
September 25, 1997

DESCRIPTION OF THE ENGAGEMENT

Standard of Value

For purposes of this valuation, the standard of value is **fair market value,** defined by the Internal Revenue Service in Revenue Ruling 59-60 as:

> "The price at which the property would change hands between a willing buyer and a willing seller when the former is not under any compulsion to buy and the latter is not under any compulsion to sell, both parties having reasonable knowledge of the relevant facts. Court decisions frequently state in addition that the hypothetical buyer and seller are assumed to be able, as well as willing, to trade and to be well informed about the property and concerning the market for such property."

Valuation of a Medical Practice

Mary Wells, M.D., P.A. is a corporation with a single stockholder. Determining the fair market value of tangible and intangible assets in a closely held medical practice requires an understanding of the operations of the Clinic and a detailed knowledge of the health care industry and the market for such practices within the industry.

OVERVIEW OF THE CLINIC AND MARKET

Background

Dr. Mary Wells began practice in Sumrall, Texas in 1983, with the opening of the current practice. The practice was incorporated in July, 1991, and has operated as a corporation since that date. Dr. Wells is the only practicing physician in the Clinic. Her curriculum vita follows:

Mary Wells, M.D. Bachelor of Science, University of Texas, 1971–1975; M.D., University of Texas School of Medicine, 1976–1980; residency, University of Texas School of Medicine, 1980–1983. Began solo practice in family medicine at Sumrall, Texas, 1983. Board certified in family medicine, 1983.

Office Personnel

The following is a listing of office personnel in the Practice:

Staff Member	Position	Status
Augusta Coleman	Administrative/Clerical	Part-Time
Bobbie Morris	Administrative/Clerical	Part-Time
Hazel M. Wells	Administrative/Clerical	Full-Time
Jezelle Doe	Administrative/Clerical	Full-Time
Kimberly Bower	Administrative/Clerical	Full-Time
Lisa Greer	Administrative/Clerical	Part-Time
Tess Frazier	Administrative/Clerical	Full-Time
Daisy Johnson	Maintenance	Full-Time
Katherine Angens	Medical Staff	Part-Time
Abigail Reeves	Medical Staff	Part-Time
Brian Kendall	Medical Staff	Full-Time
Willie Easterling	Medical Staff	Part-Time

Market Analysis

The City of Sumrall, Texas is located in the west-central part of Texas, in Jonesboro County, and about 30 miles southwest of Batesville, Texas.

The 1990 census reported 11,370 inhabitants in Jonesboro County and projections estimate the population in the year 2000 to reach 11,871. According to the Sumrall Chamber of Commerce, five primary care physicians practice in the Jonesboro County area. Based on the regional market area's estimated 1995 population of 2,695,279, there is approximately one physician for every 650 inhabitants in the service area.

One hospital is operated in the Sumrall area, Jonesboro County Hospital, a nonprofit, county-owned facility with approximately 32 beds.

In nearby Batesville, Texas, two hospitals, Regional Medical Center and City Medical Center, serve patients in Waco County and surrounding areas. Population projections estimate 50,841 inhabitants in Waco County in the year 2000.

Management estimates the Clinic's payer mix to be divided as follows:

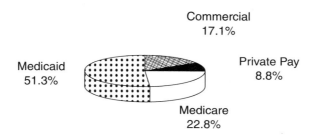

Commercial
17.1%

Medicaid
51.3%

Private Pay
8.8%

Medicare
22.8%

The health care industry in the United States has experienced significant growth in technological advancements over the past decade, while an aging population in the United States has demanded further efforts by the industry to provide a greater volume of advanced technology and services to prolong life and improve the quality of life. The developments in the industry have caused health care costs to increase dramatically over the past few years, prompting a public outcry for health maintenance and wellness at a cost-effective rate.

The past trend toward high-cost health care has resulted in limited access to health care for millions of Americans, further driving the cost of receiving adequate care beyond the reach of many elderly, indigent and uninsurable individuals. Years before the recent drive for health care reform, insurance reform has been a topic for political campaigns, although little more than legislative proposals ever came forward as a means for controlling increasing costs of coverage for the public.

President Clinton's Health Security Act of 1993 was a comprehensive, but controversial, attempt at health care reform; however, the bill and its many counterparts in both the House and Senate never materialized into law. The goals of universal health care coverage and reform of the Medicare and Medicaid systems have continued to receive the attention of both Republicans and Democrats, as well as the public as a whole. Employer efforts to reduce health care costs have created a dramatic shift to managed care in the past few years, with growth in enrollments continuing to advance at a staggering level.

Increasing numbers of providers are forming networks to offer patients a reduced cost for services. Many providers are joining health care systems to facilitate integration. Managed care plays a growing role in Texas, with its emphasis on primary care and preventive services.

This recent emphasis on health care reform and managed care at the national and state levels has greatly impacted the means by which medical practices are valued, as well as affecting the negotiated values of practices in sales transactions.

FINANCIAL ANALYSIS

Historical Income Statements

Financial statement information for Mary Wells, M.D., P.A. for the years ended December 31, 1993 through 1996, and for the eight months ended August 31, 1997, is presented in Exhibits I through K. This information was summarized from the financial statements of the Practice, but was not audited by us.

The Corporation has elected to be treated as a small business corporation under the Subchapter S rules of the Internal Revenue Service. Therefore, the Corporation passes income and losses through to its shareholder and generally does not pay tax on corporate earnings. The historical financial statements do not include provisions for corporate income taxes on earnings of the Practice.

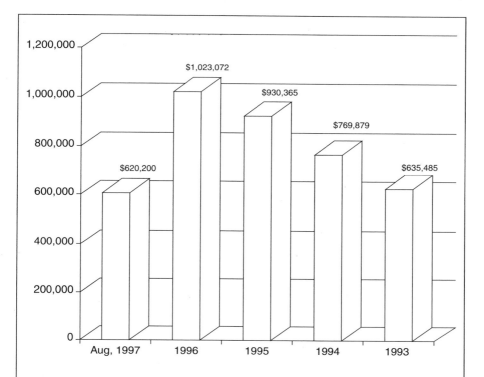

Net medical revenue for Dr. Wells' practice during the analysis period was as follows:

Revenues for the Clinic for the year ended December 31, 1997 are projected to be approximately $963,000. This represents a break in the overall trend of growth averaging over 17 percent from 1993 to 1996.

Practice overhead is compared against MGMA medians in the relationship of overhead to net medical revenue. In the periods included in the analysis, overhead ranged from a high of 46.4 percent of net medical revenue in 1993, to a low of 30.8 percent in 1995.

Adjustments to the Financial Statements

In summarizing the accompanying financial statements, we made the following adjustments:

Physician compensation and benefits and estimated physician payroll tax expenses included in non-physician benefit expense were reclassified as a physician expense.

Personal draws were added to physician compensation.

An estimated provision for depreciation was added to the 1997 expenses of the Corporation based upon tax depreciation calculations made by the Corporation's tax accountant. Internal Revenue Code Section 179 expense election, which permits certain asset costs to be immediately written off, was excluded from the depreciation adjustments.

Rent and employee benefits were estimated based on annualized 1996 amounts and added to 1997 overhead expenses.

Projected Revenues and Expenses

A comparative schedule of projected operating income is presented at Exhibit H. This schedule includes estimates of the next five years' income and expenses from operations, based heavily upon historical data and market trend analyses.

Revenues: The Clinic's records for patient encounters and revenues have generally shown an upward trend in the past five years. However, the Clinic has experienced below average accounts receivable collectibility factors, particularly attributable to the high Medicare and Medicaid payor mix. Overall revenue increases of between 2 and 4 percent can be consistently expected through the analysis period.

Dr. Wells is expected to continue to reach production levels well in excess of median levels. Estimated 1997 production for Dr. Wells is $1,375,400, which far exceeds MGMA 90th percentile levels of $526,792 for family practice physicians.

Expenses: Historical physician compensation data for 1996 is presented at Exhibit M. Provider compensation has varied over the past five years from a low of $340,465 in 1993 to a high of $703,380 in 1996. In each of these years, physician compensation has been adjusted to reflect the payment of draws to the physician-owner, which are often significantly higher than the regular salaries. These draws represent payment of profits already taxed to the shareholder. Because a significant amount of goodwill exists in this practice, a portion of the compensation and draws received by the physician-shareholder represents a return on the intangible assets in the Practice. Therefore, compensation for the projection period has been estimated based on a normalized compensation for the services rendered by the physician. This has been quantified through the use of a ratio of median provider cost, including benefits, to net medical revenues, as reported by MGMA.

Historical staff compensation levels have consistently fallen well below median norms for family practice physicians. Future compensation levels are projected to increase at about 3 percent per year, but continue to remain well below family practice median levels.

Clinic overhead is projected to increase in some areas as revenues increase and inflationary factors bring about higher costs. The Clinic has experienced unusually high expense levels in medical supplies, especially during 1997. Future medical supplies expense is projected to decline in years one and two, although remaining near historical levels and increasing as revenues increase in the Clinic.

Depreciation of assets acquired by the purchaser is based on the value expected to be allocated to those assets. In perpetuity, depreciation is anticipated to approximate capital outlay for furniture, fixtures and equipment. However, during the first year after the transaction, injection of capital is considered necessary to maintain and update the equipment of the Clinic, and thereafter, capital outlay is estimated annually at 10 percent of the purchase price estimated as allocated to fixed assets.

VALUATION PROCESS

General Background

In valuing medical practices, or any business, Internal Revenue Service mandates analysis of the following factors:

- The nature of the business and the history of the enterprise from its inception
- The economic outlook in general and the condition and outlook of the specific industry in particular
- The book value of the stock and the financial condition of the business
- The earning capacity of the company
- The dividend-paying capacity
- Whether or not the enterprise has goodwill or other intangible value
- Sales of the stock and the size of the block of stock to be valued
- The market price of stocks of corporations engaged in the same or a similar line of business having their stocks actively traded in a free and open market, either on an exchange or over-the counter

We analyzed these and other factors to determine the most appropriate methodology for the valuation of this medical practice. These methods define the stream of economic benefits and convert the benefit stream into an estimate of value.

We believe two such methods applicable to this practice are the:

1. Capitalization of Excess Earnings Method
2. Discounted Cash Flow Method

Capitalization of Excess Earnings Method

We compared the Clinic's weighted average historical earnings to expected earnings based on work-adjusted specialty norms. The difference, or excess earnings, if any, is capitalized using an excess earnings capitalization rate.

To arrive at an estimate of value, we determined the value of intangible assets of the Practice by capitalizing "excess earnings" with a capitalization rate, and added the fair market value of the Clinic's tangible net assets.

The excess earnings capitalization rate used herein is computed based on our judgment in light of the specific facts and circumstances surrounding this Practice. Because the Practice produces revenues well in excess of published norms for family practice physicians, the risk of continued productivity at these levels is somewhat higher than the risk of sustaining income at a median level. Alternatively, the history of the Practice supports the assumption that these high earnings levels can reasonably be expected to continue in the near term. In light of these facts, we have considered it necessary to establish an excess earnings capitalization rate at a level moderately higher than the discount rate used to value cash flows.

The calculations and resulting value from the use of this method is presented at Exhibit D. The value achieved under this method is $860,091.

Discounted Cash Flow Method

The discounted cash flow method is an income-based approach to the valuation of a business enterprise, and is founded on the theory that the value of a business enterprise is equivalent to the present value of a future stream of cash flows. The present value calculation is heavily dependent upon a discount rate, representing the valuator's opinion of risk associated with an ownership interest in the subject practice.

This assessment of risk is quantified through the Weighted Average Cost of Capital (WACC), which begins with the use of a build-up approach to assessing risk, then applying a calculation for the tax-affected cost of borrowed capital.

To determine an estimate of value under this method, the valuator summarizes the projections of debt-free, after-tax, future net cash flows for a projection period, then compares the present values of those streams of cash flows, and finally, adds the present value of the terminal period cash flows.

Exhibit E presents the computation of the discounted cash flow method. The development of the weighted average cost of capital rate is presented in Exhibit G. The projections used in the discounted cash flows method are reported in Exhibit H.

The value achieved using this method is $849,336.

Comparable Sales Transactions Method

This method represents a market-based approach to determining value and calculates the value of the Practice based on prices actually paid for comparable medical practices by determining the sales price as a ratio to net discretionary income available for physician compensation calculated from the comparable sales data and applying this ratio to the revenues of the medical practice being valued.

In estimating the value of the Practice under this method, we identified other family practice clinics which have actually been sold, utilizing *The Goodwill Registry* by The Health Care Group in determining the ratios of sales price to discretionary income, as presented in Exhibit F.

In light of the high productivity of the sole physician and the level of goodwill in this practice, we considered it appropriate to use the 75th percentile ratio of sales price to discretionary income in the calculation of value. The value achieved under this method is $747,727.

We did not feel that the circumstances surrounding this practice permitted the effective use of an asset-based method, because the earnings are generally driven by professional services and not by equipment or mechanized production processes; therefore, we did not utilize any methods under this approach. However, for purposes of estimating the tangible component of our value conclusion, we have performed the following calculations to estimate tangible asset values in the Practice.

Valuation of Accounts Receivable

The valuation of accounts receivable in the medical practice has been achieved through an analysis of estimated aged accounts receivable. This approach allows the valuator to assess the various components of accounts receivable for patient service revenue and assign a relative collectibility factor based upon the history of collections in the Practice and the likelihood of collection from payers at varying ages of the receivable balance.

Because the chances of collecting accounts receivable diminish with time, we have computed a factor whereby the value of the Clinic's receivables is incrementally discounted based upon the relative age of the account balance. Because collectibility differs at varying ages, we have computed the collectibility factor based upon estimated payer mix data, while placing further consideration on the historical ability of the Practice to collect its patient service charges.

The calculation of the value of clinic receivables is presented at Exhibit O. As of August 31, 1997, the value of the receivables was estimated at $102,784.

Valuation of Inventories

Inventories in medical and administrative supplies are estimated using our judgment and based on the amounts of actual expenses through August 31, 1997. As presented at Exhibit P, the value of inventories as of August 31, 1997, was $18,722.

Valuation of Property and Equipment

Tangible property and equipment of the Practice have been valued at modified book value. In accordance with the scope of our engagement, we calculated the net value of fixed assets made available to us, based upon the information available, and without an outside appraisal. Because detailed cost data and acquisition dates were not available for some individual assets, we estimated the value based on items reported in the Corporation's tax depreciation records. The value of the tangible property and equipment of Mary Wells, M.D., P.A. as of August 31, 1997 was $92,400, and is presented at Exhibit Q, subject to the limitations in the scope of our analysis and the limiting conditions presented in Exhibit A.

Liabilities of the Practice

The Clinic has no outstanding loans as of August 31, 1997.

CONCLUSIONS

We have placed different levels of reliance on the various methods presented in this report, and have reconciled the results of each, with some methods given greater relevance in our final analysis. For a medical practice, the ability to general economic benefits is assigned greater relevance; therefore, values determined under the discounted cash flows and excess earnings methods have been weighted more heavily than the market-based approach.

In our opinion, the fair market value of 100 percent of the tangible and intangible assets of the medical practice of Mary Wells, M.D., P.A. as of August 31, 1997, was $820,000.

Exhibit A
Statement of Assumptions and Limiting Conditions

Our report includes the following assumptions and limiting conditions:

1. This report may be used only for the purpose stated herein. No portion of this report may be provided to outside parties without our prior written consent.

2. Dr. Wells has represented to us that the information supplied to us was correct and complete to the best of her knowledge. Significant errors or omissions from this information could have a material effect on the opinion of value contained herein.

3. All property is assumed to be marketable and free and clear of liens, easements, or encumbrances.

4. Complete compliance with applicable laws and regulations is assumed.

5. We do not assume any responsibility for changes in the operations of the subject medical practice or in market conditions.

6. We assume no obligation to amend this report to reflect events which occur subsequent to the valuation date.

7. Some assumptions in our report will not occur as anticipated, and other unexpected events may occur. Therefore, the actual results achieved during the projection period will likely vary from the projection, and the variations may be material.

8. We have not audited or reviewed the financial data presented herein and, accordingly, do not express an opinion or any other form of assurance on it. This financial data is presented in summary form only, and does not constitute a complete presentation in accordance with generally accepted accounting principles.

Exhibit B
Valuator's Certification and Signature

I certify that, to the best of my knowledge and belief:

1. The statements of fact in this report are true and correct.

2. The reported analyses, opinions, and conclusions are limited only by the reported assumptions and limiting conditions, and are my personal, unbiased professional analyses, opinions, and conclusions.

3. I have no present or prospective interest in the subject entity or bias with respect to the parties involved.

4. My compensation is not contingent on an action or event resulting from the findings in, or the use of, this report.

5. No one provided significant professional assistance to the person signing this report.

6. My analyses, opinions, and conclusions were developed, and this report has been prepared, in conformity with the Uniform Standards of Professional Appraisal Practice and the standards of the American Institute of Certified Public Accountants.

FIRM NAME

_____

Robert Redd, CPA
Partner

Exhibit C
Professional Qualifications of Valuator

Robert Redd, CPA, Partner

Robert is a health care services partner with seven years of auditing, accounting and health care consulting experience. He has extensive experience in governmental and not-for-profit hospital auditing.

Robert received a bachelor's degree in accounting from Tennessee State University in 1992. Robert also holds a master's degree in health care administration. Robert is a Certified Public Accountant in the state of Tennessee.

Robert has supervised or managed many health care valuation engagements and has conducted audits of hospitals under Government Auditing Standards.

Exhibit D
Mary Wells, M.D., P.A.
Schedule of Capitalized Excess Earnings
Years Ended December 31, 1993 Through 1997 (Estimated)

Calculation of Physician Weighted Average Compensation:

Year	Normalized Compensation	Weighting Factor	Weighted Normalized Compensation	
1997 (est)	$ 621,067	5	$ 3,105,335	
1996	703,380	4	2,813,520	
1995	643,679	3	1,931,037	
1994	499,789	2	999,578	
1993	340,465	1	340,465	
		15	9,189,935	
Divided by Sum of Weighting Factors			15	
Weighted Average Normalized Physician Compensation				$ 612,662

Calculation of Comparative Weighted Average Compensation:

Year	Comparative Work-Adjusted Compensation	Weighting Factor	Weighted Comparative Compensation	
1997 (est)	$ 436,522	5	$ 2,182,610	
1996	463,861	4	1,855,444	
1995	421,827	3	1,265,481	
1994	318,422	2	636,844	
1993	264,171	1	264,171	
		15	6,204,550	
Divided by Sum of Weighting Factors			15	
Weighted Average Comparative Physician Compensation				413,637
Calculated Excess Earnings (Deficit)				199,025
Excess Earnings Capitalization Rate				30.8%
Indicated Intangible Value of Practice				646,185
Tangible Assets:				
Accounts Receivable				102,784
Inventories				18,722
Property and Equipment				92,400
Total Tangible Assets				213,906
Total Practice Value				**$ 860,091**

Exhibit E
Mary Wells, M.D., P.A.
Schedule of Discounted Future Cash Flows

	Base Year 1997 (Est)	Year 1	Year 2	Year 3	Year 4	Year 5	Terminal Year
Gross Revenue	$ 963,000	$ 1,008,701	$ 1,042,997	$ 1,076,373	$ 1,108,664	$ 1,139,707	
Physician Compensation	658,000	457,345	466,492	475,822	485,338	495,045	
Nonphysician Expenses	345,056	326,885	324,969	332,809	341,615	350,679	
Total Expenses	1,003,056	784,230	791,461	808,631	826,953	845,724	
Earnings Before Depreciation, Interest and Taxes (EBDIT)	(40,056)	224,471	251,536	267,742	281,711	293,983	
Less: Depreciation	(17,561)	(14,794)	(16,080)	(17,366)	(18,652)	(19,937)	
Earnings Before Taxes (EBT)	(57,617)	209,677	235,456	250,376	263,059	274,046	
Less: Effective Income Taxes (40% of Earnings)	-	(83,871)	(94,182)	(100,150)	(105,224)	(109,618)	
Debt Free Net Income	$ (57,617)	125,806	141,274	150,226	157,835	164,428	$ 166,894
Add: Depreciation		14,794	16,080	17,366	18,652	19,937	-

Exhibit E
(Continued)

	Base Year 1997 (Est)	Year 1	Year 2	Year 3	Year 4	Year 5	Terminal Year
Less: Changes in Debt Free Net Working Capital		(6,889)	(5,144)	(5,006)	(4,844)	(4,656)	-
Less: Capital Expenditures		(14,000)	(9,000)	(9,000)	(9,000)	(9,000)	-
Owner's Discretionary Cash Flow		119,711	143,210	153,586	162,643	170,709	166,894
Weighting		1	1	1	1	1	1
Weighted Average Owner's Discretionary Cash Flow		119,711	143,210	153,586	162,643	170,709	166,894
Terminal Year Capitalization Multiple							5.2632
Terminal Value							878,397
Present Value Factor for Discount Rate on Net Cash Flow		0.9106	0.7551	0.6261	0.5191	0.4305	0.4305
Present Value - Owner's Discretionary Cash Flow		$109,009	$108,132	$96,158	$84,434	$73,484	$378,119
Sum of Present Value - 5 Years	$471,217						
Add: Present Value of Terminal Year	378,119						
Business Enterprise Value	**$849,336**						

Exhibit F
Mary Wells, M.D., P.A.
Schedule of Comparable Sales Transactions

Comparable Sales Transactions:

Year	Specialty	Location	Gross Revenues	Overhead Rate	Practice Price	Goodwill Value	Tangible Value	Practice Price to Gross Revenues
1997	Family Practice	IN	$ 1,270,000	49.00%	$ 650,000	$ 490,000	$ 160,000	51.18%
1997	Family Practice	MD	609,864	38.19%	370,661	320,661	50,000	60.78%
1996	Family Practice	FL	800,000	40.00%	800,000	120,000	680,000	100.00%
1996	Family Practice	IA	1,459,467	45.20%	765,000	394,000	371,000	52.42%
1996	Family Practice	PA	725,555	44.80%	600,000	600,000	-	82.70%
1996	Family Practice	PA	800,024	45.20%	475,000	400,000	75,000	59.37%
1996	Family Practice	PA	780,135	40.10%	608,000	588,000	20,000	77.94%
1994	Family Practice	MN	1,400,000	45.00%	700,000	550,000	150,000	50.00%
1994	Family Practice	UT	1,058,081	46.55%	494,056	220,000	274,056	46.69%
1993	Family Practice	VA	1,100,000	48.00%	900,000	650,000	250,000	81.82%
Median Practice Price to Gross Revenues								60.08%
Mean Practice Price to Gross Revenues								66.29%
75th Percentile Practice Price to Gross Revenues								80.85%

219

Exhibit F
(Continued)

Subject Practice:

Year	Overhead Rate	Gross Revenues	Weighting Factor	Weighted Gross Revenues
1997 (Est)	35.84%	$ 962,774	5	$ 4,813,870
1996	31.97%	1,023,072	4	4,092,288
1995	31.11%	930,365	3	2,791,095
1994	35.49%	769,879	2	1,539,758
1993	47.23%	635,485	1	635,485
Totals			15	13,872,496
Divided by Sum of Weighting Factors				15
Weighted Average Gross Revenues				$ 924,833
Multiplied by 75th Percentile Practice Price to Gross Revenues Ratio				0.8085
Indicated Practice Value				**$ 747,727**

220

Exhibit G
Mary Wells, M.D., P.A.
Risk Build-Up Analysis

	Weighted Average Cost of Capital		Excess Earnings
Risk Free Long Term Government Bond Rate	6.6%		6.6%
Common Stock Equity Risk Premium	7.5%		7.5%
Small Stock Equity Risk Premium	3.5%		3.5%
Subjective Risk Premium	8.0%		15.0%
Net Cash Flow Discount Rate	25.6%		32.6%
Weighted Average Cost of Capital (WACC):			
Equity Portion of Book Value	75.0%		
Equity Component of WACC		19.2%	
Debt Portion of Book Value	25.0%		
Cost of Debt, After Tax	5.7%		
Debt Component of WACC		1.4%	
Weighted Average Cost of Capital		**20.6%**	
Increment of Net Cash Flow Rate over Discount Rate		0.2%	0.2%
Net Earnings Discount Rate		20.8%	32.8%
Less: Average Growth Rate		1.5%	1.5%
Net Earnings Capitalization Rate for Subsequent Year		19.3%	31.3%
Divided by: One Plus Average Growth Rate		101.5%	101.5%
Net Earnings Capitalization Rate for Current Year		**19.0%**	**30.8%**

Exhibit H
Mary Wells, M.D., P.A.
Comparative Schedule of Projected Operating Income

	Estimated 1997		Year 1		Year 2	
	Amount	Percent to Total Revenue	Amount	Percent to Total Revenue	Amount	Percent to Total Revenue
Net Revenues	$ 963,000	100.00%	$1,008,701	100.00%	$1,042,997	100.00%
Physician Payroll/ Benefits	658,000	68.32%	457,345	45.34%	466,492	44.73%
Nonphysician Payroll/ Benefits	140,590	14.60%	144,808	14.36%	147,704	14.16%
Rent & Occupancy	47,863	4.97%	47,384	4.70%	46,910	4.50%
Medical Supplies	106,194	11.03%	90,265	8.95%	85,752	8.22%
Medical Services	2,599	0.27%	2,677	0.27%	2,757	0.26%
Admin. Supplies/ Services	18,100	1.88%	14,480	1.44%	13,756	1.32%
Promotion/Marketing Expenses	-	0.00%	4,035	0.40%	4,156	0.40%
Insurance	1,637	0.17%	1,686	0.17%	1,737	0.17%
Outside Professional	17,426	1.81%	12,198	1.21%	12,564	1.20%
Informational Services	6,892	0.72%	7,099	0.70%	7,312	0.70%
Other Operating Expenses	3,755	0.39%	2,253	0.22%	2,321	0.22%
Total Expenses	1,003,056	104.16%	784,230	77.76%	791,461	75.88%
Net Operating Income	(40,056)	–4.16%	**$224,471**	**22.24%**	**$251,536**	**24.12%**
Other Income (Expense):						
Interest Income	2,648	0.28%				
Depreciation	(17,561)	–1.82%				
Net Other Income (Expense)	(14,913)	–1.54%				
Net Income Before Taxes	**$(54,969)**	–5.70%				

Exhibit H
(Continued)

	Year 3			Year 4			Year 5	
		Percent to Total			Percent to Total			Percent to Total
	Amount	Revenue		Amount	Revenue		Amount	Revenue
	$1,076,373	100.00%		$1,108,664	100.00%		$1,139,707	100.00%
	475,822	44.21%		485,338	43.78%		495,045	43.44%
	151,397	14.07%		155,939	14.07%		160,617	14.09%
	47,145	4.38%		47,381	4.27%		47,618	4.18%
	88,325	8.21%		90,975	8.21%		93,704	8.22%
	2,840	0.26%		2,925	0.26%		3,013	0.26%
	14,169	1.32%		14,594	1.32%		15,032	1.32%
	4,281	0.40%		4,409	0.40%		4,541	0.40%
	1,789	0.17%		1,843	0.17%		1,898	0.17%
	12,941	1.20%		13,329	1.20%		13,729	1.20%
	7,531	0.70%		7,757	0.70%		7,990	0.70%
	2,391	0.22%		2,463	0.22%		2,537	0.22%
	808,631	75.14%		826,953	74.60%		845,724	74.20%
	$267,742	24.86%		$281,711	25.40%		$293,983	25.80%

Exhibit I
Mary Wells, M.D., P.A.
Comparative Schedule of Normalized Revenue and Expenses
Eight Months Ended August 31, 1997 and
Years Ended December 31, 1993 Through 1996

	Eight Months Ended August 31, 1997			Year Ended December 31, 1996		
	Normalized Totals	Percent to Total Revenue	MGMA Percent to Revenue	Normalized Totals	Percent to Total Revenue	MGMA Percent to Revenue
Net Revenue	$ 620,200	100.00%	100.00%	$ 1,023,072	100.00%	100.00%
Expenses						
Physician						
Compensation						
& Benefits	537,421	86.65%	45.34%	542,211	53.00%	45.34%
Non Physician:						
Nonphysician						
Payroll/Benefits	114,028	18.39%	31.53%	142,890	13.97%	31.53%
Rent & Occupancy	27,212	4.39%	7.26%	39,321	3.84%	7.26%
Medical Supplies	67,044	10.81%	3.71%	81,338	7.95%	3.71%
Medical Services	1,620	0.26%	3.77%	3,136	0.31%	3.77%
Admin. Supplies/						
Services	11,073	1.79%	2.18%	13,395	1.31%	2.18%
Promotion/Marketing						
Expenses	500	0.08%	0.40%	297	0.03%	0.40%
Insurance	1,049	0.17%	1.80%	3,239	0.32%	1.80%
Interest	-	0.00%	0.25%	-	0.00%	0.25%
Outside						
Professional	10,800	1.74%	0.91%	19,000	1.86%	0.91%
Informational						
Services	5,831	0.94%	1.74%	10,199	1.00%	1.74%
Furniture and						
Equipment	1,700	0.27%	1.38%	-	0.00%	1.38%
Other Operating						
Expenses	2,394	0.39%	4.26%	6,877	0.67%	4.26%
Subtotal Non						
Physician	243,251	39.23%	59.19%	319,692	31.26%	59.19%
Total Expenses	780,672	125.88%	104.53%	861,903	84.26%	104.53%
Net Operating						
Income	(160,472)	-25.88%	-4.53%	161,169	15.75%	-4.53%
Other Income	1,765	0.28%		6,260	0.61%	
Depreciation	(11,707)	-1.89%		(17,561)	-1.72%	
Normalized Pre-						
Tax Net Income	**$(170,414)**	**-27.49%**		**$149,868**	**14.64%**	

224

Exhibit I
Mary Wells, M.D., P.A.
Comparative Schedule of Normalized Revenue and Expenses
Eight Months Ended August 31, 1997 and
Years Ended December 31, 1993 Through 1996

	Year Ended December 31, 1995			Year Ended December 31, 1994			Year Ended December 31, 1993	
Normalized Totals	Percent to Total Revenue	MGMA Percent to Revenue	Actual	Percent to Total Revenue	MGMA Percent to Revenue	Actual	Percent to Total Revenue	MGMA Percent to Revenue
$ 930,365	100.00%	100.00%	$ 769,879	100.00%	100.00%	$ 635,485	100.00%	100.00%
648,488	69.70%	45.34%	356,250	46.27%	41.36%	320,185	50.38%	41.57%
116,016	12.47%	31.53%	92,236	11.98%	31.26%	114,849	18.07%	29.40%
38,344	4.12%	7.26%	56,264	7.31%	7.44%	56,061	8.82%	6.79%
69,112	7.43%	3.71%	75,983	9.87%	3.92%	81,281	12.79%	3.36%
4,628	0.50%	3.77%	1,523	0.20%	4.77%	983	0.15%	4.47%
12,806	1.38%	2.18%	15,155	1.97%	2.08%	14,307	2.25%	2.08%
-	0.00%	0.40%	1,084	0.14%	0.39%	1,428	0.22%	0.35%
9,794	1.05%	1.80%	5,386	0.70%	1.72%	4,288	0.67%	2.09%
-	0.00%	0.25%	2,439	0.32%	0.36%	557	0.09%	0.53%
23,500	2.53%	0.91%	12,000	1.56%	0.62%	7,000	1.10%	0.78%
7,145	0.77%	1.74%	5,758	0.75%	1.98%	4,466	0.70%	1.78%
-	0.00%	1.38%	-	0.00%	1.18%	-	0.00%	1.38%
5,341	0.57%	4.26%	2,262	0.29%	3.58%	9,800	1.54%	3.33%
286,686	30.82%	59.19%	270,090	35.09%	59.30%	295,020	46.40%	56.34%
935,174	100.52%	104.53%	626,340	81.36%	100.66%	615,205	96.78%	97.91%
(4,089)	-0.52%	-4.53%	143,539	18.64%	-0.66%	20,280	3.19%	2.09%
4,156	0.45%		5,741	0.75%		2,428	0.38%	
(37,744)	-4.06%		(47,138)	-6.12%		(33,972)	-5.35%	
$(38,397)	-4.13%		$102,142	13.27%		$(11,264)	-1.78%	

Exhibit J
Mary Wells, M.D., P.A.
Schedule of Income and Discretionary Cash Flow
Eight Months Ended August 31, 1997

	Historical Financial Statements	Economic Adjustments	Notes	Normalized Financial Statements
Net Patient Revenue	$620,200			$620,200
Physician Benefits	9,739	527,682	1,2,3,6,8	537,421
Nonphysician Payroll/Benefits	261,185	(147,157)	2,3,7,8	114,028
Rent & Occupancy	15,400	11,812	5	27,212
Medical Supplies	67,044			67,044
Medical Services	1,620			1,620
Admin. Supplies/Services	11,073			11,073
Promotion/Marketing Expenses	500			500
Insurance	3,929	(2,880)	1	1,049
Interest	-			-
Outside Professional	10,800			10,800
Informational Services	5,831			5,831
Furniture and Equipment	1,700	11,707	4	13,407
Other Operating Expenses	2,394			2,394
Total Expenses	391,215			792,379
Pre-Tax Net Operating Income	228,985			(172,179)
Other Income (Expenses)				
Interest Income	1,765			1,765
Miscellaneous Income (Expense)	-			-
Total Other Income (Expense)	1,765			1,765
Pre-Tax Net Income	$230,750			(170,414)
Discretionary Cash Flow Adjustments:				
Depreciation		11,707	4	11,707
Net Discretionary Cash Flow				**$(158,707)**

Note 1: Physician health and life insurance premiums of $2,880 included in insurance expense have been reclassified as a physician expense.

Note 2: Physician compensation in the amount of $144,000 was reclassified from nonphysician payroll/benefits to physician compensation & benefits.

Note 3: Reasonable physician payroll tax expense has been estimated at $6,143 and reclassified from non-physician compensation.

Note 4: Provision for depreciation has been estimated based upon Clinic's 1996 tax depreciation, excluding Section 179 deduction

Note 5: Reasonable rent expense has been estimated at $11,812 based upon 1996 rent expense.

Note 6: Physician draws of $352,468 have been added to physician compensation.

Note 7: Estimated employee benefits of $25,177 have been added to nonphysician payroll/benefits based upon 1996 contributions.

Note 8: Physician pension contributions of $22,191 included in nonphysician benefits expense have been reclassified as a physician expense.

Exhibit J
(Continued)

	Historical Financial Statements	Economic Adjustments	Notes	Normalized Financial Statements
Net Patient Revenue	$1,023,072			$1,023,072
Physician Benefits	6,883	535,328	1,2,3,4,5	542,211
Nonphysician Payroll/Benefits	359,387	(216,497)	2,3,5	142,890
Rent & Occupancy	39,321			39,321
Medical Supplies	81,338			81,338
Medical Services	3,136			3,136
Admin. Supplies/Services	13,395			13,395
Promotion/Marketing Expenses	297			297
Insurance	7,559	(4,320)	1	3,239
Interest	-			-
Outside Professional	19,000			19,000
Informational Services	10,199			10,199
Furniture and Equipment	17,561			17,561
Other Operating Expenses	6,877			6,877
Total Expenses	564,953			879,464
Pre-Tax Net Operating Income	458,119			143,608
Other Income (Expenses)				
Interest Income	3,060			3,060
Miscellaneous Income (Expense)	3,200			3,200
Total Other Income (Expense)	6,260			6,260
Pre-Tax Net Income	$464,379			149,868
Discretionary Cash Flow Adjustments:				
Depreciation				17,561
Net Discretionary Cash Flow				**$167,429**

Note 1: Physician health and life insurance premiums of $4,320 included in nonphysician benefit expense have been reclassified as a physician expense.

Note 2: Physician Compensation in the amount of $180,000 was reclassified from Nonphysician Payroll/Benefits to Physician Compensation & Benefits.

Note 3: Reasonable physician payroll tax expense has been estimated at $6,497 and reclassified from non-physician compensation.

Note 4: Physician draws of $314,511 have been added to physician compensation.

Note 5: Physician pension contributions of $30,000 included in nonphysician benefits expense have been reclassified as a physician expense.

Exhibit J
(Continued)

	Historical Financial Statements	Economic Adjustments	Notes	Normalized Financial Statements
Net Patient Revenue	$930,365			$930,365
Physician Benefits	11,920	636,568	1,2,3,4,5	648,488
Nonphysician Payroll/Benefits	300,036	(184,020)	2,3,5	116,016
Rent & Occupancy	38,344			38,344
Medical Supplies	69,112			69,112
Medical Services	4,628			4,628
Admin. Supplies/Services	12,806			12,806
Promotion/Marketing Expenses	-			-
Insurance	14,114	(4,320)	1	9,794
Interest	-			-
Outside Professional	23,500			23,500
Informational Services	7,145			7,145
Furniture and Equipment	37,744			37,744
Other Operating Expenses	5,341			5,341
Total Expenses	524,690			972,918
Pre-Tax Net Operating Income	405,675			(42,553)
Other Income (Expenses)				
Interest Income	3,772			3,772
Miscellaneous Income (Expense)	384			384
Total Other Income (Expense)	4,156			4,156
Pre-Tax Net Income	$409,831			(38,397)
Discretionary Cash Flow Adjustments:				
Depreciation				37,744
Net Discretionary Cash Flow				**$ (653)**

Note 1: Physician health and life insurance premiums of $4,320 included in nonphysician benefit expense have been reclassified as a physician expense.
Note 2: Physician Compensation in the amount of $150,000 was reclassified from Nonphysician Payroll/Benefits to Physician Compensation & Benefits.
Note 3: Reasonable physician payroll tax expense has been estimated at $5,969 and reclassified from non-physician compensation.
Note 4: Physician draws of $448,228 have been added to physician compensation.
Note 5: Physician pension contributions of $28,051 included in nonphysician benefits expense have been reclassified as a physician expense.

Exhibit J
(*Continued*)

	Historical Financial Statements	Economic Adjustments	Notes	Normalized Financial Statements
Net Patient Revenue	$769,879			$769,879
Physician Benefits	9,728	346,522	1,2,3,4,5	356,250
Nonphysician Payroll/Benefits	272,549	(180,313)	2,3,5	92,236
Rent & Occupancy	56,264			56,264
Medical Supplies	75,983			75,983
Medical Services	1,523			1,523
Admin. Supplies/Services	15,155			15,155
Promotion/Marketing Expenses	1,084			1,084
Insurance	9,706	(4,320)	1	5,386
Interest	2,439			2,439
Outside Professional	12,000			12,000
Informational Services	5,758			5,758
Furniture and Equipment	47,138			47,138
Other Operating Expenses	2,262			2,262
Total Expenses	511,589			673,478
Pre-Tax Net Operating Income	258,290			96,401
Other Income (Expenses)				
Interest Income	3,741			3,741
Miscellaneous Income (Expense)	2,000			2,000
Total Other Income (Expense)	5,741			5,741
Pre-Tax Net Income	$264,031			102,142
Discretionary Cash Flow Adjustments:				
Depreciation				47,138
Net Discretionary Cash Flow				**$149,280**

Note 1: Physician health and life insurance premiums of $4,320 included in nonphysician benefit expense have been reclassified as a physician expense.

Note 2: Physician Compensation in the amount of $149,500 was reclassified from Nonphysician Payroll/Benefits to Physician Compensation & Benefits.

Note 3: Reasonable physician payroll tax expense has been estimated at $5,925 and reclassified from non-physician compensation.

Note 4: Physician draws of $161,889 have been added to physician compensation.

Note 5: Physician pension contributions of $24,888 included in nonphysician benefits expense have been reclassified as a physician expense.

Exhibit J
(Continued)

	Historical Financial Statements	Economic Adjustments	Notes	Normalized Financial Statements
Net Patient Revenue	$635,485			$635,485
Physician Benefits	4,523	315,662	1,2,3,4,5	320,185
Nonphysician Payroll/Benefits	266,861	(152,012)	2,3,5	114,849
Rent & Occupancy	56,061			56,061
Medical Supplies	81,281			81,281
Medical Services	983			983
Admin. Supplies/Services	14,307			14,307
Promotion/Marketing Expenses	1,428			1,428
Insurance	8,608	(4,320)	1	4,288
Interest	557			557
Outside Professional	7,000			7,000
Informational Services	4,466			4,466
Furniture and Equipment	33,972			33,972
Other Operating Expenses	9,800			9,800
Total Expenses	489,847			649,177
Pre-Tax Net Operating Income	145,638			(13,692)
Other Income (Expenses)				
Interest Income	2,428			2,428
Miscellaneous Income (Expense)	-			-
Total Other Income (Expense)	2,428			2,428
Pre-Tax Net Income	$148,066			(11,264)
Discretionary Cash Flow Adjustments:				
Depreciation				33,972
Net Discretionary Cash Flow				**$22,708**

Note 1: Physician health and life insurance premiums of $4,320 included in nonphysician benefit expense have been reclassified as a physician expense.

Note 2: Physician Compensation in the amount of $120,000 was reclassified from Nonphysician Payroll/ Benefits to Physician Compensation & Benefits.

Note 3: Reasonable physician payroll tax expense has been estimated at $5,311 and reclassified from non-physician compensation.

Note 4: Physician draws of $159,330 have been added to physician compensation.

Note 5: Physician pension contributions of $26,701 included in nonphysician benefits expense have been reclassified as a physician expense.

Exhibit K
Mary Wells, M.D., P.A.
Comparative Analysis of Historical Income Statements
Eight Months Ended August 31, 1997 and
Years Ended December 31, 1993 Through 1996

	Eight Months Ended August 31, 1997			Year Ended December 31, 1996		
	Actual	**Percent to Total Revenue**	**MGMA Percent to Revenue**	**Actual**	**Percent to Total Revenue**	**MGMA Percent to Revenue**
Income						
Net Patient Revenue	$620,200	100.00%	100.00%	$1,023,072	100.00%	100.00%
Expenses						
Physician Benefits	9,739	1.56%	45.34%	6,883	0.68%	45.34%
Nonphysician:						
Nonphysician						
Payroll/Benefits	261,185	42.11%	31.53%	359,387	35.13%	31.53%
Rent & Occupancy	15,400	2.48%	7.26%	39,321	3.84%	7.26%
Medical Supplies	67,044	10.81%	3.71%	81,338	7.95%	3.71%
Medical Services	1,620	0.26%	3.77%	3,136	0.31%	3.77%
Admin. Supplies/						
Services	11,073	1.79%	2.18%	13,395	1.31%	2.18%
Promotion/Marketing						
Expenses	500	0.08%	0.40%	297	0.03%	0.40%
Insurance	3,929	0.63%	1.80%	7,559	0.74%	1.80%
Interest	-	0.00%	0.25%	-	0.00%	0.25%
Outside Professional	10,800	1.74%	0.91%	19,000	1.86%	0.91%
Informational Services	5,831	0.94%	1.74%	10,199	1.00%	1.74%
Furniture and						
Equipment	1,700	0.27%	1.38%	17,561	1.72%	1.38%
Other Operating						
Expenses	2,394	0.39%	4.26%	6,877	0.67%	4.26%
Subtotal Non						
Physician	381,476	61.50%	59.19%	558,070	54.55%	59.19%
Total Expenses	391,215	63.06%	104.53%	564,953	55.23%	104.53%
Net Operating Income						
(Loss)	228,985	36.94%	-4.53%	458,119	44.77%	-4.53%
Other Income (Expenses)						
Interest Income	1,765	0.28%		3,060	0.30%	
Miscellaneous						
Income (Expense)	-	0.00%		3,200	0.31%	
Total Other Income						
(Expense)	1,765	0.28%		6,260	0.61%	
Net Income (Loss)	**$230,750**	**37.22%**		**$464,379**	**45.38%**	

Exhibit K
(Continued)

	Year Ended December 31, 1995			Year Ended December 31, 1994			Year Ended December 31, 1993		
		Percent to	MGMA		Percent to	MGMA		Percent to	MGMA
	Total	Percent to		Total	Percent to		Total	Percent to	
Actual	Revenue	Revenue	Actual	Revenue	Revenue	Actual	Revenue	Revenue	
$ 930,365	100.00%	100.00%	$769,879	100.00%	100.00%	$635,485	82.54%	100.00%
11,920	1.27%	45.34%	9,728	1.26%	41.36%	4,523	0.59%	41.57%
300,036	32.25%	31.53%	272,549	35.40%	31.26%	266,861	41.99%	29.40%
38,344	4.12%	7.26%	56,264	7.31%	7.44%	56,061	8.82%	6.79%
69,112	7.43%	3.71%	75,983	9.87%	3.92%	81,281	12.79%	3.36%
4,628	0.50%	3.77%	1,523	0.20%	4.77%	983	0.15%	4.47%
12,806	1.38%	2.18%	15,155	1.97%	2.08%	14,307	2.25%	2.08%
-	0.00%	0.40%	1,084	0.14%	0.39%	1,428	0.22%	0.35%
14,114	1.52%	1.80%	9,706	1.26%	1.72%	8,608	1.35%	2.09%
-	0.00%	0.25%	2,439	0.32%	0.36%	557	0.09%	0.53%
23,500	2.53%	0.91%	12,000	1.56%	0.62%	7,000	1.10%	0.78%
7,145	0.77%	1.74%	5,758	0.75%	1.98%	4,466	0.70%	1.78%
37,744	4.06%	1.38%	47,138	6.12%	1.18%	33,972	5.35%	1.38%
5,341	0.57%	4.26%	2,262	0.29%	3.58%	9,800	1.54%	3.33%
512,770	55.12%	59.19%	501,861	65.18%	59.30%	485,324	76.34%	56.34%
524,690	56.39%	104.53%	511,589	66.44%	100.66%	489,847	76.93%	97.91%
405,675	43.61%	-4.53%	258,290	33.56%	-0.66%	145,638	5.61%	2.09%
3,772	0.41%		3,741	0.49%		2,428	0.38%	
384	0.04%		2,000	0.26%		-	0.00%	
4,156	0.45%		5,741	0.75%		2,428	0.38%	
$409,831	44.06%		$264,031	34.31%		$148,066	5.99%	

Exhibit L

Mary Wells, M.D., P.A.

Schedule of Historical Physician Production

Years Ended December 31, 1996 Through 1997 (Estimated)

	Annualized 1997 (Est)	YTD August, 1997	1996
Physician Production			
Dr. Mary Wells	$ 1,375,400	$ 895,600	$ 1,330,330
MGMA Production Norms			
Single Specialty Family Practice Median	$ 313,230		$ 313,230
Total FTEs	1.00		1.00
Totals Applicable to Clinic	$ 313,230		$ 313,230
Family Practice 90th Percentile	$ 526,792		$ 526,792
Total FTEs	1.00		1.00
Totals Applicable to Clinic	$ 526,792		$ 526,792

Exhibit M

Mary Wells, M.D., P.A.

Schedule of Physician Compensation and Benefits

Year Ended December 31, 1996

Direct Physician Compensation:	
Salaries and bonuses	$180,000
Physician Fringe Benefits and Perquisites:	
Personal Draws	314,511
Pension Contributions	30,000
Health and Life Insurance	5,383
Automobile expenses	5,820
Payroll Taxes	6,497
Total Physician Fringes	362,211
Total Physician Compensation and Benefits Package	$542,211
MGMA Compensation Norm Analysis	
Median Family Practice, Overall	132,434
Median Family Practice, 1–2 Years in Specialty	110,100
Median Family Practice, Single Specialty	129,018
Median Family Practice, Southern Region	148,883
75th Percentile Family Practice	166,078
90th Percentile Family Practice	223,564

Exhibit N
Mary Wells, M.D., P.A.
Balance Sheet
August 31, 1997

	Clinic Financial Statements	Economic Adjustments		Adjusted Balance
Assets				
Current Assets				
Checking account	$116,914			$116,914
Accounts receivable	-	102,784	1	102,784
A/R - Employees	1,670			1,670
Inventory	-	18,722	2	18,722
Total Current Assets	118,584			240,090
Property and Equipment				
Furniture and Equipment	154,307			
Less: Accumulated Depreciation and Amortization	(136,983)			
Total Property and Equipment	17,324	75,076	3	92,400
Total Assets	$135,908			$332,490
Liabilities and Stockholders' Equity				
Current Liabilities				
Payroll Taxes Payable	$ 17,494			$ 17,494
Garnishments	160			160
Total Current Liabilities	17,654			17,654
Capital				
Retained Earnings	197,015			
Draws	(314,511)			
Net Income	230,750			
Common stock	5,000			
Total Stockholders' Equity	118,254	196,582	1,2,3	314,836
Total Liabilities and Stockholders' Equity	$135,908			$332,490

Note 1: To adjust patient accounts receivable to estimated fair market value.
Note 2: To adjust inventories to estimated fair market value.
Note 3: To allocate estimated accumulated depreciation to furniture and equipment.

Exhibit O
Mary Wells, M.D., P.A.
Schedule of Accounts Receivable Value
August 31, 1997

	Current	31 to 60 Days	61 to 90 Days	90 to 120 Days	Over 120 Days	Totals
Gross Accounts						
Receivable	$77,452	$45,221	$25,293	$18,349	$106,088	$272,403
Average Collectibility						
Factor	60.24%	53.54%	43.00%	30.45%	14.57%	37.73%
Receivables						
Valuation	**$46,654**	**$24,213**	**$10,877**	**$ 5,587**	**$ 15,453**	**$102,784**

Exhibit P
Mary Wells, M.D., P.A.
Schedule of Supply Inventory Values
August 31, 1997

	Year-to-Date 1997 Expense	Inventory Value*
Medical Supplies	$66,556	$16,639
Administrative Supplies	8,333	2,083
Totals	**$74,889**	**$18,722**

* Inventories are valued at two month's supply, using 1997 year-to-date expense amounts.

Exhibit Q
Mary Wells, M.D., P.A.
Schedule of Property and Equipment
August 31, 1997

Location	Description
Back Office	Cabinet - Metal Forms
	Chair
	Computer Terminal
	Desk
	Keyboard
	Postage Meter
	Printer
	Typewriter
Billing Office	Cabinet - File
	Chair
	Computer Terminal
	Desk
	Keyboard
Exam Room 1	Blood Pressure Machine
	Spirometer
	Stool
	Table - Exam
	Wheel Chair
Exam Room 2	Blood Pressure Machine
	Cabinet - Metal
	ENT Machine (Otoscope)
	IV Stand
	Scales
	Stool
	Table - Exam
	Testing Equipment
Exam Room 3	Blood Pressure Machine
	Cabinet - Metal
	EKG Machine
	ENT Machine
	Light
	Stool
	Table - Baby With Scale
Exam Room 4	Table - Cart
	Table - Emergency Storage
	Table - Exam
	Table - Light
	Ultra Sound Scope
Exam Room Upstairs	Copier
	Table - Exam
Lab Equipment	Abbott Cell-Dyn 1400
	Abbott IMX
	Abbott Vortaxer
	AVL 9130 Electrolytes Analyzer
	Centrifuge
	Glucometers
	Printer

Exhibit Q
(*Continued*)

Location	Description
Lab Equipment	Printer
	Refrigerator - Lab Large
	Refrigerator - Injectibles
	Select-A-Fuge 24
	Spectrum CCX
	Sperimix Rocker
Manager's Office	Bookshelf - Metal
	Cabinets - File (2)
	Chair
	Computer Terminal
	Desk
	Keyboard
Nurses Station	Desk
	Monitor - Holter
	NDIX Machine (Breathing Monitor)
	Printer
	Stool
Receptionist Area	Battery Backup
	Computer Terminal
	Copier
	Fax Machine
	File Server
	Keyboard
	Medifax Unit
	Multi Modem
	Printer
	Telephone System
Surgery Room	Auto Clave
	Circumstraint
	Electro Surgical Unit
	IV Holder
	Lamp
	Papoose Board One Large/One Small
	Stool
	Table - Exam
	Table - Tray
Waiting Room	Chairs- Arm (10)
	Magazine Rack
	Table and Chairs (4)
	Tables (3)
X-Ray Room	Cabinets - Metal X-Ray Storage (3)
	Stool
	X-Ray Machine With Table & Developer
Estimated Fair Market Value	$ 92,400

Exhibit R
Mary Wells, M.D., P.A.
Schedule of Patient Visits

Eight Months Ended August 31, 1997 and Year Ended December 31, 1996

Description of Evaluation and Management Service	CPT Codes	Year-to-Date August 31, 1997	1996
Office Visits:			
	99201	-	2
	99202	-	80
	99203	50	97
	99204	3	55
	99205	-	-
	99211	27	1,372
	99212	2,428	2,534
	99213	8,998	12,147
	99214	1	255
	99215	1	51
Hospital Observation	99217-99220	79	100
Hospital Inpatient	99221-99239	1,409	2,436
Consults	99241-99275	-	-
ER Visits	99281-99285	52	119
Critical Care	99291-99292	2	10
Nursing Facility	99301-99313	293	367
Rest Home	99321-99333	1	-
Home Visits	99341-99353	15	27
Prolonged Services	99354-99360	-	-
Case Management	99361-99373	-	1
Care Plan Oversight	99375-99376	62	356
Preventive Medicine	99381-99429	75	108
Newborn	99431-99440	88	97
Totals		13,584	20,214

Sample Time, Fee, and Expense Budget Form

Description	Assigned To	Budgeted Hours	Rate	Fee
Engagement Planning				
File Documentation				
Valuation Analysis				
Site Visit				
Report Preparation				
Review				
Client Conferences				
Other Matters				
Totals				
Travel				
Meals				
Lodging				
Telephone				
Postage, Delivery				
Other Expenses				
Total Expenses				
Total Fee and Expenses				

Illustrative Provisions for Medical Practice Valuation Engagement Letter

Addressee:

- Addressed to client's highest directly responsible level of management

Summary of Engagement:

- Description of the entity to be valued

- Interest being valued

- Standard of value

- Purpose for the valuation

- Effective date of the valuation

Limitations on Scope:

- Descriptions of any expected limitations on the scope of the engagement

- Restrictions on report as a result of scope limitations

Restrictions on Distribution of Report:

- Limitations on distribution of all or parts of report

- Parties to whom report may be disseminated

- Limitations on reproduction of report

Staffing:

- Who will be staffing the engagement

Timing:

- Timing of receipt of requested information and site visit

- Timing of delivery of report

Fee Arrangements:

- Hourly rates or flat fee arrangement

- Provisions for unexpected amendment to the fee estimate

- Billing policies and payment expectations

Other Provisions:

- Record retention policies

- Limits of liability, indemnification

- Limits on testimony with or without prior arrangements

- Response to subpoenas for data gathered during the engagement

- Signed by principal of firm

- Signed, dated by client

Note: This list is intended as a guide for provisions to be considered for a medical practice valuation engagement letter. It does not represent an all-inclusive list of engagement letter provisions, nor does it provide recommended language.

APPENDIX C

Medical Practice Valuation Information Request Form

Clinic Name: _____

Completed By: _____

Date: _____

1. Articles of incorporation and corporate by-laws, partnership, or LLC agreement

2. Curriculum vitae for physicians

3. Corporate minutes for the past five years.

4. Lease agreements.

5. Financial statements and tax returns of the medical practice for five years.

6. Charges, collections and adjustments for the past five years.

7. Aged patient accounts receivable summary balances as of the valuation date, aged current, 30, 60, 90, 120 and 180. Please also include any work-in-process not billed by the practice as of the valuation date.

8. Accounts payable listing as of the valuation date.

9. Listing of supply and drug inventories.

10. Appraisals of assets.

11. Budgets or projections.

12. Notes agreements, including notes payable and receivable

13. Real estate and personal property tax bills.

14. Strategic plan.

15. Fee schedule.

16. Fixed assets detail, including: description, date purchased, and original cost

17. Compensation of all physicians. Identify any direct or discretionary physician expenses included in the financial statements.

18. Production report or procedure stats on number of procedures performed for last full year for all CPT codes.

19. List of managed care contracts, including date relationship began, PMPM rates (if capitated), and number of patients.

21. List of referring doctors, location, and age.

22. Copy of any prior valuations of the practice or offers to purchase the practice.

23. List of competing physician practices in area.

29. Employee list, including job description, pay rate, and 1996 W-2 compensation.

Medical Practice Valuation Questionnaire

1. Clinic's legal name:

2. Type of entity (circle one): Corporation S-Corporation Proprietorship Partnership PLLC

3. Date of incorporation or formation:

4. When does your fiscal year end?

5. Do you have more than one clinic location? If yes, location(s):

6. List of related parties (subsidiaries, affiliates, or relatives) with which the medical practice does business.

7. Provide the history of the medical practice. Please attach additional pages as needed to fully describe the background of the physician and medical practice.

8. Explain any covenants-not-to-compete and similar agreements.

9. List the management of the practice and job titles.

10. Describe the condition of the medical practice's equipment.

11. Has the medical practice had difficulties complying with OSHA or CLIA regulations? Have you been cited or audited by an agency?

12. List any income currently being earned by the practice or the physician that will not be earned by a purchaser of the practice (income that will not flow to any buyer).

13. List average patients per day seen by each doctor, by category.

14. Complete practice payer mix:

    _____% Medicare

    _____% Medicaid

    _____% Commercial

    _____% PPO fee for service

    _____% HMO fee for service

    _____% Self-pay

    _____% Capitated plans

    _____% Other

    100 %

15. List the major managed care plans in the service area.

16. List Medicare senior plans currently being offered in the service area.

17. What percent of the population in the service area is enrolled in:

    Managed care plans? _____%

    Capitated plans? _____%

    Medicare HMO enrollment? _____%

18. List integrated delivery systems in the service area (e.g., IPAs, PHOs, etc.)

19. Is there Medicaid managed care in the service area? If yes, please describe.

20. Describe the medical practice's profit sharing, pension, or other retirement plan programs.

21. Describe the physician compensation formula.

22. Describe plans for major capital expenditures.

23. Provide details on any contingent liabilities, including lawsuits and pending or threatened litigation.

24. List any nonoperating and/or personal assets, such as real estate investments, aircraft, or boats.

25. Do you have a computer system for billing and patient accounts?

26. What type of computer software do you use?

27. Name, phone number, and contact person of the practice's outside accounting firm.

28. Do you have a personnel policy and procedures manual? Do you have written job descriptions for your employees?

29. Describe relevant past and expected future trends for the medical practice, such as growth patterns, mergers, or acquisitions.

30. Describe any future events that may impact the practice's income stream. For example, the growth in managed care, local competition, or a change in service reimbursements.

31. List all managed care plans in which the practice is not a participating provider and the reasons why the practice is not participating in each.

Revenue Ruling 59-60

In valuing the stock of closely held corporations, or the stock of corporations where market quotations are not available, all other available financial data, as well as all relevant factors affecting the fair market value must be considered for estate tax and gift tax purposes. No general formula may be given that is applicable to the many different valuation situations arising in the valuation of such stock. However, the general approach, methods, and factors which must be considered in valuing such securities are outlined.

Section 1. Purpose.

The purpose of this Revenue Ruling is to outline and review in general the approach, methods and factors to be considered in valuing shares of the capital stock of closely held corporations for estate tax and gift tax purposes. The methods discussed herein will apply likewise to the valuation of corporate stocks on which market quotations are either unavailable or are of such scarcity that they do not reflect the fair market value.

Sec. 2. Background and Definitions.

.01 All valuations must be made in accordance with the applicable provisions of the Internal Revenue Code of 1954 and the Federal Estate Tax & Gift Tax Regulations. Sections 2031(a), 2032 and 2512(a) of the 1954 Code (sections 811 and 1005 of the 1939 Code) require that the property to be included in the gross estate, or made the subject of a gift, shall be taxed on the basis of the value of the property at the time of death of the decedent, the alternative date if so elected, or the date of gift.

.02. Section 20.2031-1(b) of the Estate Tax Regulations (Section 81.10 of the Estate Tax Regulations 105) and Section 25.2512-1 of the Gift Tax Regulations (Section 86.19 of Gift Tax Regulations 108) define fair market value, in effect, as the price at which the property would change hands between a willing buyer and a willing seller when the former is not under any compulsion to buy and the latter is not under any compulsion to sell, both parties having reasonable knowledge of relevant facts. Court decisions frequently state in addition that the hypothetical buyer and seller are assumed to be able, as well as willing, to trade and to be well informed about the property and concerning the market for such property.

.03 Closely held corporations are those corporations the shares of which are owned by a relatively limited number of stockholders. Often the entire stock issue is held by one family. The result of this situation is that little, if any, trading in the shares takes place. There is, therefore, no established market for the stock and such sales as occur at irregular intervals seldom reflect all of the elements of a representative transaction as defined by the term "fair market value."

Sec. 3. Approach to Valuation.

.01 A determination of fair market value, being a question of fact, will depend upon the circumstances in each case. No formula can be devised that will be generally applicable to the multitude of different valuation issues arising in estate and gift tax cases. Often, an appraiser will find wide differences of opinion as to the fair market value of a particular stock. In resolving such differences, he should maintain a reasonable attitude in recognition of the fact that valuation is not an exact science. A sound valuation will be based upon all the relevant facts, but the elements of common sense, informed judgement and reasonableness must enter into the process of weighing those facts and determining their aggregate significance.

.02 The fair market value of specific shares of stock will vary as general economic conditions change from "normal" to "boom" or "depression," that is, according to the degree of optimism or pessimism with which the investing public regards the future at the required date of appraisal. Uncertainty as to the stability or continuity of the future income from a property decreases its value by increasing the risk of loss of earnings and value in the future. The value of shares of stock of a company with very uncertain future prospects is highly speculative. The appraiser must exercise his judgment as to the degree of risk attaching to the business of the corporation which issued the stock, but that judgment must be related to all of the other factors affecting value.

.03 Valuation of securities is, in essence, a prophesy as to the future and must be based on facts available at the required date of appraisal. As a generalization, the prices of stocks which are traded in volume in a free and active market by informed persons best reflect the consensus of the investing public as to what the future holds for the corporations and industries represented. When a stock is closely held, is traded infrequently, or is traded in an erratic market, some other measure of value must be used. In many instances, the next best measure may be found in the prices at which the stocks of companies engaged in the same or a similar line of business are selling in a free and open market.

Sec. 4. Factors to Consider.

.01 It is advisable to emphasize that in the valuation of the stock of closely held corporations or the stock of corporations where market quotations are either lacking or too scarce to be recognized, all available financial data, as well as all relevant factors affecting the fair market value, should be considered. The following factors, although not all-inclusive are fundamental and require careful analysis in each case:

(a) The nature of the business and the history of the enterprise from its inception.

(b) The economic outlook in general and the condition and outlook of the specific industry in particular.

(c) The book value of the stock and the financial condition of the business.

(d) The earning capacity of the company.

(e) The dividend-paying capacity.

(f) Whether or not the enterprise has goodwill or other intangible value.

(g) Sales of the stock and the size of the block of stock to be valued.

(h) The market price of stocks of corporations engaged in the same or a similar line of business having their stocks actively traded in a free and open market, either on an exchange or over-the-counter.

.02 The following is a brief discussion of each of the foregoing factors:

(a) The history of a corporate enterprise will show its past stability or instability, its growth or lack of growth, the diversity or lack of diversity of its operations, and other facts needed to form an opinion of the degree of risk involved in the business. For an enterprise which changed its form of organization but carried on the same or closely similar operations of its predecessor, the history of the former enterprise should be considered. The detail to be considered should increase with approach to the required date of appraisal, since recent events are of greatest help in predicting the future; but a study of gross and net income, and of dividends covering a long prior period, is highly desirable. The history to be studied should include, but need not be limited to, the nature of the business, its products or services, its operating and investment assets, capital structure, plant facilities, sales records and management, all of which should be considered as of the date of the appraisal, with due regard for recent significant changes. Events of the past that are unlikely to recur in the future should be discounted, since value has a close relation to future expectancy.

(b) A sound appraisal of a closely held stock must consider current and prospective economic conditions as of the date of appraisal, both in the national economy and in the industry or industries with which the corporation is allied. It is important to know that the company is more or less successful than its competitors in the same industry, or that it is maintaining a stable position with respect to competitors. Equal or even greater significance may attach to the ability of the industry with which the company is allied to compete with other industries. Prospective competition which has not been a factor in prior years should be given careful attention. For example, high profits due to the novelty of its product and the lack of competition often lead to increasing competition. The public's appraisal of the future prospects of competitive industries or of competitors within an industry may be indicated by price trends in the markets for commodities and for securities. The loss of the manager of a so-called "one-man" business may have a depressing effect upon the value of the stock of such business, particularly if there is a lack of trained personnel capable of succeeding to the management of the enterprise. In valuing the stock of this type of business, therefore, the effect of the loss of the manager on the future expectancy of the business, and the absence of management succession potentialities are pertinent factors to be taken into consideration. On the other hand, there may be factors which offset, in whole or in part, the loss of the manager's services. For instance, the nature of the business and of its assets may be such that they will not be impaired by the loss of the manager. Furthermore, the loss may be adequately covered by life insurance, or competent management might be employed on the basis of the consideration paid for the former manager's services. These, or other offsetting factors, if found to exist, should be carefully weighed against the loss of the manger's services in valuing the stock of the enterprise.

(c) Balance sheets should be obtained, preferably in the form of comparative annual statements for two or more years immediately preceding the date of appraisal, together with a balance sheet at the end of the month preceding that date, if corporate accounting will permit. Any balance sheet descriptions that are not self-explanatory, and balance sheet items comprehending diverse assets or liabilities, should be clarified in essential detail by supporting supplemental schedules. These statements usually will disclose to the appraiser:

(1) liquid position (ratio of current assets to current liabilities);

(2) gross and net book value of principal classes of fixed assets;

(3) working capital;

(4) long-term indebtedness;

(5) capital structure; and

(6) net worth.

Consideration also should be given to any assets not essential to the operation of the business, such as investments in securities, real estate, etc. In general, such nonoperating assets will command a lower rate of return than do the operating assets, although in exceptional cases the reverse may be true. In computing the book value per share of stock, assets of the investment type should be revalued on the basis of their market price and the book value adjusted accordingly. Comparison of the company's balance sheets over several years may reveal, among other facts, such developments as the acquisition of additional production facilities or subsidiary companies, improvement in financial position, and details as to recapitalizations and other changes in the capital structure of the corporation. If the corporation has more than one class of stock outstanding, the charter or certificate of incorporation should be examined to ascertain the explicit rights and privileges of the various stock issues including:

(1) voting powers,

(2) preference as to dividends, and

(3) preference as to assets in the event of liquidation.

(d) Detailed profit-and-loss statements should be obtained and considered for a representative period immediately prior to the required date of appraisal, preferably five or more years. Such statements should show

(1) gross income by principal items;

(2) principal deductions from gross income including major prior items of operating expenses, interest and other expense on each item of long-term debt, depreciation and depletion if such deductions are made, officers' salaries, in total if they appear to be reasonable or in detail if they seem to be excessive, contributions (whether or not deductible for tax purposes) that the nature of its business and its community position require the corporation to make, and taxes by principal items, including income and excess profits taxes;

(3) net income available for dividends;

(4) rates and amounts of dividends paid on each class of stock;

(5) remaining amount carried to surplus; and

(6) adjustments to, and reconciliation with, surplus as stated on the balance sheet. With profit and loss statements of this character available, the appraiser should be able to separate recurrent from nonrecurrent items of income and expense, to distinguish between operating income and investment income, and to ascertain whether or not any line of business in which the company is engaged is operated consistently at a loss and might be abandoned with benefit to the company. The percentage of

earnings retained for business expansion should be noted when dividend-paying capacity is considered. Potential future income is a major factor in many valuations of closely-held stocks, and all information concerning past income which will be helpful in predicting the future should be secured. Prior earnings records usually are the most reliable guide as to the future expectancy, but resort to arbitrary five-or-ten-year averages without regard to current trends or future prospects will not produce a realistic valuation. If, for instance, a record of progressively increasing or decreasing net income is found, then greater weight may be accorded the most recent years' profits in estimating earning power. It will be helpful, in judging risk and the extent to which a business is a marginal operator, to consider deductions from income and net income in terms of percentage of sales. Major categories of cost and expense to be so analyzed include the consumption of raw materials and supplies in the case of manufacturers, processors and fabricators; the cost of purchased merchandise in the case of merchants; utility services; insurance; taxes; depletion or depreciation; and interest.

(e) Primary consideration should be given to the dividend-paying capacity of the company rather than to dividends actually paid in the past. Recognition must be given to the necessity of retaining a reasonable portion of profits in a company to meet competition. Dividend-paying capacity is a factor that must be considered in an appraisal, but dividends actually paid in the past may not have any relation to dividend-paying capacity. Specifically, the dividends paid by a closely held family company may be measured by the income needs of the stockholders or by their desire to avoid taxes on dividend receipts, instead of by the ability of the company to pay dividends. Where an actual or effective controlling interest in a corporation is to be valued, the dividend factor is not a material element, since the payment of such dividends is discretionary with the controlling stockholders. The individual or group in control can substitute salaries and bonuses for dividends, thus reducing net income and understating the dividend-paying capacity of the company. It follows, therefore, that dividends are less reliable criteria of fair market value than other applicable factors.

(f) In the final analysis, goodwill is based upon earning capacity. The presence of goodwill and its value, therefore, rests upon the excess of net earnings over and above a fair return on the net tangible assets. While the element of goodwill may be based primarily on earnings, such factors as the prestige and renown of the business, the ownership of a trade or brand name, and a record of successful operation over a prolonged period in a particular locality, also may furnish support for the inclusion of intangible value. In some instances it may not be possible to make a separate appraisal of the tangible and intangible assets of the business. The enterprise has a value as an entity. Whatever intangible value there is, which is supportable by the facts, may be measured by the amount by which the appraised value of the tangible assets exceeds the net book value of such assets.

(g) Sales of stock of a closely held corporation should be carefully investigated to determine whether they represent transactions at arm's length. Forced or distress sales do not ordinarily reflect fair market value nor do isolated sales in small amounts necessarily control as the measure of value. This is especially true in the valuation of a controlling interest in a corporation. Since, in the case of closely held stocks, no prevailing market prices are available, there is no basis for making an adjustment for blockage. It follows, therefore, that such stocks should be valued upon a consideration of all the evidence affecting the fair market value. Although it is true that a minority interest in an unlisted corporation's stock is more difficult to sell than a similar block of listed stock, it is equally true that control of a corporation, either actual or in effect, representing as it does an added element of value, may justify a higher value for a specific block of stock.

(h) Section 2031(b) of the Code states, in effect, that in valuing unlisted securities the value of stock or securities of corporations engaged in the same or a similar line of business which are listed on an exchange should be taken into consideration along with all other factors. An important consideration is that the corporations to be used for comparisons have capital stocks which are actively traded by the public. In accordance with Section 2031(b) of the Code, stocks listed on an exchange are to be considered first. However, if sufficient comparable companies whose stocks are listed on an exchange cannot be found, other comparable companies which have stocks actively traded in on the over-the-counter market also may be used. The essential factor is that whether the stocks are sold on an exchange or over-the-counter there is evidence of an active, free public market for the stock as of the valuation date. In selecting corporations for comparative purposes, care should be taken to use only comparable companies. Although the only restrictive requirement as to comparable corporations specified in the statute is that their lines of business be the same or similar, yet it is obvious that consideration must be given to other relevant factors in order that the most valid comparison possible will be obtained. For illustration, a corporation having one or more issues of preferred stock, bonds or debentures in addition to its common stock should not be considered to be directly comparable to one having only common stock outstanding. In like manner, a company with a declining business and decreasing markets is not comparable to one with a record of current progress and market expansion.

Sec. 5. Weight to be Accorded Various Factors.

The valuation of closely held corporate stock entails the consideration of all relevant factors as stated in Section 4. Depending upon the circumstances in each case, certain factors may carry more weight than others because of the nature of the company's business. To illustrate:

(a) Earnings may be the most important criterion of value in some cases whereas asset value will receive primary consideration in others. In general, the appraiser will accord primary consideration to earnings when valuing stocks of companies which sell products or services to the public; conversely, in the investment or holding type of company, the appraiser may accord the greatest weight to the assets underlying the security to be valued.

(b) The value of the stock of a closely held investment or real estate holding company, whether or not family owned, is closely related to the value of the assets underlying the stock. For companies of this type the appraiser should determine the fair market values of the assets of the company. Operating expenses of such a company and the cost of liquidating it, if any, merit consideration when appraising the relative values of the stock and the underlying assets. The market values of the underlying assets give due weight to potential earnings and dividends of the particular items of property underlying the stock, capitalized at rates deemed proper by the investing public at the date of appraisal. A current appraisal by the investing public should be superior to the retrospective opinion of an individual. For these reasons, adjusted net worth should be accorded greater weight in valuing the stock of a closely held investment or real estate holding company, whether or not family owned, than any of the other customary yardsticks of appraisal, such as earnings and dividend paying capacity.

Sec. 6. Capitalization Rates.

In the application of certain fundamental valuation factors, such as earnings and dividends, it is necessary to capitalize the average or current results at some appropriate rate. A determination of the proper capitalization rate presents one of the most difficult problems in valuation. That there is no ready or simple solution will become apparent by a cursory check of the rates of return and dividend yields in terms of the selling prices of corporate shares listed on the major exchanges of the country. Wide variations will be found even for companies in the same industry. Moreover, the ratio will fluctuate from year to year depending upon economic conditions. Thus, no standard tables of capitalization rates applicable to closely held corporations can be formulated. Among the more important factors to be taken into consideration in deciding upon a capitalization rate in a particular case are:

(1) the nature of the business;

(2) the risk involved; and

(3) the stability or irregularity of earnings.

Sec. 7. Average of Factors.

Because valuations cannot be made on the basis of a prescribed formula, there is no means whereby the various applicable factors in a particular case can be assigned mathematical weights in deriving the fair market value. For this reason, no useful purpose is served by taking an average of several factors (for example, book value, capitalized earnings and capitalized dividends) and basing the valuation on the result. Such a process excludes active consideration of other pertinent factors, and the end result cannot be supported by a realistic application of the significant facts in the case except by mere chance.

Sec. 8. Restrictive Agreements.

Frequently, in the valuation of closely held stock for estate and gift tax purposes, it will be found that the stock is subject to an agreement restricting its sale or transfer. Where shares of stock were acquired by a decedent subject to an option reserved by the issuing corporation to repurchase at a certain price, the option price is usually accepted as the fair market value for estate tax purposes. See Rev. Rul. 54-76 C.B. 1954-1, 194. However, in such case the option price is not determinative of fair market value for gift tax purposes. Where the option, or buy and sell agreement, is the result of voluntary action by the stockholders and is binding during the life as well as at the death of the stockholders, such agreement may or may not, depending upon the circumstances of each case, fix the value for estate tax purposes. However, such agreement is a factor to be considered, with other relevant factors, in determining fair market value. Where the stockholder is free to dispose of his shares during life and the option is to become effective only upon his death, the fair market value is not limited to the option price. It is always necessary to consider the relationship of the parties, the relative number of shares held by the decedent, and other material facts, to determine whether the agreement represents a bonafide business arrangement or is a device to pass the decedent's shares to the natural objects of his bounty for less than an adequate and full consideration in money or money's worth. In this connection see Rev. Rul. 157 C. B. 1953-2, 255, and Rev. Rul. 189, C.B. 1953-2, 294.

Sec. 9. Effect on Other Documents.
Revenue Ruling 54-77, C.B. 1954-1, 187, is hereby superseded.

Revenue Ruling 65-193
Revenue Ruling 59-60, C.B. 1959-1, 237, is hereby modified to delete the statements, contained therein at Section 4.02(f), that "In some instances it may not be possible to make a separate appraisal of the tangible and intangible assets of the business. The enterprise has a value as an entity. Whatever intangible value there is, which is supportable by the facts, may be measured by the amount by which the appraised value of the tangible assets exceeds the net book value of such assets."

The instances where it is not possible to make a separate appraisal of the tangible and intangible assets of a business are rare and each case varies from the other. No rule can be devised which will be generally applicable to such cases.

Other than this modification, Revenue Ruling 59-60 continues in full force and effect.

Source: 1965-2, C. B. 370

Revenue Ruling 68 - 609

The "formula" approach may be used in determining the fair market value of intangible assets of a business only if there is no better basis available for making the determination. ARM 34, ARM 68, OD 937, and Revenue Ruling 65-192 superseded.

The purpose of this Revenue Ruling is to update and restate, under the current statute and regulations, the currently outstanding portions of ARM 34, CB 2, 31 (1920), ARM 68, CB 8, 49 (1920), and OD 937, CB 4, 43 (1921).

The question presented is whether the "formula" approach, the capitalization of earnings in excess of a fair rate of return on net tangible assets, may be used to determine the fair market value of the intangible assets of a business.

The "formula" approach may be stated as follows:

A percentage return on the average annual value of the tangible assets used in a business is determined, using a period of years (preferably not less than five) immediately prior to the valuation date. The amount of the percentage return on tangible assets, thus determined, is deducted from the average earnings of the business for such period and the remainder, if any, is considered to be the amount of the average annual earnings from the intangible assets of the business for the period. This amount (considered as the average annual earnings from intangibles), capitalized at a percentage of, say, 15 to 20 percent, is the value of the intangible assets of the business determined under the "formula" approach.

The percentage of return on the average annual value of the tangible assets used should be the percentage prevailing in the industry involved at the date of valuation, or (when the industry percentage is not available) a percentage of 8 to 10 percent may be used.

The 8 percent rate of return and the 15 percent rate of capitalization are applied to tangibles and intangibles, respectively, of businesses with a small risk factor and stable and regular earnings; the 10 percent rate of return and 20 percent rate of capitalization are applied to businesses in which the hazards of business are relatively high.

The above rates are used as examples and are not appropriate in all cases. In applying the "formula" approach, the average earnings period and the capitalization rates are dependent upon the facts pertinent thereto in each case.

The past earnings to which the formula is applied should fairly reflect the probable future earnings. Ordinarily, the period should not be less than five years, and abnormal years, whether above or below the average, should be eliminated. If the business is a sole proprietorship or partnership, there should be deducted from the earnings of the business a reasonable amount for services performed by the owner or partners engaged in the business. See Lloyd B. Sanderson Estate v. Commissioner, 42 F. 2d 160 (1930). Further, only the tangible assets entering into net worth, including accounts and bills receivable in excess of accounts and bills payable, are used for determining earnings on the tangible assets. Factors that influence the capitalization rate include

(1) the nature of the business,

(2) the risk involved, and

(3) the stability or irregularity of earnings.

The "formula" approach should not be used if there is better evidence available from which the value of intangibles can be determined. If the assets of a going business are sold upon the basis of a rate of capitalization that can be substantiated as being realistic, though it is not within the range of figures indicated here as the ones ordinarily to be adopted, the same rate of capitalization should be used in determining the value of intangibles.

Accordingly, the "formula" approach may be used for determining the fair market value of intangible assets of a business only if there is no better basis therefore available.

See also Revenue Ruling 59-60, CB 1959-1,237, as modified by Revenue Ruling 65-193, CB 1965-2, 370, which sets forth the property approach to use in the valuation of closely-held corporate stocks for estate and gift tax purposes. The general approach, methods, and factors, outlined in Revenue Ruling 59-60, as modified, are equally applicable to valuations of corporate stocks for income and other tax purposes as well as for estate and gift tax purposes. They apply also to problems involving the determination of the fair market value of business interests of any type, including partnerships and proprietorships, and of intangible assets for all tax purposes.

ARM 34, ARM 68, and OD 937 are superseded, since the positions set forth therein are restated to the extent applicable under current law in this Revenue Ruling. Revenue Ruling 65-192, CB 1965-2, 219, which contained restatements of ARM 34 and ARM 68, is also superseded.

A P P E N D I X   F

STANDARD 9

In developing a business or intangible asset appraisal, an appraiser must be aware of, understand, and correctly employ those recognized methods and procedures that are necessary to produce a credible appraisal.

Comment: STANDARD 9 is directed toward the same substantive aspects set forth in STANDARD 1, but addresses business and intangible asset appraisal.

Standards Rule 9-1

In developing a business or intangible asset appraisal, an appraiser must:

(a) be aware of, understand, and correctly employ those recognized methods and procedures that are necessary to produce a credible appraisal;

Comment: Departure from this binding requirement is not permitted. Changes and developments in the economy and in investment theory have a substantial impact on the business appraisal profession. Important changes in the financial arena, securities regulation, tax law and major new court decisions may result in corresponding changes in business appraisal practice.

(b) not commit a substantial error of omission or commission that significantly affects an appraisal;

Comment: Departure from this binding requirement is not permitted. In performing appraisal services an appraiser must be certain that the gathering of factual information is conducted in a manner that is sufficiently diligent to reasonably ensure that the data that would have a material or significant effect on the resulting opinions or conclusions are considered. Further, an appraiser must use sufficient care in analyzing such data to avoid errors that would significantly affect his or her opinions and conclusions.

(c) not render appraisal services in a careless or negligent manner, such as a series of errors that, considered individually, may not significantly affect the results of an appraisal, but which, when considered in the aggregate, would be misleading.

Comment: Departure from this binding requirement is not permitted. Perfection is impossible to attain and competence does not require perfection. However, an appraiser must not render appraisal services in a careless or negligent manner. This rule requires an appraiser to use diligence and care. The fact that the carelessness or negligence of an appraiser has not caused an error that significantly affects his or her opinions or conclusions and thereby seriously harms a client does not excuse such carelessness or negligence.

Standards Rule 9-2

In developing a business or intangible asset appraisal, an appraiser must observe the following specific appraisal guidelines:

(a) adequately identify the business enterprise, assets, or equity under consideration, define the purpose and the intended use of the appraisal, consider the elements of the appraisal investigation, consider any special limiting conditions, and identify the effective date of the appraisal;

(b) define the value being considered.

(i) if the appraisal concerns a business enterprise or equity interests, consider any buy-sell agreements, investment letter stock restrictions, restrictive corporate charter or partnership agreement clauses, and any similar features or factors that may have an influence on value.

(ii) if the appraisal concerns assets, the appraiser must consider whether the assets are:

(1) appraised separately; or

(2) appraised as parts of a going concern.

Comment: The value of assets held by a business enterprise may change significantly depending on whether the basis of valuation is acquisition or replacement, continued use in place, or liquidation.

(iii) if the appraisal concerns equity interests in a business enterprise, consider the extent to which the interests do or do not contain elements of ownership control.

Comment: Special attention should be paid to the attributes of the interest being appraised including the rights and benefits of ownership. The elements of control in a given situation may be affected by law, distribution of ownership interests, contractual relationships, and many other factors. As a consequence, the degree of control or lack of it depends on a broad variety of facts and circumstances which must be evaluated in the specific situation. Equity interests in a business enterprise are not necessarily worth the pro rata share of the business enterprise value as a whole.

Conversely, if the value of the whole is not considered, the value of the business enterprise is not necessarily a direct mathematical extension of the value of the fractional interests.

Standards Rule 9-3

In developing a business or intangible asset appraisal relating to an equity interest with the ability to cause liquidation of the enterprise, an appraiser must investigate the possibility that the business enterprise may have a higher value in liquidation than for continued operation as a going concern absent contrary provisions of law of a competent jurisdiction. If liquidation is the indicated basis of valuation, any real estate or personal property to be liquidated must be valued under the appropriate standard.

Comment: Departure from this binding requirement is not permitted. This rule requires the appraiser to recognize that continued operation of a business is not always the best premise of value as liquidation may result in a higher value. It should be noted, however, that this should be considered only when the business equity being appraised is in a position to cause liquidation. If liquidation is the appropriate premise of value, then assets such as real estate and tangible personal property must be appraised under STANDARD 1 and STANDARD 7, respectively.

Standards Rule 9-4

In developing a business or intangible asset appraisal, an appraiser must observe the following specific appraisal guidelines when applicable:

(a) consider all appropriate valuation methods and procedures.

(b) collect and analyze relevant data regarding:

    (i) the nature and history of the business;

    (ii) financial and economic conditions affecting the business enterprise, its industry, and general economy;

    (iii) past results, current operations, and future prospects of the business enterprise;

    (iv) past sales of capital stock or other ownership interests in the business enterprise being appraised;

    (v) sales of similar businesses or capital stock of publicly held similar businesses;

    (vi) prices, terms, and conditions affecting past sales of similar business assets;

Comment: This guideline directs the appraiser to study the prospective and retrospective aspects of the business enterprise and to study it in terms of the economic and industry environment within which it operates. Further, sales of securities of the business itself or similar businesses for which sufficient information is available should also be considered.

In certain circumstances, the business appraiser may also collect and analyze data regarding functional and/or economic utility or obsolescence of the business assets.

Economic obsolescence is a major consideration when assets are considered as parts of a going concern. It may also be one of the criteria in deciding that liquidation is the appropriate premise for valuation.

Standards Rule 9-5

In developing a business or intangible asset appraisal, an appraiser must:

(a) select and employ one or more approaches that apply to the specific appraisal assignments.

Comment: This rule requires the appraiser to use all relevant approaches for which sufficient reliable data are available. However, it does not mean that the appraiser must use all approaches in order to comply with the rule if certain approaches are not applicable.

(b) consider and reconcile the indications of value resulting from the various approaches to arrive at the value conclusion.

Comment: Departure from this binding requirement is not permitted. The appraiser must evaluate the relative reliability of the various indications of value. The appraiser should consider quality and quantity of data leading to each of the indications of value. The value conclusion is the result of the appraiser's judgment and not necessarily the result of a mathematical process.

STANDARD 10

In reporting the results of a business or intangible asset appraisal an appraiser must communicate each analysis, opinion, and conclusion in a manner that is not misleading.

Standards Rule 10-1

Each written or oral business or intangible asset appraisal report must:

(a) clearly and accurately set forth the appraisal in a manner that will not be misleading.

Comment: Departure from this binding requirement is not permitted.

(b) contain sufficient information to enable the intended user(s) to understand it. Any specific limiting conditions concerning information should be noted.

Comment: Departure from this binding requirement is not permitted. Any specific limiting conditions should be noted in the engagement letter as well as in the report itself. A failure to observe this rule could cause the intended users of the report to make a serious error even though each analysis, opinion, and conclusion in the report is clearly and accurately stated.

(c) clearly and accurately disclose any extraordinary assumption that directly affects the appraisal and indicate its impact on value.

Comment: Departure from this binding requirement is not permitted. This rule requires a clear and accurate disclosure of any extraordinary assumptions or conditions that directly affect an analysis, opinion, or conclusion. Examples of such extraordinary assumptions or conditions might include items such as the execution of a pending lease agreement, atypical financing, infusion of additional working capital or making other capital additions, or compliance with regulatory authority rules. The report should indicate whether the extraordinary assumption or condition has a positive, negative or neutral impact on value.

Standards Rule 10-2

Each written business or intangible asset appraisal report must comply with the following specific reporting guidelines:

(a) identify and describe the business enterprise, assets or equity being appraised.

(b) state the purpose and intended use of the appraisal.

(c) define the value to be estimated.

(d) set forth the effective date of the appraisal and the date of the report.

Comment: If the appraisal concerns equity, it is not enough to identify the entity in which the equity is being appraised without also identifying the nature of the equity, for example: the number of shares of common or preferred stock. The purpose may be to express an opinion of value but the intended use of the appraisal must also be stated.

The report date is when the report is submitted; the appraisal date or date of value is the effective date of the value conclusion.

(e) describe the extent of the appraisal process employed;

(f) set forth all assumptions and limiting conditions that affect the analyses, opinions, and conclusions.

(g) set forth the information considered, the appraisal procedures followed, and the reasoning that supports the analyses, opinions and conclusions.

(h) set forth any additional information that may be appropriate to show compliance with, or clearly identify and explain permitted departures from, the requirements of STANDARD 9.

(i) set forth the rationale for the valuation methods and procedures considered and employed.

(j) include a signed certification in accordance with Standards Rule 10-3.

Standards Rule 10-3

Each written business or intangible asset appraisal report must contain a signed certification that is similar in content to the following:
I certify that, to the best of my knowledge and belief:

- the statements of fact contained in this report are true and correct.

- the reported analyses, opinions, and conclusions are limited only by the reported assumptions and limiting conditions, and are my personal, unbiased professional analyses, opinions, and conclusions.

- I have no (or the specified) present or prospective interest in the property that is the subject of this report, and I have no (or the specified) personal interest or bias with respect to the parties involved.

- my compensation is not contingent on an action or event resulting from the analyses, opinions, or conclusions in, or the use of, this report.

- my analyses, opinions, and conclusions were developed, and this report has been prepared, in conformity with the Uniform Standards of Professional Appraisal Practice. no one provided significant professional assistance to the person signing this report. (If there are exceptions, the name of each individual providing significant professional assistance must be stated.)

Comment: Departure from this binding requirement is not permitted.

Standards Rule 10-4

To the extent that it is both possible and appropriate, each oral business or intangible asset appraisal report (including expert testimony) must address the substantive matters set forth in Standards Rule 10-2 and state conformity with Standards Rule 10-3.

Standards Rule 10-5

An appraiser who signs a business or intangible asset appraisal report prepared by another, even under the label "review appraiser", must accept full responsibility for the contents of this report.

Comment: Departure from this binding requirement is not permitted. This requirement is directed to the employer or supervisor signing the report of an employee or subcontractor. The employer or supervisor signing the report is as responsible as the individual preparing the appraisal for the content and conclusions of the appraisal and the report. Using a conditional label next to the signature of the employer or supervisor or signing a form report on the line over the words review appraiser does not exempt that individual from adherence to these Standards.

This requirement does not address the responsibilities of a review appraiser, the subject of STANDARD 3.

Glossary

COMMON VALUATION TERMINOLOGY

Capitalization rate: a rate applied to net earnings or net cash flow to determine the estimated value or the expected return of the benefit stream.

Discount rate: a rate applied to net earnings or net cash flows to determine the present value of the benefit stream. Discount rates are determined by first applying a risk-free rate as of the date of the valuation and adding to this an equity risk premium (typically the difference between an average long-term stock portfolio and the risk-free rate) to result in an average market rate of return. Other risk factors associated with the medical practice being valued are then analyzed to determine an increase or decrease in risk. Such factors considered are the size of the practice, geographical area of practice and surrounding competition, economic factors in area, changes in the industry and impact on practice, financial health of the practice, patient base and demographics, and management of the practice.

Discounted cash flow method: a method of determining the estimated value of a medical practice by first projecting its net earnings or net cash flow for a given period and then applying a discount rate to those earnings or cash flow to result in the present value of the benefit stream.

Equity risk premium: a rate used in determining the discount rate, which represents the average return on a long-term stock portfolio over the return on investment of long-term risk-free bonds.

Excess earnings method: a method of determining a practice's value attributable to intangible assets by measuring the shareholders' earnings in excess of normal operating expenses of the practice and a level of reasonable shareholder compensation. This is historically measured over a number of years. The excess earnings are multiplied by a capitalization rate of a multiplier to determine the practice's value of intangible assets.

Fair value: the amount that will fairly compensate a party who has been deprived of a benefit of an asset or an entity.

Fair market value: as defined in the Internal Revenue Service's Revenue Ruling 59-60, it is "the amount at which the property would change hands between a willing buyer and a willing seller when the former is not under compulsion to buy and the latter is not under any compulsion to sell, both parties having reasonable knowledge of the relevant facts."

Going concern value: the assumption that the practice will continue to operate in the future in an ongoing manner essentially the same as on the valuation date.

Goodwill: a component of a practice's value that represents the practice's and the physicians' relationship with its patients, peers and competitors, hospitals and other health care facilities, vendors and creditors, the community, and so on. This component is typically the amount of a practice's value that exceeds the value of the tangible assets: real estate, furniture and fixtures, equipment, supplies, and accounts receivable.

Intangible assets: the practice's assets represented by such things as patient base, medical records, reputation in the medical community, goodwill, practice name, practice location, practice phone number, practice's staff, practice's logo and signs, and so forth.

Investment value: the amount that can be calculated by injecting the invested capital and specific circumstances as planned by the investor (purchasing entity).

Liquidation value: the amount of a practice's tangible assets priced as a result of the practice's closure.

Net book value (also referred to as **net asset value**): the difference between the basis (original cost, purchase price, or other adjusted basis) and the accumulated depreciation or amortization of an asset or group of assets as of a specific point in time. The "net book value" of a medical practice is the difference between total net assets and total net liabilities. This is also called stockholders' equity, net worth, capital, and owners' equity.

Present value factor: a numerical factor based on a given interest rate (discount rate) that is used as a multiplier to determine the present value of an amount such as net cash flow or net earnings. Present value factors are used in the discounted cash flow method of valuation.

Residual value: see **Terminal value.**

Risk-free rate of return: a rate used in determining a discount rate that represents the yield (return on investment) of investments that are referred to as risk-free, typically long-term U.S. Treasury bonds for a term of 20 to 30 years.

Tangible assets: the practice's assets such as land, building, furniture, fixtures, business equipment, medical equipment, clinical and office supplies, and accounts receivable.

Terminal value: a value assigned to continuing operations of a medical practice beyond a projected timeframe in which the practice is believed to have achieved operational stability. This is also referred to as "residual value" and "perpetuity value."

Terminal year: the year in which a practice is considered to have achieved operational stability.

Weighted average cost of capital: a method used to determine the discount rate that takes into consideration a combination of the cost of debt and the cost of equity.

Index

Mergers, 3, 12
Minority interest, 171-174

Normalizing adjustments, 109-111
Note agreements, 73

Objective weighted average of value, 166–167
Offers, previous, 67
On-site inspection, 145–156
   checklist for, 157–163
Operating costs, *see* Expenses
Oral reports, 183
Overstated revenues, 31–33
Ownership interests, 175–176

Partnership agreement, 66
Payback approach, 170–171
Payer mix, 43–45, 100. *See also* Reimbursement
Payroll taxes, 138–139
Personnel, *see* Employees
Physician Practice Management Company (PPMC), 2
Physicians:
   age of, 97
   curriculum vitae of, 79, 98
   interview of, 154–155
   marketing valuation services to, 9–10
   productivity of, 38-40, 69-70
   valuation planning and, 58
Practice goodwill, 50
Practice information questionnaire, 79–80, 244–246
Practice risk, 93–94, 96–99
Practitioners' Publishing Company, 92, 184
Premiums, 171
   and control, 172–174
   and marketability, 174–175
   and ownership interests, 175–176
Present value, 119
Private inurement/benefit, 18–20

Productivity, of physicians, 38–40, 70, 76
Professional goodwill, *see* Intangible assets, examples
Profit, *see* Revenues

Questionnaire, on practice, 79–80, 244–246

Real estate, 133
Reasonableness checks, 169–171
Reconciliation of Valuation Methods, 166
   BizComps, 127
   Done Deals, 127
   Mergerstat Review, 127
   Pratt's Stats, 127
Referrals:
   information on, 77
   Medicare fraud and, 17–18
   patterns of, 42–43, 93, 96
   and productivity, 38–40
   Stark Law and, 20–22
   tax-exempt organizations and, 18–20
Referring Doctor Report, 42
Regulatory issues:
   Medicare fraud, 17–18
   private inurement/benefit, 18–20
   Stark Law, 20–22
Reimbursement, 47
   collecting information on, 69–70
   risk and, 94, 99–100
   risks to future, 40–42
Rental costs, 36–37, 67–68, 133
Replacement cost, 128
Reports:
   oral, 183
   sample, 190–238
   standards for, 177–178
   written, 178–183
Representation letter, 176
Reproduction cost, 129
Retirement plan contributions, 34

Valuation methods (*Continued*)
  market approach, 107, 125–128, 140
  misapplication of, 185
  reconciling, 166–169
Valuation process, *see also* Valuation
    methods
  beginning, 57–86
  and capitalization rate, 87–104
  checklist for, 54–56
  completing, 165–187
  and on-site inspection, 145–163
  special issues of, 23–56
Valuation services:
  marketing of, 9–10

professional standards for, 177–178,
  260–268
Value, defined, 13–16

Wall Street Journal, 92
Weighted average cost of capital
  (WACC), 102–103
Work papers, 82
Working capital, 131–132
Written reports:
  full format, 178–182, 202–238
  letter, 182–183, 190–201